Lecture Notes in Computer Science 10430

Commenced Publication in 1973
Founding and Former Series Editors:
Gerhard Goos, Juris Hartmanis, and Jan van Leeuwen

More information about this series at http://www.springer.com/series/8637

Abdelkader Hameurlain · Josef Küng
Roland Wagner · Reza Akbarinia
Esther Pacitti (Eds.)

Transactions on Large-Scale Data- and Knowledge-Centered Systems XXXIII

 Springer

Editors-in-Chief

Abdelkader Hameurlain
IRIT, Paul Sabatier University
Toulouse
France

Roland Wagner
FAW, University of Linz
Linz
Austria

Josef Küng
FAW, University of Linz
Linz
Austria

Guest Editors

Reza Akbarinia
Inria and LIRMM, University of Montpellier
Montpellier
France

Esther Pacitti
Inria and LIRMM, University of Montpellier
Montpellier
France

ISSN 0302-9743   ISSN 1611-3349   (electronic)
Lecture Notes in Computer Science
ISSN 1869-1994   ISSN 2510-4942   (electronic)
Transactions on Large-Scale Data- and Knowledge-Centered Systems
ISBN 978-3-662-55695-5   ISBN 978-3-662-55696-2   (eBook)
DOI 10.1007/978-3-662-55696-2

Library of Congress Control Number: 2017949172

Printed on acid-free paper

This Springer imprint is published by Springer Nature
The registered company is Springer-Verlag GmbH Germany
The registered company address is: Heidelberger Platz 3, 14197 Berlin, Germany

Preface

This volume contains five fully revised selected regular papers, covering a wide range of very hot topics in the field of data and knowledge management systems. These include distributed massive data streams, storage systems in fog environments, scientific workflow scheduling in multi-site clouds, cost optimization of data flows based on task-re-ordering, and fusion strategies for large-scale multi-modal image retrieval. We would like to sincerely thank the editorial board and the external reviewers for thoroughly refereeing the submitted papers and ensuring the high quality of this volume.

Special thanks go to Gabriela Wagner for her high availability and her valuable work in the realization of this TLDKS volume.

July 2017

Reza Akbarinia
Abdelkader Hameurlain
Josef Küng
Esther Pacitti
Roland Wagner

Organization

Editorial Board

Georges Hebrail	EDF R&D, France
Philippe Lamarre	LIRIS, France
Josep Lluís Larriba Pey	Universitat Politècnica de Catalunya, Spain
Florent Masseglia	Inria & Lirmm, University of Montpellier, France
Pascal Molli	University of Nantes, France
Marta Patiño-Martínez	Universidad Politècnica de Madrid, Spain
Tamer Ozsu	University of Waterloo, Canada
Fabio Port	LNCC, Brazil
Philippe Pucheral	PRISM & Inria, France
Patrick Valduriez	Inria & Lirmm, University of Montpellier, France

Contents

Lightweight Metric Computation for Distributed Massive Data Streams

Emmanuelle Anceaume[1] and Yann Busnel[2(✉)]

[1] IRISA/CNRS, Rennes, France
emmanuelle.anceaume@irisa.fr
[2] IMT Atlantique/IRISA, Rennes, France
yann.busnel@imt-atlantique.fr

Abstract. The real time analysis of massive data streams is of utmost importance in data intensive applications that need to detect as fast as possible and as efficiently as possible (in terms of computation and memory space) any correlation between its inputs or any deviance from some expected nominal behavior. The IoT infrastructure can be used for monitoring any events or changes in structural conditions that can compromise safety and increase risk. It is thus a recurrent and crucial issue to determine whether huge data streams, received at monitored devices, are correlated or not as it may reveal the presence of attacks. We propose a metric, called codeviation, that allows to evaluate the correlation between distributed massive streams. This metric is inspired from classical metric in statistics and probability theory, and as such enables to understand how observed quantities change together, and in which proportion. We then propose to estimate the codeviation in the data stream model. In this model, functions are estimated on a huge sequence of data items, in an online fashion, and with a very small amount of memory with respect to both the size of the input stream and the values domain from which data items are drawn. We then generalize our approach by presenting a new metric, the *Sketch-⋆ metric*, which allows us to define a distance between updatable summaries of large data streams. An important feature of the *Sketch-⋆ metric* is that, given a measure on the entire initial data streams, the *Sketch-⋆ metric* preserves the axioms of the latter measure on the sketch. We finally present results obtained during extensive experiments conducted on both synthetic traces and real data sets allowing us to validate the robustness and accuracy of our metrics.

Keywords: Data stream model · Correlation metric · Statistical metric · Distributed approximation algorithm

1 Introduction

Performance of many complex monitoring applications, including Internet monitoring applications, and data mining, or massively distributed infrastructures

This work has been partially funded by the French ANR project SocioPlug (ANR-13-INFR-0003) and by the DeSceNt project granted by the Labex CominLabs excellence laboratory (ANR-10-LABX-07-01).

© Springer-Verlag GmbH Germany 2017
A. Hameurlain et al. (Eds.): TLDKS XXXIII, LNCS 10430, pp. 1–39, 2017.
DOI: 10.1007/978-3-662-55696-2_1

such as sensor networks, and the Internet of Things (IoT) depend on the detection of correlated events. For instance, detecting correlated network anomalies should drastically reduce the number of false positive or negative alerts that networks operators have to currently face when using network management tools such as SNMP or NetFlow. Indeed, to cope with the complexity and the amount of raw data, current network management tools analyze their input streams in isolation [1,2]. Diagnosing flooding attacks through the detection of correlated flows should improve intrusion detection tools [3–5], while analyzing the effect of multivariate correlation should help for an early detection of Distributed Denial of Service (DDoS) [6]. Finally, the sustainable development of smart cities is expected to handle large amounts of data generated from large number of sensors with the consequent necessity for quick aggregation of the data, which could be exploited to detect correlated events. Among possible applications, smart building management systems rely on service-oriented continuous queries over sensor data streams in case of energy consumption monitoring [7], air pollution monitoring applications heavily rely on sensors to detect threshold crossings [8]. More generally, Stankovic [9] argues that the real time analysis of large and distributed data streams is of utmost importance to tackle issues related to creative knowledge, robustness, privacy, and security.

The point is that, in all these contexts, data streams arrive at nodes in a very high rate and may contain up to several billions of data items per day. Thus computing statistics with traditional methods is unpractical due to constraints on both available processing capacity and memory. Actually, two main approaches exist to monitor in real time massive data streams. The first one consists in regularly sampling the input streams so that only a limited amount of data items is locally kept. This allows for an exact computation of functions on these samples. However, accuracy of this computation with respect to the stream in its entirety fully depends on the volume of data items that has been sampled and their order in the stream. Furthermore, an adversary may easily take advantage of the sampling policy to hide its attacks among data items that are not sampled, or in a way that prevents its "malicious" data items from being correlated [10]. In contrast, the streaming approach consists in scanning, on the fly, each piece of data of the input stream, and in locally keeping only compact synopses or sketches that contain the most important information about these data. This approach enables the derivation of some data streams statistics with guaranteed error bounds without making any assumptions on the order in which data items are received at nodes.

Work on data stream analysis mainly focuses on efficient methods (data-structures and algorithms) to answer different kind of queries over massive data streams, as for example the computation of the number of different data items in a given stream [11–13]. Mostly, these methods consist in deriving statistic estimators over the data stream, in creating summary representations of streams (to build histograms, wavelets, and quantiles), and in comparing data streams. Regarding the construction of estimators, a seminal work is due to Alon et al. [14]. The authors have proposed estimators of the frequency moments F_k of a stream, which are important statistical tools that allow to quantify specificities of a data stream. Subsequently, a lot of attention has been devoted to the strongly related notion of the entropy [15] of a stream [16–18], and all notions based on entropy as the quantification of the amount of randomness of a stream (*e.g*, [17,19–21]). The construction of synopses or sketches of the data stream have been proposed for different applications (*e.g*, [22–25]). Actually in [26], the authors propose a characterization of the information divergences that are not sketchable, and prove that any distance that has not "norm-like" properties is not sketchable.

On the other hand, very few works have tackled the distributed streaming model, also called the functional monitoring problem [27], which combines features of both the streaming model and communication complexity models. As in the streaming model, the input data is read on the fly, and processed with a minimum workspace and time. In the communication complexity model, each node receives an input data stream, performs some local computation, and communicates only with a coordinator who wishes to continuously compute or estimate a given function of the union of all the input streams. The challenging issue in this model is for the coordinator to compute the given function by minimizing the number of communicated bits [27–29]. Cormode *et al.* [27] pioneer the formal study of functions in this model by focusing on the estimation of the first three frequency moments F_0, F_1 and F_2 [14]. Arackaparambil *et al.* [28] consider the empirical entropy estimation [14] and improve the work of Cormode by providing lower bounds on the frequency moments, and finally distributed algorithms for counting at any time t the number of items that have been received by a set of nodes from the inception of their streams have been proposed in [30,31].

We go a step further by studying the dispersion matrix of distributed streams. Specifically, we propose a novel metric that allows us to approximate in real time the correlation between distributed and massive streams. This metric, called the sketch codeviation, allows us to quantify how observed data items change together, and in which proportion. As shown in [32], such a network-wide traffic monitoring tool should allow monitoring applications to get significant information on the traffic behavior changes to subsequently inform more detailed detection tools on where DDoS attacks are currently active. We provide a distributed algorithm that additively approximates the codeviation among n data streams $\sigma_1, \ldots, \sigma_n$ by using a sublinear number of bits of space for each of the n nodes, sublinear in the domain size from which items values are drawn, and in the largest size of these data streams.

We then generalize our approach by proposing a novel metric, named *Sketch-⋆ metric* in the following, that reflects the relationships between any two massive data streams. Actually, the problem of detecting changes or outliers in a data stream is similar to the problem of identifying patterns that do not conform to an expected behavior, which has been an active area of research for many decades. To accurately analyze streams of data, a panel of information-theoretic measures and distances have been proposed as key measures in statistical inference and data processing problems [33]. There exist two broad classes of measures, namely the f-divergences, introduced by Csiszar, Morimoto and Ali and Silvey [34–36], and the Bregman divergences, which are very important to quantify the amount of information that separates two distributions. Among them, the most commonly used are the Kullback-Leibler (KL) divergence [37], the Jensen-Shannon divergence and the Battacharyya distance [38]. More details can be found in the comprehensive survey of Basseville [33].

Unfortunately, computing information theoretic measures of distances in the data stream model is challenging essentially because one needs to process a huge amount of data sequentially, on the fly, and by using very little storage with respect to the size of the stream. In addition the analysis must be robust over time to detect any sudden change in the observed streams.

We tackle this issue with the *Sketch-⋆ metric*. This metric allows us to efficiently and accurately estimate a broad class of distance measures between any two large data streams. Such an estimation is achieved by computing these distances only on compact synopses or sketches of streams. The *Sketch-⋆ metric* is distribution-free and makes no assumption about the underlying data volume. It is thus capable of comparing any two data streams, identifying their correlation if any, and more generally, it allows us to acquire a deep understanding of the structure of the input streams. Formalization of this metric is one of the contributions of this paper. We present an approximation algorithm that constructs a sketch of the stream from which the *Sketch-⋆ metric* is computed. As for the codeviation, this algorithm is a one-pass algorithm. It uses very basic computations, little storage space (*i.e.*, logarithmic in the size of the input stream and the number of items in the stream), and does not need any information on the structure of the input stream.

Road Map of the Paper. In Sect. 2, we present the computational model under which we analyze our algorithms and derive bounds, and recall some mathematical background that will be needed in the remaining of the paper.

We present in Sect. 3 the sketch codeviation that allows us to approximate in real time the correlation between distributed and massive streams. We give upper and lower bounds on the quality of this approximated metric with respect to the codeviation in Sect. 3.2. As in [6], we use the codeviation analysis method, which is a statistical-based method that does not rely upon any knowledge of the nominal packet distribution. We then provide in Sect. 3.3 the algorithm that computes the sketch codeviation between any two data streams. We extend this algorithm to handle distributed streams. Section 3.4 presents our distributed algorithm additively approximates the codeviation among n data streams $\sigma_1, \ldots, \sigma_n$ by using $\mathcal{O}\left((1/\varepsilon) \log(1/\delta) (\log N + \log m)\right)$ bits of space for each of the n nodes, where N is the domain size from which items values are drawn, and m is the largest size of these data streams (more formally, $m = \max_{i \in [n]} \|X_{\sigma_i}\|_1$ where X_{σ_i} is the fingerprint vector representing the items frequency in stream σ_i). We guarantee that for any $0 < \delta < 1$, the maximal error of our estimation is bounded by $\varepsilon m/N$, as shown by performance evaluation results presented in Sect. 3.5.

The *Sketch-⋆ metric*, which allows us to efficiently estimate a broad class of distances measures between any two large data streams by computing these distances only using compact synopses or sketches of the streams is introduced in Sect. 4. Formalization of the *Sketch-⋆ metric* is presented in Sect. 4.2. The description of the algorithm that approximates the *Sketch-⋆ metric* in one pass appears in Sect. 4.3. This algorithm uses very basic computations, little storage space (*i.e.*, $\mathcal{O}(t(\log N + k \log m))$ where k and t are precision parameters, and m and N are respectively the size of the input stream and the domain size from which items values are drawn), and does not need any information on the structure of the input stream. Finally, the robustness of our approach is validated with a detailed experimentation study based on both synthetic traces that range from stable streams to highly skewed ones, and real data sets.

2 Data Stream Model

2.1 Model

We present the computation model under which we analyze our algorithms and derive lower and upper bounds. We consider a set of n nodes $S_1, \ldots, S_n$ such that each node S_i receives a large sequence σ_{S_i} of data items or symbols. We assume that streams $\sigma_{S_1}, \ldots, \sigma_{S_n}$ do not necessarily have the same size, *i.e.*, some of the items present in one stream do not necessarily appear in others or their occurrence number may differ from one stream to another one. We also suppose that node S_i ($1 \leq i \leq n$) does not know the length of its input stream. Items arrive regularly and quickly, and due to memory constraints (*i.e.*, nodes can locally store only a small amount of information with respect to the size of their input stream and perform simple operations on them), need to be processed sequentially and in an online manner. Nodes cannot communicate among each other. On the other hand, there exists a specific node, called the *coordinator* in the following, with which each node may communicate [27]. We assume that communication is instantaneous. We refer the reader to [39] for a detailed description of data streaming models and algorithms. Note that in the IoT context, it may not be reasonnable to rely on a central entity. We could extend our distributed solution to a fully decentralized version by organizing sites in such a way that each one could locally aggregate the information provided by its neighbours, as done in [40].

2.2 Preliminaries

We first present notations and background that make this paper self-contained. Let σ be a stream of data items that arrive sequentially. Each data item i is drawn from the universe $\Omega = \{1, 2, \ldots, N\}$, where N is very large. A natural approach to study a data stream σ of length m is to model it as a fingerprint vector over the universe Ω, given by $X = (x_1, x_2, \ldots, x_N)$ where x_i represents the number of occurrences of data item i in σ. Note that in the following by abusing the notation, we denote this "$|\Omega|$-point distribution" by "Ω-point distribution", also known as the item frequency vector of σ. Note also that $0 \leq x_i \leq m$. We have $\|X\|_1 = \sum_{i \in \Omega} x_i$, *i.e.*, $\|X\|_1$ is the norm of X. Thus $m = \|X\|_1$. A natural approach to study a data stream σ is to model it as an empirical data distribution over the universe Ω, given by $(p_1, p_2, \ldots, p_N)$ with $p_i = x_i/m$.

2-Universal Hash Functions. In the following, we use hash functions randomly picked from a 2-universal hash family. A collection H of hash functions $h : \{1, \ldots, M\} \to \{0, \ldots, M'\}$ is said to be *2-universal* if for every $h \in H$ and for every two different items $x, y \in [M]$, $\mathbb{P}\{h(x) = h(y)\} \leq \frac{1}{M'}$, which is exactly the probability of collision obtained if the hash function assigns truly random values to any $x \in [M]$.

Randomized (ε, δ)-additively-approximation Algorithm. A randomized algorithm $\mathcal{A}$ is said to be an (ε, δ)-additively-approximation of a function ϕ on σ if, for any sequence of items in the input stream σ, $\mathcal{A}$ outputs $\hat{\phi}$ such that $\mathbb{P}\{|\hat{\phi} - \phi| > \varepsilon\} < \delta$, where $\varepsilon, \delta > 0$ are given as parameters of the algorithm.

3   Correlation Estimation Using Codeviation

3.1   Codeviation

In this paper, we focus on the computation of the deviation between any two streams using a space efficient algorithm with some error guarantee. The extension to a distributed environment $\sigma_1, \ldots, \sigma_n$ is studied in Sect. 3.4. We propose a metric over Ω-point distributions of items, which is inspired from the classical covariance metric in statistics. Such a metric allows us to qualify the dependance or correlation between two quantities by comparing their variations. As will be shown in Sect. 3.5, this metric captures shifts in the network-wide traffic behavior when a DDoS attack is active. The codeviation between any two Ω-point distributions $X = (x_1, x_2, \ldots, x_N)$, and $Y = (y_1, y_2, \ldots, y_N)$ is the real number denoted $\text{cod}(X, Y)$ defined by

$$\text{cod}(X, Y) = \frac{1}{N} \sum_{i \in \Omega} (x_i - \overline{x})(y_i - \overline{y}) = \frac{1}{N} \sum_{i \in \Omega} x_i y_i - \overline{x}\,\overline{y} \tag{1}$$

$$\text{where } \overline{x} = \frac{1}{N} \sum_{i \in \Omega} x_i \text{ and } \overline{y} = \frac{1}{N} \sum_{i \in \Omega} y_i.$$

3.2   Sketch codeviation

As presented in the Introduction, we propose a statistic tool, named the sketch codeviation, which allows to approximate the codeviation between any two data streams using compact synopses or sketches. We then give bounds on the quality of this tool with respect to the computation of the codeviation applied on full streams.

Definition 1 (Sketch codeviation). *Let X and Y be any two Ω-point distributions of items, such that $X = (x_1, \ldots, x_N)$ and $Y = (y_1, \ldots, y_N)$. Given a* *precision parameter k, we define the sketch codeviation between X and Y as*

$$\widehat{\mathrm{cod}}_k(X,Y) = \min_{\rho \in \mathcal{P}_k(\Omega)} \mathrm{cod}\left(\widehat{X}_\rho, \widehat{Y}_\rho\right)$$

$$= \min_{\rho \in \mathcal{P}_k(\Omega)} \left(\frac{1}{N}\sum_{a \in \rho}\widehat{X}_\rho(a)\widehat{Y}_\rho(a) - \left(\frac{1}{N}\sum_{a \in \rho}\widehat{X}_\rho(a)\right)\left(\frac{1}{N}\sum_{a \in \rho}\widehat{Y}_\rho(a)\right)\right)$$

where $\forall a \in \rho, \widehat{X}_\rho(a) = \sum_{i \in a} x_i$, and $\mathcal{P}_k(\Omega)$ is a k-cell partition of Ω, i.e., the set of all the partitions of the set Ω into exactly k nonempty and mutually disjoint sets (or cells).

Lemma 1. *Let $X = (x_1, \ldots, x_N)$, and $Y = (y_1, \ldots, y_N)$ be any two Ω-point distributions. We have*

$$\widehat{\mathrm{cod}}_N(X,Y) = \mathrm{cod}(X,Y)$$

Proof. It exists a unique partition ρ_N of N into exactly N nonempty and mutually disjoint sets, such that ρ_N is made of N singletons: $\rho_N = \{\{1\}, \{2\}, \ldots, \{N\}\}$. Thus for any cell $a \in \rho_N$, there exists a unique $i \in \Omega$ such that $\widehat{X}_\rho(a) = x_i$. Thus, $\widehat{X}_\rho = X$ and $\widehat{Y}_\rho = Y$. $\qquad\square$

Note that for $k > N$, it does not exist a partition of N into k nonempty parts. By convention, for $k > N$, $\widehat{\mathrm{cod}}_k(X,Y) = \widehat{\mathrm{cod}}_N(X,Y)$.

Proposition 1. *The sketch codeviation is a function of the codeviation. We have*

$$\widehat{\mathrm{cod}}_k(X,Y) = \mathrm{cod}(X,Y) + \mathcal{E}_k(X,Y)$$

where $\quad \mathcal{E}_k(X,Y) = \min_{\rho \in \mathcal{P}_k(\Omega)} \frac{1}{N}\sum_{a \in \rho}\sum_{i \in a}\sum_{j \in a \setminus \{i\}} x_i y_j.$

Proof. From Relation (1), we have

$$\widehat{\mathrm{cod}}_k(X,Y) = \min_{\rho \in \mathcal{P}_k(\Omega)}\left(\left(\frac{1}{N}\sum_{a \in \rho}\widehat{X}_\rho(a)\widehat{Y}_\rho(a)\right) - \left(\frac{1}{N}\sum_{a \in \rho}\widehat{X}_\rho(a)\right)\left(\frac{1}{N}\sum_{a \in \rho}\widehat{Y}_\rho(a)\right)\right)$$

$$= \min_{\rho \in \mathcal{P}_k(\Omega)}\left(\left(\frac{1}{N}\sum_{a \in \rho}\left(\sum_{i \in a}x_i\right)\left(\sum_{i \in a}y_i\right)\right) - \left(\frac{1}{N}\sum_{i \in \Omega}x_i\right)\left(\frac{1}{N}\sum_{j \in \Omega}y_j\right)\right)$$

$$= \min_{\rho \in \mathcal{P}_k(\Omega)}\left(\left(\frac{1}{N}\sum_{a \in \rho}\left(\sum_{i \in a}\sum_{j \in a}x_i y_j\right)\right) - \overline{x}\,\overline{y}\right)$$

$$= \mathrm{cod}(X,Y) + \min_{\rho \in \mathcal{P}_k(\Omega)}\frac{1}{N}\sum_{a \in \rho}\sum_{i \in a}\sum_{j \in a \setminus \{i\}} x_i y_j.$$

which concludes the proof. $\qquad\square$

The value $\mathcal{E}_k(X,Y)$ (which corresponds to the minimum sums over any partition ρ in $\mathcal{P}_k(\Omega)$) represents the *overestimation factor* of the sketch codeviation with respect to the codeviation.

Derivation of Lower Bounds on $\mathcal{E}_k(X,Y)$. We first show that if k is large enough, then the overestimation factor $\mathcal{E}_k(X,Y)$ is null, that is, the sketch codeviation matches exactly the codeviation.

Theorem 1 (Accuracy of the sketch codeviation). *Let X and Y be any two Ω-point distributions of items, such that $X = (x_1,\ldots,x_N)$ and $Y = (y_1,\ldots,y_N)$. If $k \geq |\operatorname{supp}(X) \cap \operatorname{supp}(Y)| + \mathbf{1}_{\operatorname{supp}(X)\smallsetminus\operatorname{supp}(Y)} + \mathbf{1}_{\operatorname{supp}(Y)\smallsetminus\operatorname{supp}(X)}$ then*

$$\widehat{\operatorname{cod}}_k(X,Y) = \operatorname{cod}(X,Y),$$

where $\operatorname{supp}(X)$, respectively $\operatorname{supp}(Y)$, represents the support of distribution X, respectively Y (i.e., the set of items in Ω that have a non null frequency $x_i \neq 0$, respectively $y_i \neq 0$, for $1 \leq i \leq N$), and notation $\mathbf{1}_A$ denotes the indicator function which is equal to 1 if the set A is not empty and 0 otherwise.

Proof. Two cases are examined.

– **Case 1:**
 Let $k = |\operatorname{supp}(X) \cap \operatorname{supp}(Y)| + \mathbf{1}_{\operatorname{supp}(X)\smallsetminus\operatorname{supp}(Y)} + \mathbf{1}_{\operatorname{supp}(Y)\smallsetminus\operatorname{supp}(X)}$. We consider a partition $\overline{\rho} \in \mathcal{P}_k(\Omega)$ defined as follows

$$\begin{cases} \forall \ell \in \operatorname{supp}(X) \cap \operatorname{supp}(Y), \{\ell\} \in \overline{\rho} \\ \operatorname{supp}(X) \smallsetminus \operatorname{supp}(Y) \in \overline{\rho} \\ \operatorname{supp}(X)^{\complement} \in \overline{\rho} \end{cases} \tag{2}$$

Then from Relation (2) we have

$$\begin{cases} \forall \ell \in \operatorname{supp}(X) \cap \operatorname{supp}(Y), \displaystyle\sum_{i \in \{\ell\}} \sum_{j \in \{\ell\}\smallsetminus\{i\}} x_i y_j = 0 \\ \forall \ell \in \operatorname{supp}(X) \smallsetminus \operatorname{supp}(Y), y_\ell = 0 \\ \forall \ell \in \operatorname{supp}(X)^{\complement}, \qquad x_\ell = 0. \end{cases}$$

Thus, $\sum_{a \in \overline{\rho}} \sum_{i \in a} \sum_{j \in a \smallsetminus \{i\}} x_i y_j = 0$. From Proposition (1), we get that $\widehat{\operatorname{cod}}_k(X,Y) = \operatorname{cod}(X,Y)$.
– **Case 2:**
 For $k > |\operatorname{supp}(X) \cap \operatorname{supp}(Y)| + \mathbf{1}_{\operatorname{supp}(X)\smallsetminus\operatorname{supp}(Y)} + \mathbf{1}_{\operatorname{supp}(Y)\smallsetminus\operatorname{supp}(X)}$ (and $k < N$), it is always possible to split one of the two last cells of $\overline{\rho}$ as defined in Relation (2) with a singleton $\{\ell\}$ such that $x_\ell = 0$ or $y_\ell = 0$.

Both cases complete the proof. □

Derivation of Upper Bounds on $\mathcal{E}_k(X,Y)$. We have shown with Theorem 1 that the sketch codeviation matches exactly the codeviation if $k \geq |\operatorname{supp}(X) \cap \operatorname{supp}(Y)| + \mathbf{1}_{\operatorname{supp}(X)\smallsetminus\operatorname{supp}(Y)} + \mathbf{1}_{\operatorname{supp}(Y)\smallsetminus\operatorname{supp}(X)}$. In this section, we characterize the upper bound of the overestimation factor, *i.e.*, the error made with respect to the codeviation, when k is strictly less than this bound. To prevent problems of measurability, we restrict the classes of Ω-point distribution under consideration. Specifically, given $m_{\mathcal{X}}$ and $m_{\mathcal{Y}}$ any positive integers, we define the two classes $\mathcal{X}$ and $\mathcal{Y}$ as $\mathcal{X} = \{X = (x_1, \ldots, x_N) \text{ such that } ||X||_1 = m_{\mathcal{X}}\}$ and $\mathcal{Y} = \{Y = (y_1, \ldots, y_N) \text{ such that } ||Y||_1 = m_{\mathcal{Y}}\}$. The following theorem derives the maximum value of the overestimation factor.

Theorem 2 (Upper bound of $\mathcal{E}_k(X,Y)$). *Let $k \geq 1$ be the precision parameter of the sketch codeviation. For any two Ω-point distributions $X \in \mathcal{X}$ and $Y \in \mathcal{Y}$, let $\mathcal{E}_k$ be the maximum value of the overestimation factor $\mathcal{E}_k(X,Y)$. Then, the following relation holds.*

$$\mathcal{E}_k = \max_{X \in \mathcal{X}, Y \in \mathcal{Y}} \mathcal{E}_k(X,Y) = \begin{cases} \dfrac{m_{\mathcal{X}} m_{\mathcal{Y}}}{N} & \text{if } k = 1, \\[2ex] \dfrac{m_{\mathcal{X}} m_{\mathcal{Y}}}{N} \left(\dfrac{1}{k} - \dfrac{1}{N} \right) & \text{if } k > 1. \end{cases}$$

Proof. For readability reason, the proof of this theorem is presented in Appendix A. □

Theorem 2 shows that for any $k \geq 1$, the maximum value $\mathcal{E}_k$ of the overestimation factor of the sketch codeviation is less than or equal to $m_{\mathcal{X}} m_{\mathcal{Y}}/N$. We now demonstrate that, given X and Y, the overestimation factor $\mathcal{E}_k(X,Y)$ is a decreasing function in k.

Lemma 2. *Let X and Y be any two Ω-point distributions. We have:*

$$\mathcal{E}_1(X,Y) \geq \mathcal{E}_2(X,Y) \geq \ldots \geq \mathcal{E}_k(X,Y) \geq \ldots \geq \mathcal{E}_N(X,Y).$$

Proof.

– **Case** $k = 1$. By assumption, $|\mathcal{P}_1(\Omega)| = 1$, *i.e.*, there exists a single partition which is the set Ω itself. Thus we directly have

$$\mathcal{E}_1(X,Y) = \frac{1}{N} \sum_{i \in \Omega} \sum_{j \in \Omega \smallsetminus \{i\}} x_i y_j. \qquad (3)$$

– **Case** $k = 2$. For any partition $\{a_1, a_2\} \in \mathcal{P}_2(\Omega)$, we have

$$\mathcal{E}_1(X,Y) = \frac{1}{N} \left(\sum_{i \in a_1} \sum_{j \in a_1 \smallsetminus \{i\}} x_i y_j + \sum_{i \in a_1} \sum_{j \in a_2} x_i y_j \right.$$

$$\left. + \sum_{i \in a_2} \sum_{j \in a_1} x_i y_j + \sum_{i \in a_2} \sum_{j \in a_2 \smallsetminus \{i\}} x_i y_j \right)$$

$$= \mathcal{E}_2^\rho(X,Y) + \frac{1}{N} \left(\sum_{i \in a_1} \sum_{j \in a_2} x_i y_j + \sum_{i \in a_2} \sum_{j \in a_1} x_i y_j \right)$$

$$\geq \mathcal{E}_2(X,Y).$$

– **Case** $2 < k < N$. Let $\overline{\rho} = \mathrm{argmin}_{\rho \in \mathcal{P}_k(\Omega)} \mathcal{E}_k^\rho(X, Y)$, *i.e.*, partition $\overline{\rho}$ minimizes the overestimation factor for a given k. Then, there exists a partition $\rho' \in \mathcal{P}_{k+1}(\Omega)$ that can be obtained by splitting a cell of $\overline{\rho}$ in two cells, and constructed as follows

$$\begin{cases} \exists a_0 \in \overline{\rho}, \exists a_1, a_2 \in \rho', \text{ such that } a_0 = a_1 \cup a_2 \\ \forall a \in \overline{\rho}, a \neq a_0 \Rightarrow \exists a' \in \rho', \text{ such that } a = a'. \end{cases}$$

By using an argument similar to the previous one, we have

$$\mathcal{E}_k(X, Y) = \mathcal{E}_{k+1}^{\rho'}(X, Y) + \frac{1}{N} \left(\sum_{i \in a_1} \sum_{j \in a_2} x_i y_j + \sum_{i \in a_2} \sum_{j \in a_1} x_i y_j \right)$$

$$\geq \mathcal{E}_{k+1}(X, Y).$$

Lemma 1 concludes the proof.   □

3.3   Approximation Algorithm

In this section, we propose a one-pass algorithm that computes the sketch codeviation between any two large input streams. By definition of the metric (*cf.* Definition 1), we need to generate all the possible k-cell partitions. The number of these partitions follows the Stirling numbers of the second kind, which is equal to $S(N, k) = \frac{1}{k!} \sum_{j=0}^{k} (-1)^{k-j} \binom{k}{j} j^N$. Therefore, $S(N, k)$ grows exponentially with N. We show in the following that generating $t = \lceil \log(1/\delta) \rceil$ random k-cell partitions, where δ is the probability of error of our randomized algorithm, is sufficient to guarantee good overall performance of the sketch codeviation metric.

Our algorithm is inspired from the Count-Min Sketch algorithm proposed by Cormode and Muthukrishnan [41]. Specifically, the Count-Min algorithm is an (ε, δ)-approximation algorithm that solves the *frequency-estimation* problem. For any item v in the input stream σ, the algorithm outputs an estimation $\hat{x}_v$ of v such that $\mathbb{P}\{|\hat{x}_v - x_v| > \varepsilon(||X||_1 - x_v)\} < \delta$, where $\varepsilon, \delta > 0$ are given as parameters of the algorithm. The estimation is computed by constructing a two-dimensional array C of $t \times k$ counters through a collection of 2-universal hash functions $\{h_\ell\}_{1 \leq \ell \leq t}$, where $k = e/\varepsilon$ and $t = \lceil \log(1/\delta) \rceil$. Each time an item v is read from the input stream, this causes one counter per line to be incremented, *i.e.*, $C[\ell][h_\ell(v)]$ is incremented for all $\ell \in [t]$.

To compute the sketch codeviation of any two streams σ_1 and σ_2, two sketches $\hat{\sigma}_1$ and $\hat{\sigma}_2$ of these streams are constructed according to the above description (*i.e.*, construction of two arrays C_{σ_1} and C_{σ_1} of $t \times k$ counters through t 2-universal hash functions $\{h_\ell\}_{1 \leq \ell \leq t}$). Note that there is no particular assumption on the length of both streams σ_1 and σ_2 (their respective length m_1 and m_2 are finite but unknown). By properties of the 2-universal hash functions $\{h_\ell\}_{1 \leq \ell \leq t}$, each line ℓ of C_{σ_1} and C_{σ_2} corresponds to the same partition ρ_ℓ of Ω, and each entry a of line ℓ corresponds to $\hat{X}_{\rho_\ell}(a)$ (*cf.* Definition 1). Therefore, when a query

---

Algorithm 1. Sketch codeviation algorithm

Input: Two input streams σ_1 and σ_2; δ and ε precision settings;

Output: The sketch codeviation $\widehat{\text{cod}}_k(\sigma_1, \sigma_2)$ between σ_1 and σ_2

1 $t \leftarrow \lceil \ln \frac{1}{\delta} \rceil$; $k \leftarrow \lceil \frac{e}{\varepsilon} \rceil$;

2 Choose t functions $h : \Omega \rightarrow [k]$, each from a 2-universal hash function family;

3 $C_{\sigma_1}[1..t][1..k] \leftarrow 0$;

4 $C_{\sigma_2}[1..t][1..k] \leftarrow 0$;

5 **for** $i \in \sigma_1$ **do**

6   **for** $\ell = 1$ **to** t **do**

7         $C_{\sigma_1}[\ell][h_\ell(i)] \leftarrow C_{\sigma_1}[\ell][h_\ell(i)] + 1$;

8 **for** $j \in \sigma_2$ **do**

9   **for** $\ell = 1$ **to** t **do**

10         $C_{\sigma_2}[\ell][h_\ell(j)] \leftarrow C_{\sigma_2}[\ell][h_\ell(j)] + 1$;

11 **On query** $\widehat{\text{cod}}(\sigma_1, \sigma_2)$ **return** $\min_{1 \le \ell \le t} \text{cod}(C_{\sigma_1}[\ell][-], C_{\sigma_2}[\ell][-])$

---

is issued to compute the sketch codeviation $\widehat{\text{cod}}$ between these two streams, the codeviation value between the ℓth line of C_{σ_1} and C_{σ_2} for each $\ell = 1 \dots t$ is computed, and the minimum value among these t ones is returned. Algorithm 1 presents the pseudo-code of our algorithm.

Theorem 3. *The sketch codeviation* $\widehat{\text{cod}}(X, Y)$ *returned by Algorithm 1 satisfies, with* $E_{\text{cod}} = \widehat{\text{cod}}(X, Y) - \text{cod}(X, Y),$

$$E_{\text{cod}} \ge 0 \text{ and } \mathbb{P}\left\{ |E_{\text{cod}}| \ge \frac{\varepsilon}{N} \left(\|X\|_1 \|Y\|_1 - \|XY\|_1 \right) \right\} \le \delta.$$

Proof. The first relation holds by Proposition 1. Regarding the second one, let us first consider the ℓ-th line of both C_{σ_1} and C_{σ_2}. We have

$$\widehat{\text{cod}}[\ell](X, Y) = \text{cod}(C_{\sigma_1}[\ell][-], C_{\sigma_2}[\ell][-])$$

$$= \frac{1}{N} \sum_{a=1}^{k} C_{\sigma_1}[\ell][a] C_{\sigma_2}[\ell][a] - \left(\frac{1}{N} \sum_{a=1}^{k} C_{\sigma_1}[\ell][a] \right) \left(\frac{1}{N} \sum_{a=1}^{k} C_{\sigma_1}[\ell][u] \right).$$

By construction of Algorithm 1, $\forall 1 \le \ell \le t, \forall i, j \in \sigma_1$ such that $h_\ell(i) = h_\ell(j) = a$, we have

$$C_{\sigma_1}[\ell][a] = x_i + \sum_{j \neq i} x_j.$$

Similarly, $\forall 1 \le \ell \le t, \forall i, j \in \sigma_2$ such that $h_\ell(i) = h_\ell(j) = a$, we have

$$C_{\sigma_2}[\ell][a] = y_i + \sum_{j \neq i} y_j.$$

Thus,

$$
\begin{aligned}
\widehat{\mathrm{cod}}[\ell](X,Y) &= \frac{1}{N} \sum_{a=1}^{k} \left(\sum_{\substack{i=1 \\ h_\ell(i)=a}}^{N} x_i \right) \left(\sum_{\substack{i=1 \\ h_\ell(i)=a}}^{N} y_i \right) \\
&\quad - \frac{1}{N} \sum_{a=1}^{k} \left(\sum_{\substack{i=1 \\ h_\ell(i)=a}}^{N} x_i \right) \frac{1}{N} \sum_{a=1}^{k} \left(\sum_{\substack{i=1 \\ h_\ell(i)=a}}^{N} y_i \right) \\
&= \frac{1}{N} \sum_{i=1}^{N} x_i y_i + \frac{1}{N} \sum_{\substack{i \neq j \\ h_\ell(i)=h_\ell(j)}} x_i y_j - \left(\frac{1}{N} \sum_{i=1}^{N} x_i \right) \left(\frac{1}{N} \sum_{i=1}^{N} y_i \right) \\
&= \mathrm{cod}(X,Y) + \frac{1}{N} \sum_{\substack{i \neq j \\ h_\ell(i)=h_\ell(j)}} x_i y_j
\end{aligned}
$$

We have

$$
\mathbb{E}\left[\widehat{\mathrm{cod}}[\ell](X,Y) \right] = \mathbb{E}\left[\mathrm{cod}(X,Y) \right] + \frac{1}{N} \sum_{i \neq j} x_i y_j \mathbb{P}\{h_\ell(i)=h_\ell(j)\}.
$$

By linearity of the expectation, we get

$$
\mathbb{E}\left[\widehat{\mathrm{cod}}[\ell](X,Y) - \mathrm{cod}(X,Y) \right] = \frac{1}{N} \sum_{i \neq j} x_i y_j \mathbb{P}\{h_\ell(i)=h_\ell(j)\}.
$$

By definition of 2-universal hash functions, we have $\mathbb{P}\{h_\ell(i) = h_\ell(j)\} \leq \frac{1}{k}$. Therefore,

$$
\mathbb{E}\left[\widehat{\mathrm{cod}}[\ell](X,Y) - \mathrm{cod}(X,Y) \right] \leq \frac{1}{Nk} \sum_{i \neq j} x_i y_j = \frac{1}{Nk} \left(\|X\|_1 \|Y\|_1 - \|XY\|_1 \right).
$$

By definition of k (*cf.* Algorithm 1), we have

$$
\mathbb{E}\left[\widehat{\mathrm{cod}}[\ell](X,Y) - \mathrm{cod}(X,Y) \right] \leq \frac{\varepsilon}{eN} \left(\|X\|_1 \|Y\|_1 - \|XY\|_1 \right)
$$

Using the Markov inequality, we obtain

$$
\mathbb{P}\left\{ |\widehat{\mathrm{cod}}[\ell](X,Y) - \mathrm{cod}(X,Y)| \geq \frac{\varepsilon}{N} \left(\|X\|_1 \|Y\|_1 - \|XY\|_1 \right) \right\} \leq \frac{1}{e}
$$

By construction $\widehat{\mathrm{cod}}(X,Y) = \min_{1 \leq \ell \leq t} \widehat{\mathrm{cod}}[\ell](X,Y)$. Thus, by definition of t (*cf.* Algorithm 1) we obtain

$$
\mathbb{P}\left\{ |\widehat{\mathrm{cod}}(X,Y) - \mathrm{cod}(X,Y)| \geq \frac{\varepsilon}{N} \left(\|X\|_1 \|Y\|_1 - \|XY\|_1 \right) \right\} \leq \left(\frac{1}{e} \right)^t = \delta
$$

that concludes the proof.   □

Lemma 3. *Algorithm 1 uses $\mathcal{O}\left((\frac{1}{\varepsilon})\log\frac{1}{\delta}(\log N + \log m)\right)$ bits of space to give an approximation of the sketch codeviation, where $m = \max(\|X\|_1, \|Y\|_1)$.*

Proof. Both matrices C_{σ_i} for $i \in \{1, 2\}$ are composed of $t \times k$ counters, where each counter uses $\mathcal{O}(\log m)$ bits of space. With a suitable choice of hash family, we can store each of the t hash functions above in $\mathcal{O}(\log N)$ space. This gives an overall space bound of $\mathcal{O}(t\log N + tk\log m)$, which proves the lemma with the chosen values of k and t. ∎

3.4 Distributed codeviation Approximation Algorithm

In this section, we propose an algorithm that computes the codeviation between a set of n distributed data streams, so that the number of bits communicated between the n sites and the coordinator is minimized. This amounts for the coordinator to compute an approximation of the codeviation matrix Σ, which is the dispersion matrix of the n data streams. As previously evoked in Sect. 2, it is possible to have a fully decentralized version of our algorithm, by for example, organizing the sites along a distributed hash table (DHT) and by taking profit of the additive property of the Count-Min data structure to allow each site to aggregate their schetch so have to progressively obtain a global view of the system. Such a possible solution appears in [40]. In the following we present the coordinator-based version for clarity of the analysis. Note however that the distributed version would have a non negligeable impact on the communication cost. This issue is left for future work.

Specifically, let $\mathbb{X} = \{X_1, X_2, \ldots, X_n\}$ be the set of Ω-point distributions $X_1, \ldots, X_n$ describing respectively the streams $\sigma_1, \ldots, \sigma_n$. We have

$$\widehat{\Sigma} = \left[\widehat{\text{cod}}(X_i, X_j)\right]_{1 \le i \le n, 1 \le j \le n}.$$

The algorithm proceeds in rounds until all the data streams have been read in their entirety. In the following, we denote by $\sigma_i^{(r)}$ the substream of σ_i received by S_i during the round r, and by d_r the number of data items in this substream.

In a bootstrap phase corresponding to round $r = 1$ of the algorithm, each site S_i computes a single sketch C_{σ_i} of the received data stream σ_i as described in lines 5–7 of Algorithm 1. Once node S_i has received d_1 data items (where d_1 should typically be set to 100 [28]), then node S_i sends $C_{\sigma_i^{(1)}}$ to the coordinator, keeps a copy of $C_{\sigma_i^{(1)}}$, and starts a new round $r = 2$. Upon receipt of $C_{\sigma_i^{(1)}}$ from any S_i, the coordinator asks all the $n - 1$ other nodes S_j to send their own sketch $C_{\sigma_j^{(1)}}$.

Once the coordinator has received all $C_{\sigma_i^{(1)}}$, for $1 \le i \le n$, it sets $\forall i \in [n], C_{\sigma_i} \leftarrow C_{\sigma_i^{(1)}}$. The coordinator builds the sketch codeviation matrix $\widehat{\Sigma} = \left[\widehat{\text{cod}}(X_i, X_j)\right]_{1 \le i \le n, 1 \le j \le n}$ such that the element in position i, j is the sketch codeviation between streams σ_i and σ_j. As the codeviation is symmetric, the codeviation matrix is a symmetric matrix, and thus only the upper-triangle and the diagonal need to be computed.

At round $r > 1$, each node S_i computes a new sketch $C_{\sigma_i^{(r)}}$ with the sequence of data streams received since the beginning of round r. Let $d_r = 2d_{r-1}$ be an upper bound on the number of received items during round r. When node S_i has received at least $d_{r-1}/2$ data items, it starts to compute the sketch codeviation between $C_{\sigma_i^{(r-1)}}$ and $C_{\sigma_i^{(r)}}$ as in line 11 of Algorithm 1. Once node S_i has received d_r data items since the beginning of round r, then it sends its current sketch $C_{\sigma_i^{(r)}}$ to the coordinator and starts a new round $r + 1$. Note that during round r, S_i regularly computes $\text{cod}\left(\sigma_i^{(r-1)}, \sigma_i^{(r)}\right)$ to detect whether significant variations in the stream have occurred before having received d_r items. This allows to inform the coordinator as quickly as possible that some attack might be undergoing. S_i might then send its current sketch $C_{\sigma_i^{(r)}}$ to the coordinator once $\text{cod}\left(\sigma_i^{(r-1)}, \sigma_i^{(r)}\right)$ has reached a sufficiently small value. An interesting question left for future work is the study of such a value. Upon receipt of the first $C_{\sigma_i^{(r)}}$ from any S_i, the coordinator asks all the $n - 1$ other nodes S_j to send it their own sketch $C_{\sigma_j^{(r)}}$. The coordinator locally updates the n sketches such as $C_{\sigma_i} \leftarrow C_{\sigma_i} + C_{\sigma_i^{(r)}}$ and updates the codeviation matrix $\widehat{\Sigma}$ on every couple of sketches.

Theorem 4. *The approximated codeviation matrix $\widehat{\Sigma}$ returned by the distributed sketch codeviation algorithm satisfies $\widehat{\Sigma} \geq \Sigma$ and*

$$\mathbb{P}\left\{ \left| \widehat{\Sigma} - \Sigma \right| \geq \frac{\varepsilon}{N} \max_{i,j \in [n]} \left(\|X_i\|_1 \|X_j\|_1 - \|X_i X_j\|_1 \right) \right\} \leq \delta.$$

Proof. The statement is derived from Theorem 3 and the fact that the expectation of a matrix is defined as the matrix of expected values. $\qquad\square$

Lemma 4 (Space complexity). *The distributed sketch codeviation algorithm gives an approximation of matrix Σ, using $\mathcal{O}\left((1/\varepsilon)\log(1/\delta)(\log N + \log m)\right)$ bits of space for each n nodes, and $\mathcal{O}\left(n \log m \left(1/\varepsilon \log(1/\delta) + n\right)\right)$ bits of space for the coordinator, where m is the maximum size among all the streams, i.e., $m = \max_{i \in [n]} \|X_i\|_1$.*

Proof. From the algorithm definition, each node maintains two sketches with space describes in Lemma 3. The coordinator maintains n matrices of $t \times k$ counters and the $n \times n$ codeviation matrix which takes $\mathcal{O}(n^2 \log m)$ bits, where $m = \max_{i \in [n]} \|X_i\|_1$. One can note that the coordinator does not need to maintain the t hash functions. $\qquad\square$

Lemma 5. (Communication complexity). *The distributed sketch codeviation algorithm gives an approximation of matrix Σ using a communication complexity of $\mathcal{O}\left(rn(1 + (1/\varepsilon)\log(m/2)\log(1/\delta))\right)$ bits, where r is the number of the last round and m is the maximum size of the streams.*

Proof. Suppose that the number of rounds of the algorithm is equal to r. At each round, the size of the substream on each node is at most doubled, and then lower or equal to $\frac{\|X_i\|_1}{2}$. An upper bound of number of bits sent by any node during a round r is trivially given by $(1/\varepsilon)\log(m/2)\log(1/\delta)$ where $m = \max_{i \in [n]} \|X_i\|_1$. Finally, at each end of round, the coordinator sends 1 bit to at most $n-1$ nodes. $\square$

Lemma 6 (Time complexity). *The time complexity of sketch codeviation is $\mathcal{O}(\log 1/\delta)$ per update in the reading phase of the stream, and $\mathcal{O}(1/\varepsilon \log 1/\delta)$ per query.*

Proof. Based on the pseudo-code provided in Algorithm 1, an update requires to hash the item, then retrieve and increase a cell for each row, thus the update time complexity is $O(\log 1/\delta)$. On the other hand, a query requires to sum the scalar product of each row, by retrieving each cell of the both data structure. The query time complexity is then $O(1/\varepsilon \log 1/\delta)$. $\square$

3.5 Performance Evaluation

We have implemented the distributed sketch codeviation algorithm and have conducted a series of experiments on different types of streams and for different parameters settings. We have fed our algorithm with both real-world data sets and synthetic traces. Real data give a realistic representation of some existing monitoring applications, while the latter ones allow to capture phenomenons which may be difficult to obtain from real-world traces, and thus allow to check the robustness of our metric. Synthetic traces of streams have been generated from 13 distributions showing very different shapes, that is the Uniform distribution (referred to as distribution 0 in the following), the Zipfian or power law one with parameter α from 1 to 5 (referred to as distributions $1, \ldots, 5$), the Poisson distribution with parameter λ from $N/2^1$ to $N/2^5$ (distributions $6, \ldots, 11$), and the Binomial and the Negative Binomial ones (distributions 12 and 13). All the streams generated from these distributions have a length of around $100,000$ items, and contain no more than $1,000$ distinct items. Real data have been downloaded from the repository of Internet network traffic [42]. We have used 5 large traces among the available ones. Two of them represent two weeks logs of HTTP requests to the Internet service provider ClarkNet WWW server – ClarkNet is a full Internet access provider for the Metro Baltimore-Washington DC area – the other two ones contain two months of HTTP requests to the NASA Kennedy Space Center WWW server, and the last one represents seven months of HTTP requests to the WWW server of the University of Saskatchewan, Canada. In the following these data sets will be respectively referred to as ClarkNet, NASA, and Saskatchewan traces. We have used as data items the source hosts of the HTTP requests. Table 1 presents some statistics of these five data traces, in term of stream size (*cf.* "# items"), number of distinct items in each stream (*cf.* "# distinct") and the number of occurrences of the most frequent item (*cf.* "max. freq."). Note that all these benchmarks share a Zipfian behavior, with a lower α for the University of Saskatchewan.

Table 1. Statistics of the five real data traces.

Data trace	Trace	# items (m)	# distinct (n)	max. freq
NASA (July)	0	1,891,715	81,983	17,572
NASA (August)	1	1,569,898	75,058	6,530
ClarkNet (August)	2	1,654,929	90,516	6,075
ClarkNet (September)	3	1,673,794	94,787	7,239
Saskatchewan	4	2,408,625	162,523	52,695

Experimental Evaluation of the Sketch codeviation. Figures 1 and 2 summarize the results obtained by feeding our distributed codeviation algorithm with respectively synthetics traces and real datasets. The isopeths on the left of respectively Figs. 1 and 2 represent the $n \times n$ codeviation matrix computed by storing in memory the streams in their entirety. The isopeths on the right of respectively Figs. 1 and 2 correspond to the $n \times n$ sketch codeviation matrix returned by the distributed algorithm based on sketches of size $k = \log N$. Both the x-axis and the y-axis represent the 13 synthetic streams on Fig. 1, and the 5

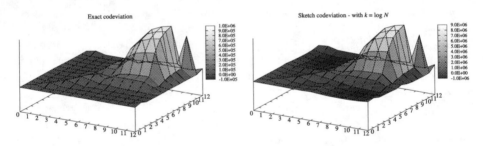

Fig. 1. Synthetic traces – The isopleth on the left has been computed with all the items in memory, while the one on the right has been computed by the distributed algorithm from sketches of length $k = \log N$.

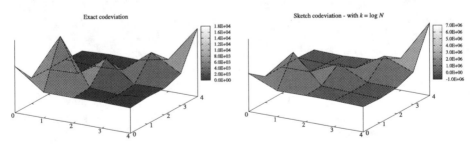

Fig. 2. Real datasets – The isopleth on the left has been computed with all the items in memory, while the one on the right has been computed by the distributed algorithm from sketches of length $k = \log N$.

real data sets on Fig. 2, while the z-axis represents the value of each cell matrix in both figures.

These results clearly show that our distributed algorithm is capable of efficiently and accurately quantifying how observed data streams change together and in which proportion whatever the shape of the input streams. Indeed, by using sketches of size $k = \log N$, one obtains isopeths very similar to the ones computed with all the items stored in memory. Note that the order of magnitude exhibited by the sketch codeviation matrix is due to the overestimation factor and remains proportional to the exact one. Both results from synthetic traces and real datasets lead to the same conclusions. The following experimental results focus on the detection of attacks.

Detection of Different Profiles of Attacks. Figure 3 shows how efficiently our approximation distributed algorithm detects different scenarii of attacks in real time. Specifically, we compute at each round of the distributed protocol, the distance between the codeviance matrix Σ constructed from the streams under investigation and the mean of covariance matrices $\mathbb{E}(\Sigma_N)$ computed under normal situations. This distance has been proposed in [6]. Specifically, given two square matrices M and M' of size n, consider the distance as follows:

$$\|M - M'\| = \sqrt{\sum_{i=1}^{n}\sum_{j=1}^{n}(M_{i,j} - M'_{i,j})^2}.$$

We evaluate at each round r, the variable d_r defined by

$$d_r = \|\Sigma_r - \mathbb{E}(\Sigma_N)\|.$$

Interestingly, Jin and Yeung [6] propose to detect abnormal behaviors with respect to normal ones as follows. First they analyze normal traffic-wide behaviors, and estimate at the end of analysis, a point c and a constant a for d_r satisfying $|d_r - c| < a, \forall r \in \mathbb{N}^*$. The constant a is selected as the upper threshold of the i.i.d $|d_r - c|$. Then when investigating the potential presence of DDoS attacks over the network, they consider as abnormal any traffic pattern that shows for any r, $|d_r - c| > a$. Because we think that it is not tractable to characterize what is a normal network-wide traffic *a priori*, we adapt this definition by considering the past behavior of the traffic under investigation. Specifically, at any round $r > 1$, the distance is computed between the current codeviance matrix Σ_r and the mean one $\mathbb{E}(\Sigma_r)$ corresponding to previous rounds $1, \ldots, r-1, r$. That is $\mathbb{E}(\Sigma_r) = ((r-1)\mathbb{E}(\Sigma_{r-1}) + \Sigma_r)/r$. As shown in Fig. 3(b), this distance provides better results than the ones obtained with the original distance [6], which is depicted in Fig. 3(a).

Based on these distances, we have fed our distributed algorithm with different patterns of traffic. Specifically, Fig. 3 shows the distance between the codeviance matrix and the mean ones (respectively based on normal ones for Fig. 3(a) and on past ones for Fig. 3(b)). These distances are depicted, as a function of time,

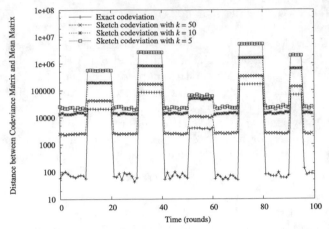

(a) With $\mathbb{E}(\Sigma_N)$ computed on "normal" traffic behavior

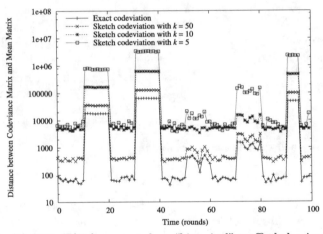

(b) With $\mathbb{E}(\Sigma_r)$ computed on "historical" traffic behavior

Fig. 3. Distance between the codeviation matrix and the mean of the past ones when all the 10 synthetic traces follow different distributions as a function of the rounds of the protocol, with $\delta = 10^{-5}$.

when the codeviance is exactly computed and when it is estimated with our distributed algorithm with different values of k. What can be seen is that, albeit there are up to two orders of magnitude between the exact codeviance matrix and the estimated one, the shape of the codeviance variations are for most of them similar, especially in Fig. 3(b). Different attack scenarii are simulated. From round 0 to 10, all the 10 synthetic traces follow the same nominal distribution (*e.g.*, a Poisson distribution). Then from round 10 to 20 a targeted attack is launched by flooding a single node (*i.e.*, one among the ten traces follows a Zipfian distribution with $\alpha = 4$). This gives rise to a drastic and abrupt increase of the distance. As can be shown, the estimated covariance exactly follows the exact one, which is a very good result. Then after coming back to a "normal" traffic, half of the traces are replaced by Zipfian ones (from round 30 to 40), representing a flooding attack toward a group of nodes. As for the previous attack, the covariance matrices are highly impacted by this attack. From round 50 to 60, traces follow a Zipfian distribution with $\alpha = 1$ which represents unbalanced network traffic but should not be completely representative of attacks. On the other hand, in the fourth and fifth attack periods, all the traces follow a Zipfian distribution with different values of $\alpha \geq 2$, which clearly shows a flooding attack toward a group of targeted nodes.

From these experiments, one could extract the value of the upper threshold a. For instance, a should be set to $1,000$ for the exact codeviation and for the sketch codeviation with $k = 50$, which lead to detect all the DDoS attacks. Considering the sketch codeviation with $k = 10$ (respectively $k = 5$), a should be set to $10,000$ (respectively $50,000$) in order to detect all these attacks.

The main lesson drawn from these results is the good performance of our distributed algorithm whatever the pattern of the attack.

4   Sketch-⋆ metric

We generalize the above approach by proposing the Sketch-⋆ metric that reflects the relationships between any two discrete probability distributions in the context of massive data streams. To accurately analyze streams of data, a panel of information-theoretic measures and distances have been proposed to answer the specificities of the analyses. Among them, the most commonly used are the Kullback-Leibler (KL) divergence [37], or more generically, the f-divergences, introduced by Csiszar, Morimoto and Ali & Silvey [34–36], the Jensen-Shannon divergence and the Battacharyya distance [38]. After having recalled the formal definitions of these metrics, we introduce the Sketch-⋆ metric specification, and then present a space and computation-efficient algorithm to compute any generalized metric ϕ between the summaries of any two stream σ_1 and σ_2, such that this computation preserves all the properties of ϕ computed on σ_1 and σ_2. We finally show the robustness of our approach through extensive simulations.

4.1   Metrics and Divergences

This section is devoted to the description of a collection of metrics.

Metric Definitions. The classical definition of a metric is based on a set of four axioms.

Definition 2 (Metric). *Given a set X, a metric is a function $d\colon X \times X \to \mathbb{R}$ such that, for any $x, y, z \in X$, we have:*

$$\text{Non-negativity:} \quad d(x, y) \geq 0 \tag{4}$$

$$\text{Identity of indiscernibles:} \quad d(x, y) = 0 \Leftrightarrow x = y \tag{5}$$

$$\text{Symmetry:} \quad d(x, y) = d(y, x) \tag{6}$$

$$\text{Triangle inequality:} \quad d(x, y) \leq d(x, z) + d(z, y) \tag{7}$$

In the context of information divergence, usual distance functions are not precisely metric. Indeed, most of divergence functions do not verify the 4 axioms, but only a subset of them. For instance, a pseudometric is a function that verifies the axioms of a metric with the exception of the identity of indiscernible, while a premetric is a pseudometric that relax both the symmetry and the triangle inequality axioms.

Definition 3 (Pseudometric). *Given a set X, a **pseudometric** is a function that verifies the axioms of a metric with the exception of the* identity of indiscernible, *which is replaced by*

$$\forall x \in X, d(x, x) = 0.$$

Note that this definition allows that $d(x, y) = 0$ for some $x \neq y$ in X.

Definition 4 (Quasimetric). *Given a set X, a **quasimetric** is a function that verifies all the axioms of a metric with the exception of the* symmetry *(cf. Relation 6).*

Definition 5 (Semimetric). *Given a set X, a **semimetric** is a function that verifies all the axioms of a metric with the exception of the* triangle inequality *(cf. Relation 7).*

Definition 6 (Premetric). *Given a set X, a **premetric** is a pseudometric that relax both the* symmetry *and* triangle inequality *axioms.*

Definition 7 (Pseudoquasimetric). *Given a set X, a **pseudoquasimetric** is a function that relax both the* identity of indiscernible *and the* symmetry *axioms.*

Note that the latter definition simply corresponds to a premetric satisfying the triangle inequality. Remark also that all the generalized metrics preserve the *non-negativity* axiom.

Two classes of generalized metrics, usually denoted as *divergences*, that allow to measure the separation of distributions have been proposed, namely the class of f-divergences and the class of Bregman divergences.

f**-divergence.** The class of f-divergences provides a set of relations that is used to measure the "distance" between two distributions p and q. Mostly used in the context of statistics and probability theory, a f-divergence $\mathcal{D}_f$ is a premetric that guarantees monotonicity and convexity.

Definition 8 (f-divergence). *Let p and q be two Ω-point distributions. Given a convex function $f : (0, \infty) \to \mathbb{R}$ such that $f(1) = 0$, the f-divergence of q from p is*

$$\mathcal{D}_f(p||q) = \sum_{i \in \Omega} q_i f\left(\frac{p_i}{q_i}\right),$$

where by convention, we assume that $0f(\frac{0}{0}) = 0$, $af(\frac{0}{a}) = a\lim_{u \to 0} f(u)$, and $0f(\frac{a}{0}) = a\lim_{u \to \infty} f(u)/u$ if these limits exist.

Property 1 (Monotonicity). Given κ an arbitrary transition probability that respectively transforms two Ω-point distributions p and q into p_κ and q_κ, we have:

$$\mathcal{D}_f(p||q) \geq \mathcal{D}_f(p_\kappa||q_\kappa).$$

Property 2 (Convexity). Let p_1, p_2, q_1 and q_2 be four Ω-point distributions. Given any $\lambda \in [0, 1]$, we have:

$$\mathcal{D}_f\left(\lambda p_1 + (1-\lambda)p_2||\lambda q_1 + (1-\lambda)q_2\right) \leq \lambda \mathcal{D}_f(p_1||q_1) + (1-\lambda)\mathcal{D}_f(p_2||q_2).$$

Bregman Divergence. Initially proposed in [43], the Bregman divergences are a generalization of the notion of distance between points. This class of generalized metrics always satisfies the non-negativity and identity of indecernibles. However they do not always satisfy the triangle inequality and their symmetry depends on the choice of the differentiable convex function F. Specifically,

Definition 9 (Bregman divergence (BD)). *Given a continuously-differentiable and strictly convex function F defined on a closed convex set C, the Bregman divergence of p from q is*

$$\mathcal{B}_F(p||q) = F(p) - F(q) - \langle \nabla F(q), (p - q)\rangle.$$

where the operator $\langle \cdot, \cdot \rangle$ denotes the inner product, and $\nabla F(q)$ is the gradient of F at q.

In the context of data stream, it is possible to reformulate this definition as follows. Specifically,

Definition 10 (Decomposable BD). *Let p and q be any two Ω-point distributions. Given a strictly convex function $F : (0, 1] \to \mathbb{R}$, the Bregman divergence of q from p is defined as*

$$\mathcal{B}_F(p||q) = \sum_{i \in \Omega}\left(F(p_i) - F(q_i) - (p_i - q_i)F'(q_i)\right).$$

The Bregman divergence verifies non-negativity and convexity properties in its first argument, but not necessarily in the second argument. Another interesting property is given by thinking of the Bregman divergence as an operator of the function F.

Property 3 (Linearity). Let F_1 and F_2 be any two strictly convex and differentiable functions. Given any $\lambda \in [0, 1]$, we have that

$$\mathcal{B}_{F_1 + \lambda F_2}(p||q) = \mathcal{B}_{F_1}(p||q) + \lambda \mathcal{B}_{F_2}(p||q).$$

Classical Metrics. Based on these definitions, we present several commonly used metrics in Ω-point distribution context. These specific metrics are used in the evaluation part presented in Sect. 4.4.

Kullback-Leibler divergence. The Kullback-Leibler (KL) divergence [37], also called the relative entropy, is a robust metric for measuring the statistical difference between two data streams. The KL divergence owns the special feature that it is both a f-divergence and a Bregman one (with $f(t) = F(t) = t \log t$).

Given p and q two Ω-point distributions, the Kullback-Leibler divergence is defined as

$$\mathcal{D}_{KL}(p||q) = \sum_{i \in \Omega} p_i \log \frac{p_i}{q_i}. \tag{8}$$

Jensen-Shannon divergence. The Jensen-Shannon divergence (JS) is a symmetrized version of the Kullback-Leibler divergence. Also known as information radius (IRad) or total divergence to the average, it is defined as

$$\mathcal{D}_{JS}(p||q) = \frac{1}{2} D_{KL}(p||\ell) + \frac{1}{2} D_{KL}(q||\ell), \tag{9}$$

where $\ell = \frac{1}{2}(p+q)$. Note that the square root of this divergence is a metric.

Bhattacharyya distance. The Bhattacharyya distance is derived from his proposed measure of similarity between two multinomial distributions, also known as the Bhattacharya coefficient (BC) [38]. It is a semimetric as it does not verify the triangle inequality. It is defined as

$$\mathcal{D}_B(p||q) = -\log(BC(p,q)) \text{ where } BC(p,q) = \sum_{i \in \Omega} \sqrt{p_i q_i}.$$

Note that the famous Hellinger distance [44] is equal to $\sqrt{1 - BC(p,q)}$ verifies it.

4.2   Sketch-⋆ Metric

We now present a method to sketch two input data streams σ_1 and σ_2, and to compute any generalized metric ϕ between these sketches such that this computation preserves all the properties of ϕ computed on σ_1 and σ_2.

Definition 11 (Sketch-⋆ metric). *Let p and q be any two Ω-point distributions. Given a precision parameter k, and any generalized metric ϕ on the set of all Ω-point distributions, there exists a Sketch-⋆ metric $\widehat{\phi}_k$ defined as follows*

$$\widehat{\phi}_k(p||q) = \max_{\rho \in \mathcal{P}_k(\Omega)} \phi(\widehat{p}_\rho||\widehat{q}_\rho).$$

We recall that, again, $\forall a \in \rho$, $\widehat{p}_\rho(a) = \sum_{i \in a} p_i$ and where $\mathcal{P}_k(\Omega)$ is the set of all partitions of Ω into exactly k nonempty and mutually exclusive cells.

Remark 1. Note that for $k > N$, it does not exist a partition of Ω into k non-empty parts. By convention, we consider that $\widehat{\phi}_k(p||q) = \phi(p||q)$ in this specific context.

In this section, we focus on the preservation of axioms and properties of a generalized metric ϕ by the corresponding *Sketch-$\star$ metric* $\widehat{\phi}_k$.

Axioms Preserving

Theorem 5. *Given any generalized metric ϕ then, for any $k \in \mathbb{N}$, the corresponding Sketch-$\star$ metric $\widehat{\phi}_k$ preserves all the axioms of ϕ.*

Proof. The proof is directly derived from Lemmata 7, 8, 9 and 10.   □

Lemma 7 (Non-negativity). *Given any generalized metric ϕ verifying the Non-negativity axiom then, for any $k \in \mathbb{N}$, the corresponding Sketch-$\star$ metric $\widehat{\phi}_k$ preserves the Non-negativity axiom.*

Proof. Let p and q be any two Ω-point distributions. By definition,

$$\widehat{\phi}_k(p||q) = \max_{\rho \in \mathcal{P}_k(\Omega)} \phi(\widehat{p}_\rho||\widehat{q}_\rho)$$

As for any two k-point distributions, ϕ is positive we have $\widehat{\phi}_k(p||q) \geq 0$ that concludes the proof.   □

Lemma 8 (Identity of indiscernible). *Given any generalized metric ϕ verifying the Identity of indiscernible axiom then, for any $k \in \mathbb{N}$, the corresponding Sketch-$\star$ metric $\widehat{\phi}_k$ preserves the Identity of indiscernible axiom.*

Proof. Let p be any Ω-point distribution. We have

$$\widehat{\phi}_k(p||p) = \max_{\rho \in \mathcal{P}_k(\Omega)} \phi(\widehat{p}_\rho||\widehat{p}_\rho) = 0,$$

due to the Identity of indiscernible axiom on ϕ.

Consider now two Ω-point distributions p and q such that $\widehat{\phi}_k(p||q) = 0$. Metric ϕ verifies both the non-negativity axiom (by construction) and the Identity of indiscernible axiom (by assumption). Thus we have $\forall \rho \in \mathcal{P}_k(\Omega), \widehat{p}_\rho = \widehat{q}_\rho$, leading to

$$\forall \rho \in \mathcal{P}_k(\Omega), \forall a \in \rho, \sum_{i \in a} p(i) = \sum_{i \in a} q(i). \tag{10}$$

Moreover, for any $i \in \Omega$, there exists a partition $\rho \in \mathcal{P}_k(\Omega)$ such that $\{i\} \in \rho$. By Eq. 10, $\forall i \in \Omega, p(i) = q(i)$, and so $p = q$.

Combining the two parts of the proof leads to $\widehat{\phi}_k(p||q) = 0 \Longleftrightarrow p = q$, which concludes the proof of the Lemma.   □

Lemma 9 (Symmetry). *Given any generalized metric ϕ verifying the Symmetry axiom then, for any $k \in \mathbb{N}$, the corresponding Sketch-$\star$ metric $\widehat{\phi}_k$ preserves the Symmetry axiom.*

Proof. Let p and q be any two Ω-point distributions. We have

$$\widehat{\phi}_k(p||q) = \max_{\rho \in \mathcal{P}_k(\Omega)} \phi(\widehat{p}_\rho||\widehat{q}_\rho).$$

Let $\overline{\rho} \in \mathcal{P}_k(\Omega)$ be a k-cell partition such that $\phi(\widehat{p}_{\overline{\rho}}||\widehat{q}_{\overline{\rho}}) = \max_{\rho \in \mathcal{P}_k(\Omega)} \phi(\widehat{p}_\rho||\widehat{q}_\rho)$. We get

$$\widehat{\phi}_k(p||q) = \phi(\widehat{p}_{\overline{\rho}}||\widehat{q}_{\overline{\rho}}) = \phi(\widehat{q}_{\overline{\rho}}||\widehat{p}_{\overline{\rho}}) \leq \widehat{\phi}_k(q||p).$$

By symmetry, considering $\underline{\rho} \in \mathcal{P}_k(\Omega)$ such that $\phi(\widehat{q}_{\underline{\rho}}||\widehat{p}_{\underline{\rho}}) = \max_{\rho \in \mathcal{P}_k(\Omega)} \phi(\widehat{q}_\rho||\widehat{p}_\rho)$, we also have $\widehat{\phi}_k(q||p) \leq \widehat{\phi}_k(p||q)$, which concludes the proof. $\square$

Lemma 10 (Triangle inequality). *Given any generalized metric ϕ verifying the Triangle inequality axiom then, for any $k \in \mathbb{N}$, the corresponding Sketch-$\star$ metric $\widehat{\phi}_k$ preserves the Triangle inequality axiom.*

Proof. Let p, q and r be any three Ω-point distributions. Let $\overline{\rho} \in \mathcal{P}_k(\Omega)$ be a k-cell partition such that $\phi(\widehat{p}_{\overline{\rho}}||\widehat{q}_{\overline{\rho}}) = \max_{\rho \in \mathcal{P}_k(\Omega)} \phi(\widehat{p}_\rho||\widehat{q}_\rho)$. We have

$$
\begin{aligned}
\widehat{\phi}_k(p||q) &= \phi(\widehat{p}_{\overline{\rho}}||\widehat{q}_{\overline{\rho}}) \\
&\leq \phi(\widehat{p}_{\overline{\rho}}||\widehat{r}_{\overline{\rho}}) + \phi(\widehat{r}_{\overline{\rho}}||\widehat{q}_{\overline{\rho}}) \\
&\leq \max_{\rho \in \mathcal{P}_k(\Omega)} \phi(\widehat{p}_\rho||\widehat{r}_\rho) + \max_{\rho \in \mathcal{P}_k(\Omega)} \phi(\widehat{r}_\rho||\widehat{q}_\rho) \\
&= \widehat{\phi}_k(p||r) + \widehat{\phi}_k(r||q)
\end{aligned}
$$

that concludes the proof. $\square$

Properties Preserving

Theorem 6. *Given a f-divergence ϕ then, for any $k \in \mathbb{N}$, the corresponding Sketch-$\star$ metric $\widehat{\phi}_k$ is also a f-divergence.*

Proof. From Theorem 5, $\widehat{\phi}_k$ preserves the axioms of the generalized metric. Thus, $\widehat{\phi}_k$ and ϕ are in the same equivalence class. Moreover, from Lemma 11, $\widehat{\phi}_k$ verifies the monotonicity property. Thus, as the f-divergence is the only class of decomposable information *monotonic* divergences (*cf.* [35]), $\widehat{\phi}_k$ is also a f-divergence. $\square$

Theorem 7. *Given a Bregman divergence ϕ then, for any $k \in \mathbb{N}$, the corresponding Sketch-$\star$ metric $\widehat{\phi}_k$ is also a Bregman divergence.*

Proof. From Theorem 5, $\widehat{\phi}_k$ preserves the axioms of the generalized metric. Thus, $\widehat{\phi}_k$ and ϕ are in the same equivalence class. Moreover, the Bregman divergence is characterized by the property of transitivity (*cf.* [45]) defined as follows. Given p, q and r three Ω-point distributions such that $q = \Pi(L|r)$ and $p \in L$, with Π is a selection rule according to the definition of Csiszár in [45] and L is a subset of the Ω-point distributions, we have the Generalized Pythagorean Theorem:

$$\phi(p||q) + \phi(q||r) = \phi(p||r).$$

Moreover the authors in [46] show that the set Γ_N of all discrete probability distributions over N elements $(\{x_1, \ldots, x_N\})$ is a Riemannian manifold, and it owns another different dually flat affine structure. They also show that these dual structures give rise to the generalized Pythagorean theorem. This is verified for the coordinates in Γ_N and for the dual coordinates [46]. Combining these results with the projection theorem [45, 46], we obtain that

$$
\begin{aligned}
\widehat{\phi}_k(p||r) &= \max_{\rho \in \mathcal{P}_k(\Omega)} \phi(\widehat{p}_\rho||\widehat{r}_\rho) \\
&= \max_{\rho \in \mathcal{P}_k(\Omega)} (\phi(\widehat{p}_\rho||\widehat{q}_\rho) + \phi(\widehat{q}_\rho||\widehat{r}_\rho)) \\
&= \max_{\rho \in \mathcal{P}_k(\Omega)} \phi(\widehat{p}_\rho||\widehat{q}_\rho) + \max_{\rho \in \mathcal{P}_k(\Omega)} \phi(\widehat{q}_\rho||\widehat{r}_\rho) \\
&= \widehat{\phi}_k(p||q) + \widehat{\phi}_k(q||r)
\end{aligned}
$$

Finally, by the characterization of Bregman divergence through transitivity [45], and reinforced with Lemma 13 statement, $\widehat{\phi}_k$ is also a Bregman divergence.   □

In the following, we show that the *Sketch-⋆ metric* preserves the properties of divergences.

Lemma 11 (Monotonicity). *Given any generalized metric ϕ verifying the Monotonicity property then, for any $k \in \mathbb{N}$, the corresponding Sketch-⋆ metric $\widehat{\phi}_k$ preserves the Monotonicity property.*

Proof. Let p and q be any two Ω-point distributions. Given $c < N$, consider a partition $\mu \in \mathcal{P}_c(\Omega)$. As ϕ is monotonic, we have $\phi(p||q) \geq \phi(\widehat{p}_\mu||\widehat{q}_\mu)$ [47]. We split the proof into two cases:

Case (1). Suppose that $c \geq k$. Computing $\widehat{\phi}_k(\widehat{p}_\mu||\widehat{q}_\mu)$ amounts in considering only the k-cell partitions $\rho \in \mathcal{P}_k(\Omega)$ that verify

$$
\forall b \in \mu, \exists a \in \rho : b \subseteq a.
$$

These partitions form a subset of $\mathcal{P}_k(\Omega)$. The maximal value of $\phi(\widehat{p}_\rho||\widehat{q}_\rho)$ over this subset cannot be greater than the maximal value over the whole $\mathcal{P}_k(\Omega)$. Thus we have

$$
\widehat{\phi}_k(p||q) = \max_{\rho \in \mathcal{P}_k(\Omega)} \phi(\widehat{p}_\rho||\widehat{q}_\rho) \geq \widehat{\phi}_k(\widehat{p}_\mu||\widehat{q}_\mu).
$$

Case (2). Suppose now that $c < k$. By definition, we have $\widehat{\phi}_k(\widehat{p}_\mu||\widehat{q}_\mu) = \phi(\widehat{p}_\mu||\widehat{q}_\mu)$. Consider $\rho' \in \mathcal{P}_k(\Omega)$ such that $\forall a \in \rho', \exists b \in \mu, a \subseteq b$. It then exists a transition probability that respectively transforms $\widehat{p}_{\rho'}$ and $\widehat{q}_{\rho'}$ into $\widehat{p}_\mu$ and $\widehat{q}_\mu$. As ϕ is monotonic, we have

$$
\begin{aligned}
\widehat{\phi}_k(p||q) &= \max_{\rho \in \mathcal{P}_k(\Omega)} \phi(\widehat{p}_\rho||\widehat{q}_\rho) \\
&\geq \phi(\widehat{p}_{\rho'}||\widehat{q}_{\rho'}) \\
&\geq \phi(\widehat{p}_\mu||\widehat{q}_\mu) = \widehat{\phi}_k(\widehat{p}_\mu||\widehat{q}_\mu).
\end{aligned}
$$

Finally for any value of c, $\widehat{\phi}_k$ guarantees the monotonicity property. This concludes the proof.   □

Lemma 12 (Convexity). *Given any generalized metric ϕ verifying the Convexity property then, for any $k \in \mathbb{N}$, the corresponding Sketch-$\star$ metric $\widehat{\phi}_k$ preserves the Convexity property.*

Proof. Let p_1, p_2, q_1 and q_2 be any four Ω-point distributions. Given any $\lambda \in [0,1]$, we have:

$$\widehat{\phi}_k \left(\lambda p_1 + (1-\lambda)p_2 || \lambda q_1 + (1-\lambda)q_2 \right)$$
$$= \max_{\rho \in \mathcal{P}_k(\Omega)} \phi \left(\lambda \widehat{p_1}_\rho + (1-\lambda)\widehat{p_2}_\rho || \lambda \widehat{q_1}_\rho + (1-\lambda)\widehat{q_2}_\rho \right)$$

Let $\overline{\rho} \in \mathcal{P}_k(\Omega)$ such that

$$\phi \left(\lambda \widehat{p_1}_{\overline{\rho}} + (1-\lambda)\widehat{p_2}_{\overline{\rho}} || \lambda \widehat{q_1}_{\overline{\rho}} + (1-\lambda)\widehat{q_2}_{\overline{\rho}} \right)$$
$$= \max_{\rho \in \mathcal{P}_k(\Omega)} \phi \left(\lambda \widehat{p_1}_\rho + (1-\lambda)\widehat{p_2}_\rho || \lambda \widehat{q_1}_\rho + (1-\lambda)\widehat{q_2}_\rho \right).$$

As ϕ verifies the Convexity property, we have:

$$\widehat{\phi}_k \left(\lambda p_1 + (1-\lambda)p_2 || \lambda q_1 + (1-\lambda)q_2 \right)$$
$$= \phi \left(\lambda \widehat{p_1}_{\overline{\rho}} + (1-\lambda)\widehat{p_2}_{\overline{\rho}} || \lambda \widehat{q_1}_{\overline{\rho}} + (1-\lambda)\widehat{q_2}_{\overline{\rho}} \right)$$
$$\leq \lambda \phi(\widehat{p_1}_{\overline{\rho}} || \widehat{q_1}_{\overline{\rho}}) + (1-\lambda)\phi(\widehat{p_2}_{\overline{\rho}} || \widehat{q_2}_{\overline{\rho}})$$
$$\leq \lambda \left(\max_{\rho \in \mathcal{P}_k(\Omega)} \phi(\widehat{p_1}_\rho || \widehat{q_1}_\rho) \right) + (1-\lambda) \left(\max_{\rho \in \mathcal{P}_k(\Omega)} \phi(\widehat{p_2}_\rho || \widehat{q_2}_\rho) \right)$$
$$= \lambda \widehat{\phi}_k(p_1 || q_1) + (1-\lambda)\widehat{\phi}_k(p_2 || q_2)$$

that concludes the proof. □

Lemma 13 (Linearity). *The Sketch-$\star$ metric definition preserves the Linearity property.*

Proof. Let F_1 and F_2 be two strictly convex and differentiable functions, and any $\lambda \in [0,1]$. Consider the three Bregman divergences generated respectively from F_1, F_2 and $F_1 + \lambda F_2$.

Let p and q be two Ω-point distributions. We have:

$$\widehat{\mathcal{B}}_{F_1 + \lambda F_{2\,k}}(p||q) = \max_{\rho \in \mathcal{P}_k(\Omega)} \mathcal{B}_{F_1 + \lambda F_2}(\widehat{p}_\rho || \widehat{q}_\rho)$$
$$= \max_{\rho \in \mathcal{P}_k(n)} \left(\mathcal{B}_{F_1}(\widehat{p}_\rho || \widehat{q}_\rho) + \lambda \mathcal{B}_{F_2}(\widehat{p}_\rho || \widehat{q}_\rho) \right)$$
$$\leq \widehat{\mathcal{B}}_{F_{1\,k}}(p||q) + \lambda \widehat{\mathcal{B}}_{F_{2\,k}}(p||q)$$

As F_1 and F_2 are two strictly convex functions, and taken a leaf out of the Jensen's inequality, we have:

$$\widehat{\mathcal{B}}_{F_{1\,k}}(p||q) + \lambda \widehat{\mathcal{B}}_{F_{2\,k}}(p||q) \leq \max_{\rho \in \mathcal{P}_k(\Omega)} \left(\mathcal{B}_{F_1}(\widehat{p}_\rho || \widehat{q}_\rho) + \lambda \mathcal{B}_{F_2}(\widehat{p}_\rho || \widehat{q}_\rho) \right)$$
$$= \widehat{\mathcal{B}}_{F_1 + \lambda F_{2\,k}}(p||q)$$

that concludes the proof. □

Algorithm 2. *Sketch-⋆ metric* algorithm

    Input: Two input streams σ_1 and σ_2; the distance ϕ, k and t settings;

    Output: The distance $\hat{\phi}$ between σ_1 and σ_2

1 Choose t functions $h : \Omega \rightarrow [k]$, each from a 2-universal hash function family;

2 $C_{\sigma_1}[1...t][1...k] \leftarrow 0$;

3 $C_{\sigma_2}[1...t][1...k] \leftarrow 0$;

4 **for** $i \in \sigma_1$ **do**

5   **for** $\ell = 1$ **to** t **do**

6         $C_{\sigma_1}[\ell][h_\ell(i)] \leftarrow C_{\sigma_1}[\ell][h_\ell(i)] + 1$;

7 **for** $j \in \sigma_2$ **do**

8   **for** $\ell = 1$ **to** t **do**

9         $C_{\sigma_2}[\ell][h_\ell(j)] \leftarrow C_{\sigma_2}[\ell][h_\ell(j)] + 1$;

10 **On query** $\hat{\phi}_k(\sigma_1 \| \sigma_2)$ **return** $\max_{1 \leq \ell \leq t} \phi(C_{\sigma_1}[\ell][-], C_{\sigma_2}[\ell][-])$;

To summarize, we have shown that the *Sketch-⋆ metric* preserves all the axioms of a metric as well as the properties of f-divergences and Bregman divergences. We now show how to efficiently implement such a metric.

4.3   Approximation Algorithm

In this section, we propose an algorithm that computes the *Sketch-⋆ metric* in one pass on the stream.

    To compute the *Sketch-⋆ metric* of two streams σ_1 and σ_2, two sketches $\hat{\sigma}_1$ and $\hat{\sigma}_2$ of these streams are constructed as in Sect. 3.3. Note that again there is no particular assumption on the length of both streams σ_1 and σ_2. That is their respective length is finite but unknown. Algorithm 2 presents the pseudo-code of our algorithm.

Lemma 14. *Given parameters k and t, Algorithm 2 gives an approximation of the Sketch-⋆ metric, using*

$$\mathcal{O}\left(t(\log N + k \log m)\right) \ \text{bits of space.}$$

Proof. The matrices C_{σ_i}, for any $i \in \{1, 2\}$, are composed of $t \times k$ counters, which uses $\mathcal{O}(\log m)$. On the other hand, with a suitable choice of hash family, we can store the hash functions above in $\mathcal{O}(t \log N)$ space. □

4.4   Performance Evaluation

Settings of the Experiments. We have also implemented our *Sketch-⋆ metric* and have conducted a series of experiments on different types of streams and for different parameters settings. We have fed our algorithm with both real-world data sets and synthetic traces. We have varied all the significant parameters of our algorithm, that is, the maximal number of distinct data items N in each stream, the number of cells k of each generated partition, and the number of generated partitions t. For each parameters setting, we have conducted and averaged 100 trials of the same experiment, leading to a total of more than $300,000$ experiments for the evaluation of our metric. As in Sect. 3.5, we feed our algorithm with the same synthetic traces and the real data downloaded from the repository of Internet network traffic [42].

Main Lessons Drawn from the Experiments. In this section, we evaluate the accuracy of the *Sketch-⋆ metric* by comparing $\widehat{\phi}_k(p||q)$ with $\phi_k(p||q)$, for $\phi \in$ {Kullback-Leibler, Jensen-Shannon, Bhattacharyya}, and for p and q generated from the 7 distributions and the 5 real data sets. Distances computed from the sketches of the stream are referred to as *Sketch* in the legend of the graphs, while the ones computed from the full streams are mentioned as *Ref*. Due to space constraints, only a subset of the results are presented in the paper.

Figure 4 shows the accuracy of our metric as a function of the different input streams and the different generalized metrics applied on these streams. The first noticeable remark is that *Sketch-⋆ metric* behaves perfectly well when the two compared streams follow the same distribution, whatever the generalized metric ϕ used. This can be observed from both synthetic traces (*cf.* Fig. 4(a) with both p and q following the Pascal distribution, Fig. 4(b) with both p and q following the Binomial distribution, Fig. 4(c) with both p and q following the Zipf–$\alpha = 1$ distribution, and Fig. 4(d) with both p and q uniformly distributed), and real data sets (*cf.* Figs. 4(e) and (f) with the NASA (July and August) and ClarkNet (August and September) traces).

This tendency is further observed when the distributions of input streams are close to each other (*e.g.*, Zipf–$\alpha = 2, 4$ and Pascal distributions, or Uniform and Zipf–$\alpha = 1$). This makes the *Sketch-⋆ metric* a very good candidate as a parametric method for making distribution parameters inference. Another interesting result is shown when the two input streams exhibit a totally different shape. Specifically, let us consider Figs. 4(a) and (d). Sketching the Uniform distribution leads to k-cell partitions whose value is well distributed, that is, for a given partition ϕ, all the k cell values have with high probability the same value. Now, when sketching the Pascal distribution, the repartition of the data items in the cells of any given partitions is such that a few number of data items (those with high frequency) populate a very few number of cells. However, the values of these cells is very large compared to the other cells, which are populated by a large number of data items whose frequency is small. Thus, the contribution of data items exhibiting a small frequency and sharing the cells of highly frequent items is biased compared to the contribution of the other items. Thus although the input streams show a totally different shape, the accuracy of $\widehat{\phi}_k$ is only slightly lowered in these scenarios which makes it a very powerful tool to compare any two different data streams. The same observation holds with real data sets. When the shapes of the input streams are different (which is the case for Saskatchewan with respect to the 4 other input streams), the accuracy of the

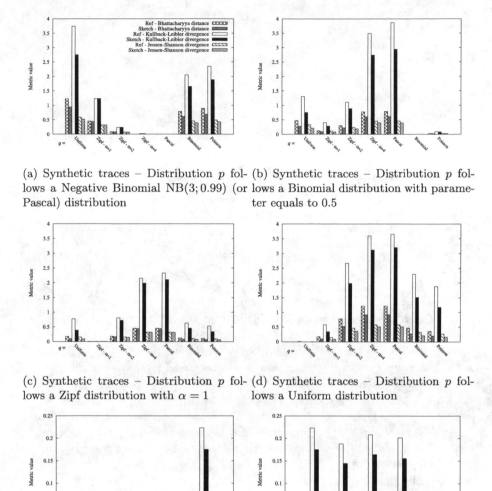

(a) Synthetic traces – Distribution p follows a Negative Binomial NB$(3; 0.99)$ (or Pascal) distribution

(b) Synthetic traces – Distribution p follows a Binomial distribution with parameter equals to 0.5

(c) Synthetic traces – Distribution p follows a Zipf distribution with $\alpha = 1$

(d) Synthetic traces – Distribution p follows a Uniform distribution

(e) Real datasets – The input stream p is the NASA (August) trace

(f) Real datasets – The input stream p is the Saskatchewan trace

Fig. 4. Comparison between the *Sketch-⋆ metric* and the ϕ metric as a function of the input stream q either generated from a distribution or real traces. For synthetic traces, $m = 200,000$ and $N = 4,000$. Parameters of the count-min sketch data structure are $k = 200$ and $t = 4$. All the histograms share the same legend, but for readability reasons, this legend is only indicated on histogram (a).

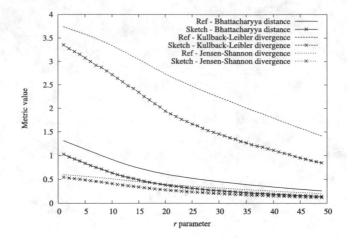

Fig. 5. Comparison between the *Sketch-⋆ metric* and the ϕ metric as a function of the parameters of the Negative Binomial distribution $NB(r, N/(2r + N))$, where distribution p follows a Uniform distribution and q follows the Negative Binomial distribution $NB(r, N/(2r + N))$.

Sketch-⋆ metric decreases a little bit but in a very small proportion. Notice that the scales on the y-axis differ significantly in Figs. 4(a)–(d) and in Figs. 4(e)–(f).

We can also observe the strong impact of the non-symmetry of the Kullback-Leibler divergence on the computation of the distance (computed on full streams or on sketches) with a clear influence when the input streams follow a Pascal and Zipf–$\alpha = 1$ distributions (see Figs. 4(a) and (c)).

Figure 5 summarizes the good properties of $\widehat{\phi}_k$ by illustrating how, for any generalized metric ϕ, and for any variations in the shape of the two input distributions, $\widehat{\phi}_k$ remains close to ϕ. Recall that increasing values of the r parameter of the Negative Binomial distribution makes the shape of the distribution flatter, while maintaining the same mean value.

Figure 6 presents the impact of the number of cells per generated partition on the accuracy of the-⋆ metric on both synthetic traces and real data. It clearly shows that by increasing k the number of data items per cell in the generated partition shrinks and thus the absolute error on the computation of the distance decreases. The same feature appears when the number N of distinct data items in the stream increases. Indeed, when N increases (for a given k), the number data items per cell augments and thus the precision of our metric decreases. This gives rise to a shift of the inflection point, as illustrated in Fig. 6(b) as data sets have almost twenty to forty times more distinct data items than the synthetic ones. As aforementioned, the input streams exhibit very different shapes which explain the strong impact of k. Note also that k has the same influence on the *Sketch-⋆ metric* for all the generalized distances ϕ.

Finally, it is interesting to note that the number t of generated partitions has a slight influence on the accuracy of our metric The reason comes from the

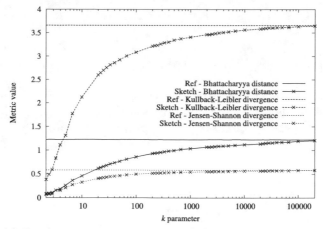

(a) Synthetic traces – Distribution p follows a Uniform distribution and q follows a Negative Binomial NB$(3; 0.99)$ one

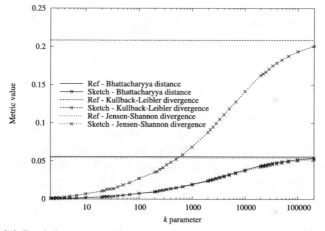

(b) Real datasets – The input stream p is the ClarkNet (August) trace and q is the Saskatchewan one

Fig. 6. Comparison between the *Sketch-⋆ metric* and the ϕ metric as a function of the number of cells k per partition (the number of partitions t of the count-min sketch data structure is set to 4). For synthetic traces, $m = 200,000$ and $N = 4,000$.

use of 2-universal hash functions, which guarantee for each of them and with high probability that data items are uniformly distributed over the cells of any partition. As a consequence, augmenting the number of such hash functions has a weak influence on the accuracy of the metric.

5   Conclusion and Future Works

In this paper we have proposed a novel metric, named the sketch codeviation, that allows to approximate the deviation between any number of distributed streams. We have given upper and lower bounds on the quality of this metric, and have provided an algorithm that additively approximates it using very little space. Beyond its theoretical interest, the sketch codeviation can be exploited in many applications. As discussed in the introduction, large scale monitoring applications are quite straightforward application domains, but we might also use it in Internet of Things applications, where it must be interesting to track the temporal and spatial correlations that may exist between the different streams produced by devices in such applications.

In order to generalized this approach, we have introduced another new metric, the *Sketch-⋆ metric*, that allows to compute any generalized metric ϕ on the summaries of two large input streams. We have presented a simple and efficient algorithm to sketch streams in the same way and compute this metric on these sketches. We have then shown that it behaves pretty well whatever the considered input streams. We are convinced of the indisputable interest of such a metric in various domains including Internet of Things statistical usages as network monitoring and information retrieval [7], and we think that it should pertinent in machine learning, and data mining applications as discussed in [9].

Regarding future works, we plan to characterize our metric among Rényi divergences [48], also known as α-divergences, which generalize different divergence classes. We also plan to consider a fully distributed setting, where each site would be in charge of analyzing its own streams and then would propagate its results to the other sites of the system for comparison or merging (without any coordinator). An immediate application of such a tool would be to detect massive attacks in a decentralized manner (*e.g.*, by identifying specific connection profiles as with worms propagation, and massive port scan attacks or by detecting sudden variations in the volume of received data), which perfectly fits with IoT constraints.

A   Derivation of Upper Bounds on $\mathcal{E}_k(X, Y)$

We have shown with Theorem 1, that the sketch codeviation matches exactly the codeviation if $k \geq |\operatorname{supp}(X) \cap \operatorname{supp}(Y)| + \mathbf{1}_{\operatorname{supp}(X) \smallsetminus \operatorname{supp}(Y)} + \mathbf{1}_{\operatorname{supp}(Y) \smallsetminus \operatorname{supp}(X)}$. In this section, we characterize the upper bound of the overestimation factor, *i.e.*, the error made with respect to the codeviation, when k is strictly less than this bound. To prevent problems of measurability, we restrict the classes of Ω-point distribution under consideration. Specifically, given $m_{\mathcal{X}}$ and $m_{\mathcal{Y}}$ any positive integers, we define the two classes $\mathcal{X}$ and $\mathcal{Y}$ as $\mathcal{X} = \{X = (x_1, \ldots, x_N)$ such that $||X||_1 = m_{\mathcal{X}}\}$ and $\mathcal{Y} = \{Y = (y_1, \ldots, y_N)$ such that $||Y||_1 = m_{\mathcal{Y}}\}$. The following theorem derives the maximum value of the overestimation factor.

Theorem 2 (Upper bound of $\mathcal{E}_k(X, Y)$). *Let $k \geq 1$ be the precision parameter of the sketch codeviation. For any two Ω-point distributions $X \in \mathcal{X}$ and $Y \in \mathcal{Y}$, let $\mathcal{E}_k$ be the maximum value of the overestimation factor $\mathcal{E}_k(X, Y)$. Then, the following relation holds.*

$$\mathcal{E}_k = \max_{X \in \mathcal{X}, Y \in \mathcal{Y}} \mathcal{E}_k(X, Y) = \begin{cases} \dfrac{m_X m_Y}{N} & \text{if } k = 1, \\[3mm] \dfrac{m_X m_Y}{N} \left(\dfrac{1}{k} - \dfrac{1}{N} \right) & \text{if } k > 1. \end{cases}$$

Proof. The first part of the proof is directly derived from Lemma 15. Using Lemmata 16 and 17, we obtain the statement of the theorem. $\qquad\square$

Lemma 15. *For any two Ω-point distributions $X \in \mathcal{X}$ and $Y \in \mathcal{Y}$, the maximum value $\mathcal{E}_1$ of the overestimation factor is exactly*

$$\mathcal{E}_1 = \max_{X \in \mathcal{X}, Y \in \mathcal{Y}} \mathcal{E}_1(X, Y) = \frac{m_X m_Y}{N}.$$

Proof. $\forall X \in \mathcal{X}, \forall Y \in \mathcal{Y}$, we are looking for the maximal value of $\mathcal{E}_1(X, Y)$ under the following constraints:

$$\begin{cases} 0 \leq x_i \leq m_X & \text{with } 1 \leq i \leq N, \\ 0 \leq y_i \leq m_Y & \text{with } 1 \leq i \leq N, \\ \sum_{i=1}^{N} x_i = m_X, \\ \sum_{i=1}^{N} y_i = m_Y. \end{cases} \tag{11}$$

In order to relax one constraint, we set $x_N = m_X - \sum_{i=1}^{N-1} x_i$. We rewrite $\mathcal{E}_1(X, Y)$ as a function f such that

$$f(x_1, \ldots, x_{N-1}, y_1, \ldots, y_N) = \sum_{i=1}^{N-1} \sum_{j=1, j \neq i}^{N} x_i y_j + \left(m_X - \sum_{i=1}^{N-1} x_i \right) \sum_{i=1}^{N-1} y_i.$$

The function f is differentiable on its domain $[0..m_X]^{N-1} \times [0..m_Y]^N$. Thus we get

$$\frac{\mathrm{d}f}{\mathrm{d}x_i}(x_1, \ldots, x_{N-1}, y_1, \ldots, y_N) = \sum_{j=1, j \neq i}^{N} y_j - \sum_{j=1}^{N-1} y_j = y_N - y_i.$$

We need to consider the following two cases:

1. $y_N > y_i$. Function f is strictly increasing, and its maximum is reached for $x_i = m_X$ (f is a Schur-convex function). By Relation 11, $\forall j \in \Omega \setminus \{i\}, x_j = 0$.
2. $y_N \leq y_i$. Function f is decreasing, and its minimum is reached at $x_i = 0$.

By symmetry on Y, the maximum of $\mathcal{E}_1(X, Y)$ is reached for a distribution for which exactly one y_i is equal to m_Y, and all the others y_j are equal to zero, which corresponds to the Dirac distribution. On the other hand, if the spike element of Y is the same as the one of X, then $\mathcal{E}_1(X,Y) = 0$, which is clearly not the maximum.

Thus, for all $X \in \mathcal{X}$ and $Y \in \mathcal{Y}$, the maximum $\mathcal{E}$ of the overestimation factor when $k = 1$ is reached for two Dirac distributions X^δ and Y^δ respectively centered in i and j with $i \neq j$, which leads to $\mathcal{E}_1 = \dfrac{1}{N} \displaystyle\sum_{i=1}^{N} \sum_{j=1, j \neq i}^{N} x_i^\delta y_j^\delta = \dfrac{m_{\mathcal{X}} m_{\mathcal{Y}}}{N}$.

$\square$

We now show that for any $k > 1$, the maximum value of overestimation factor of the sketch codeviation between X and Y is obtained when both X and Y are uniform distributions.

Lemma 16. *Let X_U and Y_U be two uniform Ω-point distributions, i.e., $X_U = (x_1, \ldots, x_N)$ with $x_i = \dfrac{||X_U||_1}{N}$ for $1 \leq i \leq N$ and $Y_U = (y_1, \ldots, y_N)$ with $y_i = \dfrac{||Y_U||_1}{N}$ for $1 \leq i \leq N$. Then for any $k > 1$, the value of the overestimation factor is given by*

$$\mathcal{E}_k(X_U, Y_U) = \frac{||X_U||_1 ||Y_U||_1}{N} \left(\frac{1}{k} - \frac{1}{N} \right).$$

Proof. By definition, $\mathcal{E}_k(X_U, Y_U)$ represents for a given k the minimum overestimation factor for all k-cell partitions of Ω, and in particular for any regular partition for which all the k cells of the partition contain the same number $\frac{N}{k}$ of elements. In such a partition, all the k disjoint cells of the cross product matrix share the same value $\dfrac{||X_U||_1 ||Y_U||_1}{N^2}$. Therefore each cell a has the same weight equal to $\dfrac{||X_U||_1 ||Y_U||_1}{N^2} \left(\dfrac{N^2}{k^2} - \dfrac{N}{k} \right)$, leading to

$$\mathcal{E}_k(X_U, Y_U) = \frac{k}{N} \frac{||X_U||_1 ||Y_U||_1}{N^2} \left(\frac{N^2}{k^2} - \frac{N}{k} \right)$$

$$= \frac{||X_U||_1 ||Y_U||_1}{N} \left(\frac{1}{k} - \frac{1}{N} \right)$$

which concludes the proof. $\square$

Lemma 17. *Let $X \in \mathcal{X}$ and $Y \in \mathcal{Y}$ be any two Ω-point distributions. Then the maximum value of the overestimation factor of the sketch codeviation when $k > 1$ is exactly*

$$\mathcal{E}_k = \max_{X \in \mathcal{X}, Y \in \mathcal{Y}} \mathcal{E}_k(X, Y) = \frac{m_{\mathcal{X}} m_{\mathcal{Y}}}{N} \left(\frac{1}{k} - \frac{1}{N} \right).$$

Proof. Given $X \in \mathcal{X}$ and $Y \in \mathcal{Y}$ any two Ω-point distributions, let us denote $\mathcal{E}_k^\rho(X, Y) = \frac{1}{N} \sum_{a \in \rho} \sum_{i \in a} \sum_{j \in a \smallsetminus \{i\}} x_i y_j$.

Consider the partition $\overline{\rho} = \operatorname{argmin}_{\rho \in \mathcal{P}_k(\Omega)} \mathcal{E}_k^\rho(X, Y)$ with $k > 1$. We introduce the operator $\widetilde{\cdot}$ that operates on Ω-point distributions. This operator is defined as follows

- If it exists $a \in \bar{p}$ such that $\exists \ell, \ell' \in a$ with $y_\ell \geq y_{\ell'}$ and $x_{\ell'} > 0$, then operator $\tilde{\ }$ is applied on the pair (ℓ, ℓ') of X so that we have $\begin{cases} \tilde{x}_\ell = x_\ell + 1 \\ \tilde{x}_{\ell'} = x_{\ell'} - 1 \end{cases}$.
- Otherwise, $\exists a, a' \in \bar{p}$ with $\exists \ell \in a, \exists \ell' \in a', x_\ell \geq x_{\ell'} > 0$. Then operator $\tilde{\ }$ is applied on the pair (ℓ, ℓ') of X so that we have $\begin{cases} \tilde{x}_\ell = x_\ell + 1 \\ \tilde{x}_{\ell'} = x_{\ell'} - 1 \end{cases}$.
- Finally, X is kept unmodified for all the other items, i.e., $\forall i \in \Omega \setminus \{\ell, \ell'\}, \tilde{x}_i = x_i$.

It is clear that any Ω-point distributions can be constructed from the uniform one, using several iterations of this operator. Thus we split the proof into two parts. The first one supposes that both Ω-point distributions X and Y are uniform while the second part considers any two Ω-point distributions.

Case 1. Let X_U and Y_U be two uniform Ω-point distributions, i.e., $X_U = (x_1, \ldots, x_N)$ with $x_i = \frac{\|X_U\|_1}{N}$ for $1 \leq i \leq N$ and $Y_U = (y_1, \ldots, y_N)$ with $y_i = \frac{\|Y_U\|_1}{N}$ for $1 \leq i \leq N$.

We split the analysis into two sub-cases: the class of partitions in which x_ℓ and $x_{\ell'}$ belong to the same cell a of a given k-partition ρ, and the class of partitions in which they are located into two separated cells a and a'. Suppose first that the $\tilde{\ }$ operator is applied on X_U. Then the overestimation factor is given by

$$\mathcal{E}_k(\widetilde{X}_U, Y_U) = \min(E, E') \text{ with } \begin{cases} E = \min\limits_{\substack{\rho \in \mathcal{P}_k(\Omega) \text{ s.t.} \\ \exists a \in \rho, \ell, \ell' \in a}} \mathcal{E}_k^\rho(\widetilde{X}_U, Y_U) \\ \\ E' = \min\limits_{\substack{\rho \in \mathcal{P}_k(\Omega) \text{ s.t.} \\ \exists a, a' \in \rho, a \neq a' \\ \wedge \ell \in a \wedge \ell' \in a'}} \mathcal{E}_k^\rho(\widetilde{X}_U, Y_U). \end{cases} \tag{12}$$

Let us consider the first term E. We have

$$E = \min_{\substack{\rho \in \mathcal{P}_k(\Omega) \text{ s.t.} \\ \exists a \in \rho, \ell, \ell' \in a}} \left(\sum_{b \in \rho \setminus \{a\}} \sum_{i \in b} \sum_{j \in b \setminus \{i\}} \tilde{x}_i y_j + \sum_{i \in a} \sum_{j \in a \setminus \{i\}} \tilde{x}_i y_j \right)$$

$$= \min_{\substack{\rho \in \mathcal{P}_k(\Omega) \text{ s.t.} \\ \exists a \in \rho, \ell, \ell' \in a}} \left(\sum_{b \in \rho \setminus \{a\}} \sum_{i \in b} \sum_{j \in b \setminus \{i\}} \frac{m_X m_Y}{N^2} + \sum_{i \in a \setminus \{\ell, \ell'\}} \sum_{j \in a \setminus \{i\}} \frac{m_X m_Y}{N^2} \right.$$

$$\left. + \sum_{j \in a \setminus \{\ell\}} \left(\frac{m_X}{N} + 1\right)\frac{m_Y}{N} + \sum_{j \in a \setminus \{\ell'\}} \left(\frac{m_X}{N} - 1\right)\frac{m_Y}{N} \right)$$

$$= \min_{\substack{\rho \in \mathcal{P}_k(\Omega) \text{ s.t.} \\ \exists a \in \rho, \ell, \ell' \in a}} \left(\mathcal{E}_k^\rho(X_U, Y_U) \right).$$

According to the second term E', we have.

$$E' = \min_{\substack{\rho \in \mathcal{P}_k(\Omega) \text{ s.t.} \\ \exists a, a' \in \rho, a \neq a' \\ \wedge \ell \in a \wedge \ell' \in a'}} \left(\sum_{\substack{b \in \rho \\ \smallsetminus \{a, a'\}}} \sum_{i \in b} \sum_{\substack{j \in b \\ \smallsetminus \{i\}}} \frac{m_X m_Y}{N^2} + \sum_{i \in a \smallsetminus \{\ell\}} \sum_{j \in a \smallsetminus \{i\}} \frac{m_X m_Y}{N^2} \right.$$

$$\left. + \sum_{i \in a' \smallsetminus \{\ell'\}} \sum_{j \in a' \smallsetminus \{i\}} \frac{m_X m_Y}{N^2} + \sum_{j \in a \smallsetminus \{\ell\}} \left(\frac{m_X}{N} + 1 \right) \frac{m_Y}{N} + \sum_{j \in a' \smallsetminus \{\ell'\}} \left(\frac{m_X}{N} - 1 \right) \frac{m_Y}{N} \right)$$

$$= \min_{\substack{\rho \in \mathcal{P}_k(\Omega) \text{ s.t.} \\ \exists a, a' \in \rho, a \neq a' \\ \wedge \ell \in a \wedge \ell' \in a'}} \left(\mathcal{E}_k^\rho(X_U, Y_U) + \frac{m_Y}{N} \left(|a| - |a'| \right) \right).$$

Thus, $\mathcal{E}_k(\widetilde{X}_U, Y_U) \leq \mathcal{E}_k(X_U, Y_U)$. By symmetry, we have $\mathcal{E}_k(X_U, \widetilde{Y}_U) \leq \mathcal{E}_k(X_U, Y_U)$.

Case 2. In the rest of the proof, we show that for any X and Y, we have $\mathcal{E}_k(\widetilde{X}, Y) \leq \mathcal{E}_k(X, Y)$. Again, we split the proof into two sub-cases according to Relation 12. We get for the first term,

$$\min_{\substack{\rho \in \mathcal{P}_k(\Omega) \text{ s.t.} \\ \exists a \in \rho, \ell, \ell' \in a}} \mathcal{E}_k^\rho(\widetilde{X}, Y) = \min_{\substack{\rho \in \mathcal{P}_k(\Omega) \text{ s.t.} \\ \exists a \in \rho, \ell, \ell' \in a}} \left(\mathcal{E}_k^\rho(X, Y) + \sum_{j \in a \smallsetminus \{\ell\}} y_j - \sum_{j \in a \smallsetminus \{\ell'\}} y_j \right)$$

$$= \min_{\substack{\rho \in \mathcal{P}_k(\Omega) \text{ s.t.} \\ \exists a \in \rho, \ell, \ell' \in a}} \left(\mathcal{E}_k^\rho(X, Y) + y_{\ell'} - y_\ell \right).$$

For the second term, we have

$$\min_{\substack{\rho \in \mathcal{P}_k(\Omega) \text{ s.t.} \\ \exists a, a' \in \rho, a \neq a' \\ \wedge \ell \in a \wedge \ell' \in a'}} \mathcal{E}_k^\rho(\widetilde{X}, Y) = \min_{\substack{\rho \in \mathcal{P}_k(\Omega) \text{ s.t.} \\ \exists a, a' \in \rho, a \neq a' \\ \wedge \ell \in a \wedge \ell' \in a'}} \left(\mathcal{E}_k^\rho(X, Y) + \sum_{j \in a \smallsetminus \{\ell\}} y_j - \sum_{j \in a' \smallsetminus \{\ell'\}} y_j \right).$$

By definition of the operator, if it exists $a \in \overline{\rho}$ such that $\exists \ell, \ell' \in a$, then $y_\ell \geq y_{\ell'}$ and so $\mathcal{E}_k^{\overline{\rho}}(\widetilde{X}, Y) \leq \mathcal{E}_k^{\overline{\rho}}(X, Y)$. Otherwise, ℓ and ℓ' are in two separated cells of $\overline{\rho}$, implying that $x_\ell \geq x_{\ell'}$. We then have $\sum_{j \in a \smallsetminus \{\ell\}} y_j \leq \sum_{j \in a' \smallsetminus \{\ell'\}} y_j$. Indeed, suppose that by contradiction

$$x_\ell \sum_{j \in a' \smallsetminus \{\ell'\}} y_j + x_{\ell'} \sum_{j \in a \smallsetminus \{\ell\}} y_j < x_\ell \sum_{j \in a \smallsetminus \{\ell\}} y_j + x_{\ell'} \sum_{j \in a' \smallsetminus \{\ell'\}} y_j.$$

Let $\overline{\rho}'$ be the partition corresponding to the partition $\overline{\rho}$ in which ℓ and ℓ' have been swapped. Then we obtain $\mathcal{E}_k^{\overline{\rho}'}(X, Y) < \mathcal{E}_k^{\overline{\rho}}(X, Y)$, which is impossible by assumption on $\overline{\rho}$. Thus, in both cases we have $\mathcal{E}_k(\widetilde{X}, Y) \leq \mathcal{E}_k^{\overline{\rho}}(\widetilde{X}, Y) \leq \mathcal{E}_k^{\overline{\rho}}(X, Y) = \mathcal{E}_k(X, Y)$. By symmetry, we also have $\mathcal{E}_k(X, \widetilde{Y}) \leq \mathcal{E}_k(X, Y)$.

Thus we have shown that the maximum of any overestimation factor is reached for the uniform Ω-point distribution. Lemma 16 concludes the proof. $\square$

References

1. Lakhina, A., Crovella, M., Diot, C.: Mining anomalies using traffic feature distributions. In: Proceedings of the ACM Conference on Applications, Technologies, Architectures, and Protocols for Computer Communications (SIGCOMM) (2005)
2. Qiu, T., Ge, Z., Pei, D., Wang, J., Xu, J.: What happened in my network: mining network events from router syslogs. In: Proceedings of the 10th ACM Conference on Internet Measurement (IMC) (2010)
3. Yeung, D.S.: Covariance-matrix modeling and detecting various flooding attacks. IEEE Trans. Syst. Man Cybernet. Part A **37**(2), 157–169 (2007)
4. Zhu, Y., Fu, X., Graham, B., Bettati, R., Zhao, W.: On flow correlation attacks and countermeasures in mix networks. In: Martin, D., Serjantov, A. (eds.) PET 2004. LNCS, vol. 3424, pp. 207–225. Springer, Heidelberg (2005). doi:10.1007/11423409_13
5. Ganguly, S., Garafalakis, M., Rastogi, R., Sabnani, K.: Streaming algorithms for robust, real-time detection of ddos attacks. In: Proceedings of the 27th International Conference on Distributed Computing Systems (ICDCS) (2007)
6. Jin, S., Yeung, D.: A covariance analysis model for ddos attack detection. In: 4th IEEE International Conference on Communications (ICC), vol. 4, pp. 1882–1886 (2004)
7. Pinarer, O., Gripay, Y., Servigne, S., Ozgovde, A.: Energy enhancement of multi-application monitoring systems for smart buildings. In: Krogstie, J., Mouratidis, H., Su, J. (eds.) CAiSE 2016. LNBIP, vol. 249, pp. 131–142. Springer, Cham (2016). doi:10.1007/978-3-319-39564-7_14
8. Boubrima, A., Matigot, F., Bechkit, W., Rivano, H., Ruas, A.: Optimal deployment of wireless sensor networks for air pollution monitoring. In: 24th International Conference on Computer Communication and Networks (ICCCN), Las Vegas, USA, August 2015
9. Stankovic, J.A.: Research directions for the internet of things. IEEE Internet Things J. **1**(1), 3–9 (2014)
10. Anceaume, E., Busnel, Y., Gambs, S.: Uniform and ergodic sampling in unstructured peer-to-peer systems with malicious nodes. In: Lu, C., Masuzawa, T., Mosbah, M. (eds.) OPODIS 2010. LNCS, vol. 6490, pp. 64–78. Springer, Heidelberg (2010). doi:10.1007/978-3-642-17653-1_5
11. Bar-Yossef, Z., Jayram, T.S., Kumar, R., Sivakumar, D., Trevisan, L.: Counting distinct elements in a data stream. In: Rolim, J.D.P., Vadhan, S. (eds.) RANDOM 2002. LNCS, vol. 2483, pp. 1–10. Springer, Heidelberg (2002). doi:10.1007/3-540-45726-7_1
12. Flajolet, P., Martin, G.N.: Probabilistic counting algorithms for data base applications. J. Comput. Syst. Sci. **31**(2), 182–209 (1985)
13. Kane, D.M., Nelson, J., Woodruff, D.P.: An optimal algorithm for the distinct element problem. In: Proceedings of the Symposium on Principles of Databases (PODS) (2010)
14. Alon, N., Matias, Y., Szegedy, M.: The space complexity of approximating the frequency moments. In: Proceedings of the Twenty-Eighth Annual ACM Symposium on Theory of Computing (STOC), pp. 20–29 (1996)
15. Cover, T., Thomas, J.: Elements of Information Theory. Wiley, New York (1991)
16. Chakrabarti, A., Cormode, G., McGregor, A.: A near-optimal algorithm for computing the entropy of a stream. In. ACM-SIAM Symposium on Discrete Algorithms, pp. 328–335 (2007)

17. Lall, A., Sekar, V., Ogihara, M., Xu, J., Zhang, H.: Data streaming algorithms for estimating entropy of network traffic. In: Proceedings of the Joint International Conference on Measurement and Modeling of Computer Systems (SIGMETRICS). ACM (2006)
18. Anceaume, E., Busnel, Y., Gambs, S.: On the power of the adversary to solve the node sampling problem. Trans. Large-Scale Data Knowl. Centered Syst. (TLDKS) **11**, 102–126 (2013)
19. Anceaume, E., Busnel, Y.: An information divergence estimation over data streams. In: Proceedings of the 11th IEEE International Symposium on Network Computing and Applications (NCA) (2012)
20. Chakrabarti, A., Ba, K., Muthukrishnan, S.: Estimating entropy and entropy norm on data streams. In: Durand, B., Thomas, W. (eds.) STACS 2006. LNCS, vol. 3884, pp. 196–205. Springer, Heidelberg (2006). doi:10.1007/11672142_15
21. Guha, S., McGregor, A., Venkatasubramanian, S.: Streaming and sublinear approximation of entropy and information distances. In: Proceedings of the Seventeenth Annual ACM-SIAM Symposium on Discrete Algorithms (SODA), pp. 733–742 (2006)
22. Rivetti, N., Busnel, Y., Querzoni, L.: Load-aware shedding in stream processing systems. In: Proceedings of the 10th ACM International Conference on Distributed Event-Based Systems (DEBS), Ivine, CA, USA, June 2016
23. Rivetti, N., Anceaume, E., Busnel, Y., Querzoni, L., Sericola, B.: Online scheduling for shuffle grouping in distributed stream processing systems. In: Proceedings of the 17th ACM/IFIP/USENIX 13th International Conference on Middleware (Middleware), Trento, Italie, December 2016
24. Charikar, M., Chen, K., Farach-Colton, M.: Finding frequent items in data streams. Theor. Comput. Sci. **312**(1), 3–15 (2004)
25. Cormode, G., Garofalakis, M.: Sketching probabilistic data streams. In: Proceedings of the 2007 ACM SIGMOD International Conference on Management of Data, pp. 281–292 (2007)
26. Guha, S., Indyk, P., Mcgregor, A.: Sketching information divergences. Mach. Learn. **72**(1–2), 5–19 (2008)
27. Cormode, G., Muthukrishnan, S., Yi, K.: Algorithms for distributed functional monitoring. In: Proceedings of the 19th Annual ACM-SIAM Symposium On Discrete Algorithms (SODA) (2008)
28. Arackaparambil, C., Brody, J., Chakrabarti, A.: Functional monitoring without monotonicity. In: Proceedings of the 36th ACM International Colloquium on Automata, Languages and Programming (ICALP) (2009)
29. Gibbons, P.B., Tirthapura, S.: Estimating simple functions on the union of data streams. In: Proceedings of the Thirteenth Annual ACM Symposium on Parallel Algorithms and Architectures (SPAA), pp. 281–291 (2001)
30. Haung, Z., Yi, K., Zhang, Q.: Randomized algorithms for tracking distributed count, frequencies and ranks. In: Proceedings of 31st ACM Symposium on Principles of Database Systems (PODS) (2012)
31. Liu, Z., Radunović, B., Vojnovic, M.: Continuous distributed counting for non-monotonic streams. In: Proceedings of 31st ACM Symposium on Principles of Database Systems (PODS) (2012)
32. Yuan, J., Mills, K.: Monitoring the macroscopic effect of DDoS flooding attacks. IEEE Trans. Dependable Secure Comput. **2**(4), 324–335 (2005)
33. Basseville, M., Cardoso, J.F.: On entropies, divergences, and mean values. In: Proceedings of the IEEE International Symposium on Information Theory (1995)

34. Ali, S.M., Silvey, S.D.: General class of coefficients of divergence of one distribution from another. J. Roy. Stat. Soc. Ser. B (Methodological) **28**(1), 131–142 (1966)
35. Csiszár, I.: Information measures: a critical survey. In: Transactions of the Seventh Prague Conference on Information Theory, Statistical Decision Functions, Random Processes, Dordrecht, D. Riedel, pp. 73–86 (1978)
36. Morimoto, T.: Markov processes and the h-theorem. J. Phys. Soc. Jpn. **18**(3), 328–331 (1963)
37. Kullback, S., Leibler, R.A.: On information and sufficiency. Ann. Math. Stat. **22**(1), 79–86 (1951)
38. Bhattacharyya, A.: On a measure of divergence between two statistical populations defined by their probability distributions. Bull. Calcutta Math. Soc. **35**, 99–109 (1943)
39. Muthukrishnan, S.: Data Streams: Algorithms and Applications. Now Publishers Inc., Hanover (2005)
40. Anceaume, E., Busnel, Y., Rivetti, N.: Estimating the frequency of data items in massive distributed streams. In: Proceedings of the 4th IEEE Symposium on Network Cloud Computing and Applications (NCCA), pp. 59–66 (2015)
41. Cormode, G., Muthukrishnan, S.: An improved data stream summary: the count-min sketch and its applications. J. Algorithms **55**(1), 58–75 (2005)
42. The Internet Traffic Archive. Lawrence Berkeley National Laboratory. http://ita.ee.lbl.gov/html/traces.html
43. Bregman, L.M.: The relaxation method of finding the common point of convex sets and its application to the solution of problems in convex programming. USSR Comput. Math. Math. Phys. **7**(3), 200–217 (1967)
44. Hellinger, E.: Neue begründung der theorie quadratischer formen von unendlichvielen veränderlichen. J. Reine Angew. Math. **136**, 210–271 (1909)
45. Csiszár, I.: Why least squares and maximum entropy? an axiomatic approach to inference for linear inverse problems. Ann. Stat. **19**(4), 2032–2066 (1991)
46. Amari, S.I., Cichocki, A.: Information geometry of divergence functions. Bull. Pol. Acad. Sci. Techn. Sci. **58**(1), 183–195 (2010)
47. Amari, S.I.: α-divergence is unique, belonging to both f-divergence and bregman divergence classes. IEEE Trans. Inf. Theor. **55**(11), 4925–4931 (2009)
48. Renyi, A.: On measures of information and entropy. In: Proceedings of the 4th Berkeley Symposium on Mathematics, Statistics and Probability, pp. 547–561 (1960)

Performance Analysis of Object Store Systems in a Fog and Edge Computing Infrastructure

Bastien Confais[1]([⊠]), Adrien Lebre[2], and Benoît Parrein[3]

[1] CNRS, LS2N, UMR 6004, Polytech Nantes, Nantes, France
bastien.confais@univ-nantes.fr
[2] Inria, LS2N, UMR 6004, Institut Mines Télécom Atlantique, Nantes, France
adrien.lebre@inria.fr
[3] Université de Nantes, LS2N, UMR 6004, Polytech Nantes, Nantes, France
benoit.parrein@polytech.univ-nantes.fr

Abstract. Fog and Edge computing infrastructures have been proposed as an alternative to the current Cloud Computing facilities to address the latency issue for some applications. The main idea is to deploy smaller data-centers at the edge of the backbone in order to bring Cloud Computing resources closer to the end-usages. While a couple of works illustrated the advantages of such infrastructures in particular for Internet of Things (IoT) applications, the way of designing elementary services that can take advantage of such massively distributed infrastructures has not been yet discussed. In this paper, we propose to deal with such a question from the storage point of view. First, we propose a list of properties a storage system should meet in this context. Second, we evaluate through performance analysis three "off-the-shelf" object store solutions, namely Rados, Cassandra and InterPlanetary File System (IPFS). In particular, we focus (i) on access times to push and get objects under different scenarios and (ii) on the amount of network traffic that is exchanged between the different geographical sites during such operations. We also evaluate how the network latencies influence the access times. Experiments are conducted using the Yahoo Cloud System Benchmark (YCSB) on top of the Grid'5000 testbed. Finally, we show that adding a Scale-Out NAS system on each site improves the access times of IPFS and reduces the amount of traffic between the sites when objects are read locally by reducing the costly DHT access. The simultaneous observation of different Fog sites also constitutes the originality of this work.

1 Introduction

The advent of smartphones, tablets as well as Internet of Things (IoT) devices revolutionized the ways people are consuming IT services. Lots of applications take advantage of the Internet and Cloud Computing solutions to extend devices' capabilities in terms of computations as well as storage. However, reaching data centers (DCs) operated by giant actors such as Amazon, Google and Microsoft implies significant penalties in terms of network latency, preventing a large amount of services to be deployed [59]. The Fog Computing paradigm [9] has

© Springer-Verlag GmbH Germany 2017
A. Hameurlain et al. (Eds.): TLDKS XXXIII, LNCS 10430, pp. 40–79, 2017.
DOI: 10.1007/978-3-662-55696-2_2

been proposed to overcome such a limitation: dedicated servers are deployed in micro/nano DCs geographically spread at the edge of the network so that it becomes possible to execute latency dependent applications as close as possible to the end-usages and keep non sensitive ones in traditional Cloud DCs. Previously, Content Delivery Networks (CDN) used a similar approach to reduce access time to data for the end users [39].

Also known as Edge Computing, the advantages of such infrastructures have been described through several scenarios [2,20]. In this paper, we propose to check if storage systems designed for Cloud infrastructures may be used in a Fog environment. Concretely, we discuss an empirical analysis of three storage systems with the ultimate goal of delivering a system such as the Simple Storage Service (S3) of Amazon. S3 is one of the most used services offered by Amazon and a building block for hundreds of Cloud services [38]. We believe that providing such a storage service for Fog/Edge Computing infrastructures can pave the way toward new services as well as IoT applications. In terms of use cases, we have in mind to provide to a mobile end user a perfect seamless storage experience towards different residential sites *e.g.*, home, public transportation, office. The three storage systems, we studied are Rados [52] which is the object storage module of the Ceph project, Cassandra [30], a high performance key value store and InterPlanetary File System (IPFS) [7], an object store which uses the concepts brought by BitTorrent protocol. We selected these three systems because *(i)* they do not rely on a central server and *(ii)* they propose software abstractions for the definition of geographical *sites*. They also propose strategies to enable users to place data near the users, mitigating the traffic exchanged between each site and reducing the impact each site may have on the others.

The contributions of our work are *(i)* the definition of Fog/Edge computing model with a list of dedicated requirements for storage service, *(ii)* an overview of the three evaluated storage systems namely Rados, Cassandra and IPFS with a specific Fog adaptation, *(iii)* a deep performance analysis of the three systems in a Fog context. We evaluate the performance in case of local and remote access. More precisely, we measure access times and amount of network traffic exchanged between the sites. We determined for each system what are the key settings that have an influence on the access times. A last contribution is *(iv)* to show that the impact of using a DHT in IPFS can be partially prevented by using a scale out NAS system deployed on each site. We prove that such a system is able to mitigate the amount of inter-sites network traffic as well as the access times when clients read objects stored locally. Experiments have been conducted on top of Grid'5000 [6] by considering several data manipulation scenarios leveraging Yahoo Cloud Service Benchmark (YCSB) [16], a well-known benchmark tool particularly designed to benchmark object stores [3,4]. Moreover, we used a benchmark we developed to measure the access times of each object. Similar to YCSB, this benchmark enabled us to see how objects are accessed in IPFS.

The remaining of the paper is organized as follows. Section 2 defines the Fog/Edge computing model we consider and gives a list of characteristics a data store service should have in such a context. Section 3 presents an overview of the three storage systems. Evaluations are discussed in Sect. 4. In Sect. 5, we introduce a coupling between IPFS and a Scale-Out NAS. Section 6 discusses the related works. Finally, Sect. 7 concludes this study and highlights some perspectives.

2 Fog and Edge Computing Model

In this section, we present the Fog/Edge architecture we are considering. Then, after listing some use cases the Fog can benefit, we present a list of characteristics we claim an object storage system should have in such a context.

2.1 Fog/Edge Networking

Industrials[1] as well as academics [9,22,23] argue in favor of a new model of distributed computing composed of IT resources spread from the Cloud to the Extreme Edge. Such an infrastructure follows a hierarchical topology from the point of views of distance and power capabilities: Cloud facilities are the farthest elements in terms of network latencies but the ones that provide the largest computing and storage capabilities. Edge/Extreme Edge devices can benefit from local computing and storage resources but those resources are limited in comparison to the Cloud ones. Finally, Fog sites can be seen as intermediate facilities that offer a tradeoff between distance and power capabilities of IT resources [8,23]. Moreover, Fog sites can complement each other to satisfy the needs between user's devices and Cloud Computing centers [12]. According to Bonomi *et al.* [9], the Fog infrastructure is organized in several layers with a Cloud infrastructure at the top. We consider all the sites of Fog be part of the same layer.

Figure 1 illustrates such a description. The Fog platform is composed of a significant number of sites that can be geographically spread over a large area. We also argue that users may benefit that some sites of Fog may be mobile. Placing a Fog facility in a train for example, allows the users to stay connected to the same site of Fog with a stable latency despites of the mobility of the train. Each site hosts a limited number of servers that offer storage and computing capabilities. Nonetheless, according to Firdhous *et al.* [22], Fog nodes should have enough resources to handle intensive user requests. End-users devices (smartphones, tablets, laptops) as well as IoT devices can reach a Fog site with a rather low latency. Devices located in the Edge are directly connected to the Fog whereas those located in the Extreme Edge have to cross a local network to reach the Fog. Fog sites are interconnected and the single distributed storage system makes them transparent from the users point of view.

We consider that the latency between Fog sites (noted L_{Core}) is up to 50 ms (mean latency of a Wide Area Network link [34]) for a static site of Fog and is up to 200 ms for a mobile one. We also consider the latency between users

---

[1] https://www.openfogconsortium.org/.

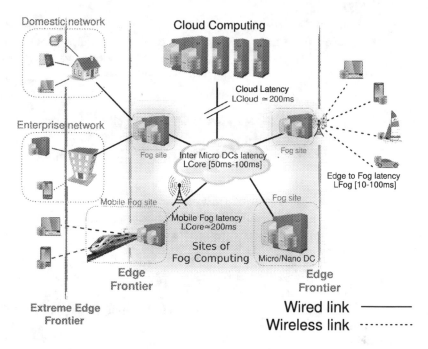

Fig. 1. Overview of a Cloud, Fog and Edge infrastructure.

and their site (noted L_{Fog}) is comprised between 10 ms and 100 ms (latency of a local wireless link [29,46]). The latency to reach a Cloud infrastructure (noted L_{Cloud}) from the clients is important (about 200 ms) [22,45] and moreover unpredictable [59].

2.2   Fog and Edge Computing: Use Cases

Many use cases have been proposed for the Fog. Yannuzzi *et al.* [54] show the Cloud Computing cannot address all the use cases and discuss the tradeoff the Fog has to solve, especially between the mobility support, the access times constraints and the amount of data that needs to be stored/computed. They show the Cloud cannot satisfy this tradeoff and a dual approach Fog/Cloud is necessary. A lot of papers propose the smart vehicles or the smart traffic light [8,9,55] as use cases that can benefit the Fog architecture. Hong *et al.* [25] have developed a programming model for the Fog and they used it to monitor vehicle traffic. Tang *et al.* [47] propose to use the Fog in the context of smart city, especially to monitor pipelines. We also found some use cases in the health field. Dubey *et al.* [20] use the Fog to make quick decisions from the values collected from sensors. Zao *et al.* [58] compute EEG pattern detection on the Fog. Finally, Fog can be used for networking services. Vaquero *et al.* [49] deploy Network Function Virtualisation (NFV) in the Fog. Virtual machines have the role of network appliances such as router, firewall and so on. The paper argue, the Fog can reduce the load of some network paths, especially the ones reaching the Cloud. Yi *et al.* [56] propose among a list of use cases, to use the Fog for data caching. In this paper, we study how a datastore system can be developed to benefit from Fog/Edge specifics.

2.3 Storage Requirements

Our objective is to study how a storage service such as a S3 object store system should be designed to deal with a Fog Computing infrastructure. The first requirement for such a system is the scalability that is required to consider the huge number of sites the Fog is composed of. Contrary to the common distributed file systems, object stores are not concerned by the problematic of storing the global namespace in a scalable way and therefore are more adapted to a Fog Computing infrastructure. We advocate that a Fog Computing storage service should meet the following properties:

- data locality (enabling low access time);
- network containment between sites;
- possibility to access data in case of service/network partitioning;
- support for users mobility;
- scalability with a large number of sites, users and objects stored.

Low access time is the main characteristic behind the motivation for the Fog paradigm. The idea of **data locality** is to favor local accesses each time it is possible. Each put into the storage service should be handled by the closest site, assuming that the closest site can deliver the best performance. The data locality property also addresses security and privacy concerns [57].

Network containment is the idea that an action on one site does not impact the other sites negatively. In other words, if one site faces a peak of activity, the performance of other sites should not change. We believe that such a criterion can be delivered by mitigating data transfers between sites each time an operation is performed. The verification of this property assumes the simultaneous observations among all the Fog sites.

The third feature is related to the **partitioning of the storage service** that can occur each time one site is disconnected from the other ones. While replication strategies between sites can ensure data availability, we claim that a Fog storage service should be able to run, at least, in a degraded/disconnected mode in order to tolerate local accesses and provide appropriate mechanisms to reconsolidate the service once the disconnection is completed.

Mobility support is another property we have identified. The idea is to enable data to follow transparently its usages. To illustrate such a feature, you can imagine a user moving from one radio base station to another one. In such a situation, the storage service should be able to relocate solicited data in a transparent manner from the previous site to the new one. Such a transparent relocation of data will mitigate remote accesses and allows the system to satisfy the aforementioned low access characteristic.

Scalability is the last property. The system has to scale to a large number of sites, with a lot of clients connected to these sites, storing a lot of objects. Performance should not be impacted by the increase of the number of sites.

According to the Brewer's theorem [11], a storage system cannot have strong consistency if each request is answered in a finite time and if the system supports the service partitioning. For this reason, we underline that discussing consistency model of the storage service we target is behind-the-scope of this first study. For the moment and for the sake of simplicity, we consider objects like files and documents of one user with no parallel and concurrent accesses.

3   Off-the-Shelf Distributed Storage Systems

Due to the complexity of modern distributed storage systems, it is important to evaluate if any of the existing systems may be used. Distributed Hash Table (DHT), gossiping and hashing are the main mechanisms used by distributed object stores in charge of storing the location of the objects. Among the different solutions that are available, we selected Rados [52], Cassandra [30] and IPFS [7]. We chose these systems because they provide software abstractions that enable the definition of areas that can be mapped to geographical sites, and thus may be adapted to a Fog Context.

Distributed file systems such as PVFS [13], Lustre [19], HDFS [44], RozoFS [40] and "other" WANWide-like proposals [26,48] have not been selected because they are not appropriated to the Fog Computing infrastructure we target. They are all designed around the concept of an entity in charge of maintaining the storage namespace in a "centralized" manner, preventing conceptually to cope with Fog Computing requirements we previously described. Especially, the network containment property cannot be satisfied because writing or reading on a local site requires remote access to the metadata server. This justify our coupling of IPFS with a Scale-Out NAS system in Sect. 5. We present in the following paragraphs, an overview of the three selected storage systems and analyze quantitatively whether and how they can fit to the Fog/Edge context.

3.1   Rados

Rados [52] is an object distributed storage solution which uses the CRUSH algorithm [51] to locate data in the infrastructure without requiring any remote communication from the clients. Conceptually speaking, this constitutes the main interest of Rados for Fog storage solutions.

General Overview. Rados uses two kinds of nodes: Object Storage Daemons (OSD) and Monitors. The formers are used to store data whereas the latters maintain a tree (*i.e.*, the "clustermap") describing the cluster's topology. Among the monitors, one is elected as the master and is in charge of maintaining a consistency view of the clustermap (**the Paxos algorithm** [31] is used to guarantee that there is only one master monitor). Before accessing data, each client

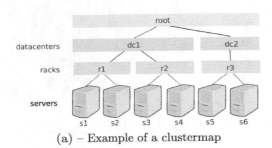

1. select the "root" node
2. select 2 "datacenters"
3. select 1 "rack"
4. select 1 "server"

(a) – Example of a clustermap   (b) – Example of a placement rule

Fig. 2. Example of a clustermap (a) and a placement rule (b) placing two replicates of the data in two servers located in two different datacenters.

retrieves the **clustermap** from one monitor. The clustermap is used by the CRUSH algorithm to locate objects.

In addition to the clustermap, the CRUSH algorithm relies on placement rules that describe how selecting the "n" leaf nodes from the clustermap used to store the object. Figure 2(a) depicts an example of a clustermap. It describes a topology containing two data centers with two racks in the first DC and one rack in the second DC. Each rack contains two servers. Figure 2(b) shows a placement rule to force two replicas to be located in two different data centers.

The location of an object is performed by hashing its name (key) in order to determine the placement group it belongs to. The placement groups (PG) are sets of objects for which all replicas are placed on the same devices. CRUSH is then executed on the identifier of the "placement group" to determine the location of the object. With the clustermap given in Fig. 2(a) and the rule in Fig. 2(b), the placement is performed as follows: *(i)* the root node of the clustermap is selected; *(ii)* 2 children nodes are chosen: in our example "dc1" and "dc2" are automatically selected because they are the only candidates; *(iii)* one rack is selected is each DC, for example "r1" and "r3" in our example; *(iv)* finally, one server is selected in each rack, *e.g.*, the two replicas will be placed on the servers "s5" and "s2".

Figure 3 shows the sequence diagram of the message exchanges we observe in a Rados deployment in a multi-sites context, respectively from a client Fig. 3(a), an OSD Fig. 3(b) and a monitor Fig. 3(c) point of view. In addition to the exchanges between the monitors, Rados uses a large number of keepalives messages between the different nodes. This enables the system to swiftly react in case of failure. We will reuse this Figure in the next section explaining how Rados can be adapted in a Fog infrastructure.

Finally, we highlight that when the network is partitioned, only the data located in the partition where a master monitor can still be elected, is available. This partition does not necessarily exist if none of the parts contains a majority of monitors. In other words, clients belonging to the partition containing a master monitor can access the clustermap and thus any object that is reachable. On the other partitions, because clients cannot get the clustermap they cannot locate and cannot access any object.

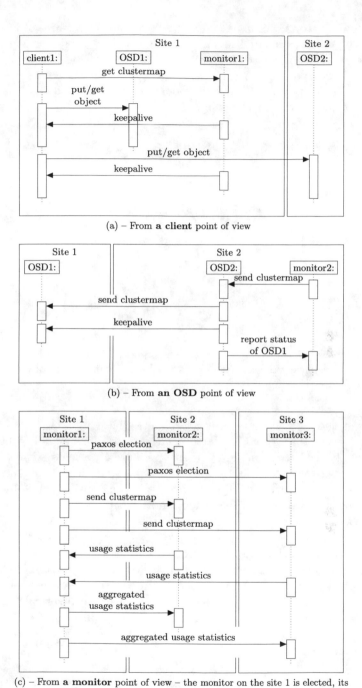

(a) – From **a client** point of view

(b) – From **an OSD** point of view

(c) – From **a monitor** point of view – the monitor on the site 1 is elected, its
clustermap is used by all nodes

Fig. 3. Sequence diagrams of the network traffics observed in Rados.

Fog Considerations. Rados allows administrators to organize objects within pools. Each pool is associated to settings like a replication factor and a "placement rule" describing where the replicas of the objects belonging to the pool are stored. Each "pool" defines a **namespace**, thus, to write or read an object, clients must provide the name of the pool. To retrieve an object, users must know the couple (pool, object_name).

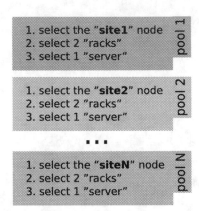

Fig. 4. Example of placement rules associated to pools adapted to a Fog context. The site storing the replicas is specified in each rule. In this example, all objects belonging to a "pool N" are stored on the "site N".

To favor the data locality property we introduced in Sect. 2.3, we propose to use placement rules to constraint objects of a particular pool to be located in one specific DC (*i.e.*, one specific site). Figure 4 presents some placement rules associated to pools. With a pool associated to each site, the drawback is the objects of a user cannot be moved easily. If a user moves, its objects have to be placed in another pool located in another site. So, the user must know in which pool it stores its data. Moreover, this approach implies that all data movements are initiated by the user. For example, an administrator cannot make the decision to move the objects from one location to another one because the user will not be able to find them. The user will continue to use the previous pool which contained its objects and not the new one. A solution for this problem could be to create a pool per user. By changing the placement rule the pool is using, data are automatically relocated to fit the new placement rule. However, this approach is not scalable when the number of users becomes significant as it will considerably increase the size of the clustermap (the list of pools and the placement rules being stored in the clustermap, its size will grow according to the number of pools/users leading to important network overheads each time the clustermap will be exchanged). The limitation in terms of mobility is also another drawback of this approach: because a pool can only be attached to one site, a user cannot store its data across distinct locations. Each time a user moves from one location to another one, it has to request the relocation of its whole pool. In other words, there is no mechanism that enables users/administrators to relocate only the solicited objects. The larger the pool, the more expensive the relocation operation is, facing potentially ping/pong effects where data goes back and forth between sites.

From the Fig. 3 the inter-sites overhead is a mix of Paxos' messages, distributions of clustermap, and usage statistics sent between the monitors. The inter-sites covers also some report of OSD status. To mitigate as much as possible this overhead, we propose to place one monitor per site. This minimizes the report of OSD status between the sites as well as the overhead related to the clustermap retrievals but it maximizes the amount of usage statistics sent between monitors. We do not have checked if the amount of network traffic between the sites becomes less important when fewer monitors are used. But for sure, with fewer monitors, the amount of network traffic vary with the number of clients because some of them have to contact a remote monitor to get the clustermap. We point out the placement of the monitors does not affect the keepalive sent from the OSDs to their neighbours, as depicted in Fig. 3(b). Having one monitor per site avoids the status reporting from the OSD to the monitor becomes an inter-sites traffic. Nevertheless, **the Paxos protocol limits the number of monitors that can be used in Rados and therefore the scalability of the system**.

To conclude, the main adaptations we propose for Rados to fit to the Fog requirements are:

1. Creating a "pool" per user with placement rule for data locality and for mobility support.
2. Placing a monitor per site to limit exchanges of metadata.

We now consider Cassandra as a second possible solution.

3.2   Cassandra

Cassandra [30] is a key value store system that uses gossip and hashing to place the data.

General Overview. Cassandra is organized as a **one-hop Distributed Hash Table (DHT)**. The set of values the object keys are defined on is divided into ranges that are distributed among the nodes composing the system. A **gossip protocol** is used to distribute the topology of the system, the status of the nodes and the ranges affected to them. Each second, each host sends a gossip packet to another one randomly selected. Once gossiped data is received, storage nodes can locate any object without any extra communication. They simply hash the object name and look for using the gossiped data, the node which is responsible for the key.

A quorum, specified by users defines the number of replicas that has to be read or written for each request to validate the operation. Depending on the values used in this quorum, Cassandra can provide different levels of consistency.

This quorum provides a trade-off between access time and data consistency. When the network is partitioned, data can be accessed as long as the client is able to retrieve as many replicas as required by the quorum. As an example, if they are two replicas, one in each network partition and the quorum specified is to retrieve the two replicas for strong consistency, the request of the client will fail because the quorum cannot be satisfied.

Moreover, Cassandra exposes the same notion of "pools" as the one proposed by Rados. Entitled "keyspaces", they define **different namespaces**. Each "keyspace" is associated to a replication factor and to a "replication strategy" defining where the replicas are stored. Like Rados, users have to specify the keyspace's name they want to use when they perform an operation.

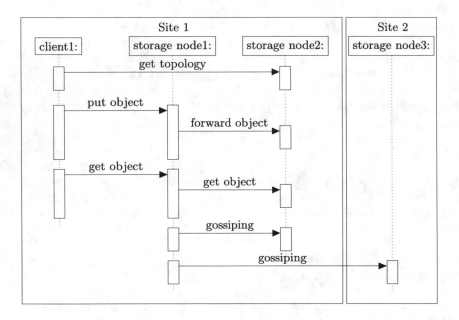

Fig. 5. Sequence diagrams of the network traffics observed in Cassandra.

The major exchanges related to the Cassandra protocol are illustrated on Fig. 5: Clients retrieve the topology from the server they connect to. Then they open a connection with some nodes composing the cluster. Several strategies are proposed to select the server used to send a request. By default, requests are balanced in a round-robin way. Clients send requests alternatively to the servers they are connected to. Each request is then forwarded to the server, which has to handle it (the server is determined based on the aforementioned strategy).

Fog Considerations. As described Cassandra proposes different strategies to locate data throughout the infrastructure. The "NetworkTopologyStrategy" is a placement strategy that specifies how many replicas should be stored on each data center (in our case on each site). For the purpose of our analysis, we configure this strategy in order to have only one copy of an object in a particular site throughout the whole system. Such a strategy enables Cassandra to mitigate the traffic between sites (the different versions of a given object are all located in the same site, limiting the traffic related to synchronize them) and provides the data locality criteria we want to favor. We highlight that having one copy of the data also guarantees strong consistency like proposed by Rados.

With "keyspaces", we have exactly the same problematic with Cassandra we have with the "pools" of Rados. We have to determine how to create the "keyspaces" in the cluster. If a "keyspace" per site is created, the user will have to remember in which "keyspace" each object is stored. Moreover, in case of mobility, the "keyspace" storing the objects will change. With a "keyspace" per user, it avoids users to remember where objects are located but it may not be scalable because "keyspace" list, associated to their replication strategy is replicated on all the nodes. Moreover, in Rados, "pools" settings are propagated from the monitors to the OSDs. In Cassandra, monitors do not exist. The list of "keyspaces" and the replication strategies associated to them is spread on all the storages nodes. To keep this list consistent between the nodes, the operation of creating a "keyspace" requires a lock on all the nodes. The creation of "keyspaces" does not work in a failure context, if some nodes are unavailable.

Moreover, the "replication strategy" associated to a "keyspace" can be modified. However, similar to Rados, the relocation requires explicit administration operations to redefine the replication strategy. Thus, **the mobility is not well-supported by Cassandra**.

Regarding the network traffic in Fig. 5, the gossip messages are the only overhead that goes throughout the different sites. This traffic is independent on the sites activities. But the network traffic inside the sites can vary depending on the size of the sites. Because of the forwarding mechanism previously described, the more nodes a site has, the more the traffic inside the site. With a lot of nodes clients will send their requests to the node which stores the needed object with a lower probability. Thus, the forward mechanism will be more used increasing the amount of network traffic inside each site.

To conclude, the main adaptations we propose for Cassandra are:

1. Creating a "keyspace" per user;
2. Using the "NetworkTopologyStrategy" placement strategy for data locality.

3.3   InterPlanetary File System

InterPlanetary File System [7] has been built on the **BitTorrent protocol** [32] and a **Kademlia DHT** [35]. BitTorrent and Kademlia are both being well-known protocols for their ability to scale to a large number of nodes. While the BitTorrent protocol is used to manipulate objects between the different peers of the system in an efficient manner, the Kademlia DHT is in charge of storing the objects' location. We underline that it is only the locations and not the content of the objects that are stored in the DHT. Such a management of the data locations is an important difference in comparison to Rados and Cassandra that have designed dedicated mechanisms to locate objects without extra communication from the clients point of view.

IPFS uses **immutable objects**. Modifying an existing object lead to creating a new one. Because objects are immutable, it is easier to maintain the consistency between all replicas. Moreover, the BitTorrent protocol that is used to pull the data enables IPFS to retrieve the same object from several sources simultaneously [41].

Contrary to Rados and Cassandra, users cannot choose the object's names. The name of an object depends on its content. Indeed, the name of an object is a checksum of the object. That is also a consequence of the object immutability.

Figure 6 shows the major message exchanges of IPFS. When a client wants to put an object, the client sends the object to a node. This node saves the object locally and then puts the location of the object in the Kademlia DHT. Reciprocally, when a client wants to get an object, it has to contact one peer of IPFS. This peer checks if it stores the object locally. In this case, the object is

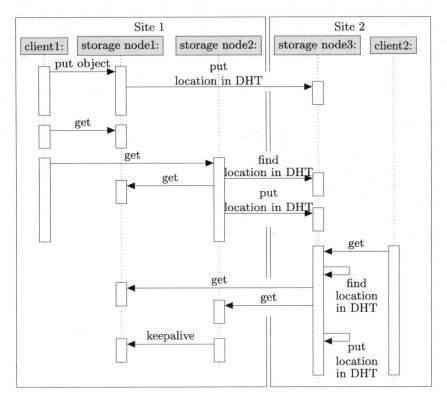

Fig. 6. Sequence diagram of the network traffic observed in IPFS from **a client** point of view. The read from "client2" on "storage node2" can only be performed after the object was relocated on this storage node, at the end of the read from "client1".

directly send to the client. Otherwise, the IPFS node will use the Kademlia DHT
to determine the node in charge of delivering the object. Based on the Kademlia
reply, the request is forwarded to the correct node. This node will send the object
to the initial IPFS peer that will make a copy before serving the client. Thanks
to such an approach, **IPFS supports the mobility of data in a native
fashion**. This node reports the existence of its new replica in the DHT, so that
a future read can be satisfied by this node, closer to the client. Storage nodes
send regularly keepalive messages to maintain the DHT. The DHT contains the
location of all the replicas of all the objects. In case of remote reading, the DHT
is accessed two times: a first time to retrieve the location of the needed object
and a second time to update the location, in order to reflect the existence of the
new replica.

Fog Considerations. By its design, IPFS favors to store objects locally: only
the use of the Kademlia DHT leads to inter-sites traffic. In conclusion, there is
no specific adaptation to achieve with IPFS in order to better fit the Fog requirements than the default configuration. IPFS can work partially in disconnected
mode as long as both the object location can be found in the Kademlia DHT
and the node storing the object is reachable.

3.4 Fog Characteristics Met for the Object Stores

Table 1 summarizes how do Rados, Cassandra and IPFS fit the requirements
that have been defined in Sect. 2.3. As discussed previously, the data locality
property in Rados and Cassandra can lead to scalability problems if a pool or a
keyspace is created for each user. Also, these two systems support the mobility
partially because they require an administration intervention. Rados supports
partially the network containment characteristic because its use of the CRUSH
algorithm. Finally, the Paxos algorithm does not make Rados scalable.

In the next part, we perform performance evaluation of the three systems
but Rados can only be used as a reference point because of it lacks of scalability
and functionality in a Fog context.

Table 1. Summary of Fog characteristics *a priori* met for 3 different object stores.

	Rados	Cassandra	IPFS
Data locality	**Yes**	**Yes**	Yes
Network containment	**Partially**	Yes	**No**
Disconnected mode	**Partially**	Yes	**Partially**
Mobility support	**Partially**	**No**	Natively
Scalability	**No**	Yes	Yes

4 Benchmark of Rados, Cassandra and IPFS

This section discusses the different evaluations we performed. Experiments settings are given in Sect. 4.1. Section 4.2 analyzes a first set of experiments that aimed to evaluate the network containment property. A second set of experiments that enabled us to investigate remote access performance (*i.e.*, when objects are accessed from a remote Fog site) is discussed in Sect. 4.3.

4.1 Material and Method

The material and method we used for the benchmark are described in the following.

Testbed Description. Experiments have been performed on the Grid'5000 testbed [6], using the "Paravance" cluster hosted in the city of Rennes (Dell powerEdge, Intel Xeon, 16 cores, 128 GB RAM, 10 Gbps Ethernet).

The Fog architecture we emulated as well as the way we deployed the different systems are presented in Fig. 7. Each Fog site is composed of two storage servers and one additional server is deployed to deliver the Monitor service for Rados experiments. Finally, each site has its own local client. Latencies between servers is set using the Linux traffic control utility (`tc`). Unless otherwise specified, we use $L_{Fog} = 10$ ms and $L_{Core} = 50$ ms. The latency between the servers located on a same site is considered low and has been set to 0.5 ms. The throughput of the network links is set to 10 Gbps, both for intra and inter-sites links. More details about the physical topology are given on the Grid'5000 website: https://www.grid5000.fr/mediawiki/index.php/Rennes:Network.

There are two reasons to simplify the network model by considering only the latency in this work. The first reason is the network latency is a good measure of the geographical distance. According to Dabek *et al.* [18] by example, "inter-host RTT is dominated by geographic distance". We consider the geographical distance between the sites is more important than the distance for a client to reach

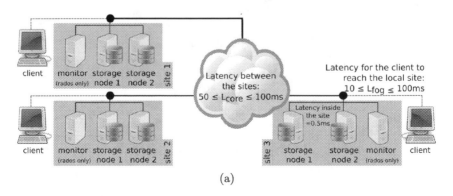

(a)

Fig. 7. Topology used to deploy Rados, Cassandra and IPFS in a Fog environment. Monitors are only deployed for Rados.

its site. Therefore, we set $L_{Core} > L_{Fog}$. The second reason is network impairment can be considered as an increase of the latency. Indeed, according to the Nielsen's law [36] and more recent studies [24] the latency is a predominant criterion that results from network impairments such as network congestion, packet losses, retransmission and so on. Finally, according to Padhye et al., increasing the latency has also an impact on the throughput achievable by TCP [37].

The definition of placement strategies such as described in Sects. 3.1 and 3.2 has been achieved respectively for Rados and Cassandra. This enabled us to write all data locally (we remind that data is written on the server the client contacts for IPFS). We configured the replication strategy of each system in order to get only one copy of each object. This modification enabled us to get a minimal boundary of access times. We believe the replication for fault tolerance can only increase the access times. We assume that a given technic of replication may impact the access times of the three systems in the same way. Therefore, to get the best access times as possible, we disabled it. We also modified the code of IPFS to avoid the intensive replication strategy it uses for metadata: by default for each object, it inserts ten copies of the corresponding metadata in the Kademlia DHT. We disabled this mechanism in order to get only one copy. Disabling all replications mechanisms allowed us to remove any possible bias in our analysis of pros/cons of the storage protocols used in each of the three systems.

Finally, the metrics we measured are the time taken to perform each operation on each site and the amount of network traffic sent between them on the experiment period. All file system partitions are unmounted between each experiment to avoid cache effects between consecutive executions.

YCSB Benchmark and Workloads. The Yahoo Cloud System Benchmark [16] (YCSB) has been used to evaluate the three systems. YCSB proposes different workloads depending (i) on the amount of data written, (ii) the size of the objects, (iii) the proportions of read, update and delete operations and also (iv) on how the objects selection is achieved. Our experiments performed write and read accesses of different sizes: clients connect the storage systems, execute write and then read operations to finally close their connection. Neither update nor delete operations are performed. The object sizes have been chosen to be representative to real scenarios [5]. Because different object stores can be suited for different object sizes, we chose to perform our tests using three sizes: 256 KB, 1 MB and 10 MB. Objects sizes of 256 KB correspond to online gaming and web hosting whereas 10 MB can be the size of object used in enterprise backup. 1 MB is an intermediate value. The number of objects used is varying from 1 to 100 per site to show how the systems react under a high load. The number of threads used by YCSB is equal to the number of objects so that all objects are written in a parallel way. In the reading phase, each object is read once and only once thanks to the "sequential" request distribution provided by YCSB. We did not use the default "zipfian" or "uniform" distributions because an object can be read several times, favoring IPFS due to the automatic relocation of data. We point out that the "sequential" distribution does not mean the objects are read sequentially by the client. It means that function returning to the different threads the name of the objects they have to read, this function reads the list of the objects sequentially.

We considered scenarios using 1, 7 and 11 sites simultaneously (*i.e.*, an instance of YCSB is launched on each client of each site). Although Fog environment can be composed of a more significant number of sites, we highlight that performing experiments up to 11 sites is enough to identify several issues the storage systems face to in this context. Each experiment has been performed at least 10 times (10 trials) to get stability in results. Unless precised, the standard deviation is not presented in our discussion as it corresponds in most cases to few hundredths of seconds. Gathered access times correspond to the time to write or read one object (*i.e.*, the time we discuss does not take into account the establishment and closing of connections). This choice is mainly due to the Cassandra client that requires a significant amount of time to open and close connections with the Fog site.

Last but not the least, we highlight that we had to implement a module for IPFS[2]. This module uses the "java-ipfs-api" library proposed by the IPFS developers. To prevent any bias in our study, the IPFS module sends requests in a random way between the servers of the site. This means that one object can have been written on one server and then a read request can be sent to the other server of the site. This behavior is required to avoid accessing the same server and thus never contacting the Kademlia DHT (as described in Sect. 3.3, if the client contacts the server that stores the requested object, the request can be satisfied without contacting the DHT).

4.2   Local Access Analysis

All clients (one per site) execute the scenario simultaneously: they write objects on their site and read them. The goal is to evaluate data locality as well as network containment properties of the three systems. This last property has been evaluated by measuring the amount of network traffic exchanged between the site and by analyzing how the object access time is impacted when the number of sites grows.

Writing and Reading Times. Tables 2(a), (b) and (c) show respectively for Rados, Cassandra and IPFS, the mean times to complete either a write or a read operation. For each of the three systems, we can see that the access times are in the same order of magnitude with respect to the number of sites composing the Fog/Edge infrastructure. As an example, it takes 0.96 s per object when 100 objects of 1 MB are written on 1 site and 1.05 s using 11 sites for Rados (represented both in bold in the table). Values for Cassandra follow the same trend. By using a mechanism that enables the location of each object without requiring a remote request, the object access time for Rados and Cassandra is not impacted by the number of sites composing the Fog/Edge infrastructure. As

---

[2] The source code is available at https://github.com/bconfais/YCSB.

Table 2. Mean time (seconds) to write or read one object with Rados (a), Cassandra (b) and IPFS (c) using 1, 7 and 11 sites. Bold values are particularly discussed in the text.

		Mean **writing** time (seconds)				Mean **reading** time (seconds)		
	Number / Size	256 KB	1 MB	10 MB	Number / Size	256 KB	1 MB	10 MB
1 site	1	0.42	0.78	3.40	1	0.39	0.74	2.53
	10	0.35	0.71	3.24	10	0.34	0.64	2.27
	100	0.35	**0.96**	9.45	100	0.32	0.62	5.83
7 sites	1	0.44	0.85	3.44	1	0.40	0.77	2.50
	10	0.35	0.68	3.42	10	0.34	0.64	2.34
	100	0.34	1.01	9.41	100	0.32	0.62	6.06
11 sites	1	0.43	0.82	3.74	1	0.40	0.76	2.56
	10	0.36	0.72	3.62	10	0.34	0.65	2.24
	100	0.36	**1.05**	9.50	100	0.32	0.61	**5.80**

(a) – Rados

		Mean **writing** time (seconds)				Mean **reading** time (seconds)		
	Number / Size	256 KB	1 MB	10 MB	Number / Size	256 KB	1 MB	10 MB
1 site	1	0.36	0.72	1.74	1	0.34	0.64	1.78
	10	0.21	0.53	1.89	10	0.16	0.46	1.81
	100	0.46	1.26	9.75	100	0.45	1.10	8.85
7 sites	1	0.36	0.67	1.92	1	0.30	0.56	1.75
	10	0.22	0.56	2.11	10	0.18	0.42	1.67
	100	0.56	1.28	9.97	100	0.38	0.96	8.89
11 sites	1	0.38	0.67	1.91	1	0.31	0.62	1.80
	10	0.21	0.57	2.06	10	0.17	0.43	1.70
	100	0.55	1.32	9.76	100	0.40	0.97	**11.75**

(b) – Cassandra

		Mean **writing** time (seconds)				Mean **reading** time (seconds)		
	Number / Size	256 KB	1 MB	10 MB	Number / Size	256 KB	1 MB	10 MB
1 site	1	0.42	0.69	1.69	1	0.23	0.26	0.57
	10	0.24	0.34	1.81	10	0.14	0.25	0.50
	100	0.35	1.23	**12.20**	100	0.22	0.61	**3.95**
7 sites	1	0.41	0.62	1.69	1	0.22	0.36	0.59
	10	0.22	0.43	1.85	10	0.18	0.32	0.51
	100	0.40	1.32	11.54	100	0.25	0.66	3.94
11 sites	1	0.41	0.65	1.65	1	0.26	0.37	0.64
	10	0.24	0.33	1.93	10	0.19	0.26	0.49
	100	0.35	1.16	**11.86**	100	0.22	0.61	**3.93**

(c) – IPFS

discussed later, most of the inter-sites network traffics are sent asynchronously and thus does not impact negatively the performance.

For IPFS, the results are rather surprising as we expected to observe performance degradations for Fog and Edge infrastructures composed of a significant number of sites: the probability to contact a remote site for determining the location of an object increases with respect to the number of sites and accessing the DHT adds a penalty to the object access time. However, we did not observe such an overhead (12.20 vs 11.86 s to write one object in the 100×10 MB workload using 3 and 11 sites). Diving into details, we discovered that an object insertion leads to two operations. The first one that consists of storing the object locally on the server is done in a synchronous manner. The second one that consists of pushing the metadata in the Kademlia DHT is performed in an asynchronous manner that is after answering the client. This means that the impact of storing the meta information on a remote server is not visible for write operations. Only read operations can lead to request the DHT is a synchronous manner. However, because of the topology we used, the number of manipulated objects and the number of sites is not important enough to observe performance penalties (3.95 vs 3.93 s to read one object in the 100×10 MB workload using 3 and 11 sites). For each client, half of the objects previously created will be retrieved without accessing the DHT. A specific experiment on the overhead of the DHT is discussed in more details in Sect. 5.

Tables show also that access times are faster for reading than writing for the three systems. There are several reasons for this. The first reason is the hard drives used to store the objects does not have the same performance in writing and in reading. The second reason is that inserting an object requires to compute its hash to determine the node of the DHT which has to store its location. Hash computation also explains that the access time grows with the size of the object: the larger the object, the longer is the access time. Finally, we can observe that accessing to a large number of objects in parallel on each client degrades the performance (0.49 vs 3.93 s for the workloads 10×10 MB and 10×100 MB in reading with 11 sites). This trend is due to the load on each client that increases to perform the different computations. In addition to determining the hash, Rados and Cassandra clients should compute the object locations. For IPFS, we noticed that the client can only perform two requests simultaneously. This means that even if the YCSB module we implemented, generates 100 requests in parallel (using 100 threads), the IPFS client can only handle them two by two. This weak parallelism leads to worse performance.

To summarize, Rados and Cassandra have stable access times, and only the load on each client seems to penalize the performance. For IPFS, additional experiments should be performed to better quantify the Kademlia DHT impacts on the access times. This is done in Sect. 5.

Inter-sites Traffic Analysis. Figures 8 and 9 show the amount of network traffic sent between sites for the 7 and 11 sites scenarios. First, it is noteworthy that the traffic quantity exchanged between sites is relatively small in comparison

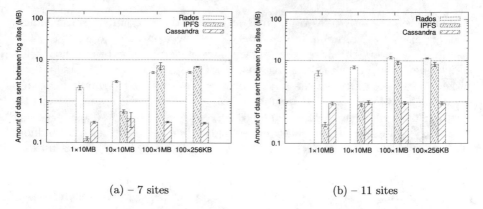

(a) – 7 sites   (b) – 11 sites

Fig. 8. Cumulated amount of network traffic exchanged between all the sites while clients **write** objects on their sites. The scale is logarithmic and the error bar represents the standard deviation.

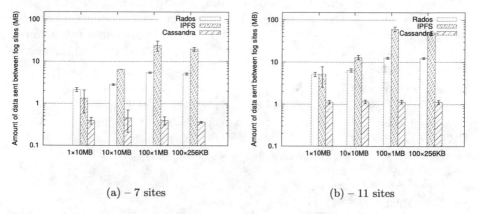

(a) – 7 sites   (b) – 11 sites

Fig. 9. Cumulated amount of network traffic exchanged between all the sites while clients **read** objects located on their sites. The scale is logarithmic and the error bar represents the standard deviation.

to the amount of data stored (less than 2%). Even if this amount of inter-sites network traffic is low, it could have an important impact on the access times.

For Rados, the amount of traffic that is exchanged between sites is similar for writing and reading and depends on the number of object manipulated and not their size (by adding sites, we increase the number of clients and thus the total number of objects manipulated). As previously described in Fig. 3(c), storage nodes send status and statistics to monitors that increases the amount of network traffic. As discussed in Sect. 3.1, it is possible to reduce the number of monitors (we used one monitor per site). While it will decrease the network overheads related to monitors, it will increase the traffic related to the OSD status reporting and clustermap retrievals.

For IPFS, the inter-sites traffic corresponds to the Kademlia DHT messages that are used to determine and update object locations. Because the DHT is distributed among the sites, these operations generate network traffic. More traffic is exchanged for read accesses because in this case, the DHT is accessed twice: one time to retrieve the object location and a second time to announce the availability of the replica created on the server. We will see in Sect. 5 that this network traffic can be reduced for IPFS.

For Cassandra, the amount of traffic increases in a linear way with the number of nodes because each second every node sends a gossip packet to another one, as explained in Sect. 3.2. Because some traffics can be asynchronous and do not impact the access times, we computed the correlations between the amount of network traffic sent and the access times for read operations on the 7 sites scenario: 0.13 for Rados, −0.46 for Cassandra and 0.98 for IPFS. It confirms for Rados and Cassandra, the network traffic does not impact the access times. For IPFS, the correlation is higher because nodes have to wait an answer from the DHT before relocating the object and sending it to the client.

To conclude, only Cassandra has a good behaviour in term of network traffic exchanged during a local access. The amount of network traffic is indeed lower than 1.5 MB using 11 sites. Details about all network traffic (intra and inter-sites) are given in Appendix A.

Impact of Inter-sites Latency (L_{Core}). In this experiment, we want to determine how the network latency between the different sites impacts the object access times. In particular, we want to quantify whether accessing the Kademlia DHT for IPFS is critical. The value of L_{Fog} is set to 10 ms (like in the previous experiment) and the value of L_{Core} has been successively defined to 50 ms, 75 ms and 100 ms. We executed the 7 sites scenario but instead of manipulating 100 objects we increased this number up to 400. The goal was to generate a sufficient number of requests to the DHT. Figure 10 shows the average time for writing and reading one object depending on the L_{Core} value. Regarding write accesses, the curves show that increasing the latency between Fog sites does not impact the performance. This is because there is no synchronous exchange for write operations as discussed in the previous paragraphs. Regarding read operations, we can observe for IPFS the penalty of accessing the DHT for a large number of objects (the curve increases from 9.74 s to 15.67 s according to L_{Core}). We also experimented with L_{Core} greater than 100 ms but Rados stopped to work because it was unable to perform the Paxos election.

Impact Latency Access to the Fog (L_{Fog}). Similarly to L_{Core}, we wanted to evaluate the impact of the L_{Fog} latency (the latency between clients located at the Edge and the servers in the site to which they belong). Clients can use wireless links that can be shared among a lot of users with packet loss and congestion, increasing the latency. The value of L_{Core} has been set to 50 ms while increasing the value of L_{Fog} from 2 ms to 100 ms. The latency between the servers of one site has not been modified (0.5 ms).

Figure 11 shows the average access time to write one object for Rados, Cassandra and IPFS as a function of the L_{Fog} value (trends being similar in writing

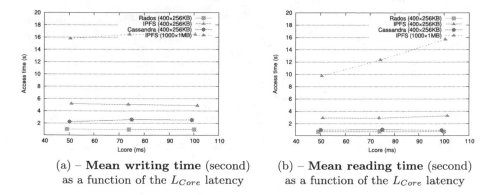

(a) – **Mean writing time** (second)
as a function of the L_{Core} latency

(b) – **Mean reading time** (second)
as a function of the L_{Core} latency

Fig. 10. Mean access time to **write** and **read** one object when the value of L_{Core} latency vary from 50 ms to 100 ms A workload of 400×256 KB is used on 7 sites. For IPFS a workload of 1000×1 MB is also used.

and reading, we only draw the results for the write operation). Curves show that the latency L_{Fog} has an impact for the three systems. However, we expected that the impact of L_{Fog} would be the same for the three systems because for writing, the client just sends the data to a storage server of the site it belongs to. It appears that L_{Fog} latency has a bigger impact on Cassandra. Its access times are increased from 1.28 to 11.91 s ($\times 9.30$) whereas with Rados, access times are only increased from 1.01 to 5.02 s ($\times 4.97$) Fig. 12 depicts this protocol: when a client writes an object, it first selects a server (with CRUSH for Rados, in a round-robin way for Cassandra and randomly for IPFS) and sends the object. All traffic behind this exchange is not governed by the L_{Fog} metric. To understand why the impact of Cassandra is more important than for Rados and IPFS.

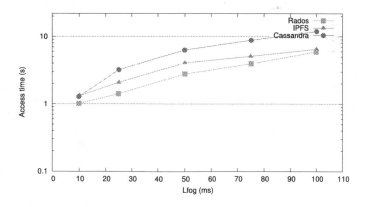

Fig. 11. Access time to write and read one object when the value of L_{fog} latency vary from 10 ms to 100 ms. Values in writing and reading are the same. A workload of 100×1 MB and a topology composed of 7 sites are used. Scale is semi-logarithmic on the y-axis.

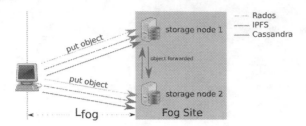

Fig. 12. Traffic sent by the client when writing for the three systems. The forward for Cassandra is not impacted by L_{fog} latency.

Indeed, the only extra traffic in writing for Cassandra is the forward that is performed between the servers of the site and thus, that is not impacted by the L_{Fog} latency. We also tried to use the "TokenAware" policy of Cassandra avoiding the forwarding mechanism but the result is not convincing. Further experiments are mandatory but left for future work.

Summary. These experiments evaluated the behaviour of the systems while manipulating objects stored locally (*i.e.*, on the closest site). Rados and IPFS get good performance in terms of access times but the amount of network traffic sent between the sites is linear to the number of objects accessed, which is a limiting factor. We observed the L_{Core} latency is not critical for the two systems although it should stay below 100 ms for Rados. For Cassandra, access times are higher but the amount of network traffic sent between the sites depends only on the total number of storage nodes. This allows Cassandra to scale to a large number of accessed objects. However, Cassandra seems to be more impacted by high network latencies between the nodes than the other systems.

In the next part, we discuss experiments that write objects on one site and read them from another one.

4.3 Remote Reading Evaluation

The second experiment aims to evaluate the mobility criteria. Concretely, we want to analyze what are the impacts on the completion times (the time to read or write one object) when a client writes data on its local site and another client reads it from another location. We use the same topology as in the previous experiments with 7 sites. Rados, Cassandra and IPFS nodes are deployed in the same way but only two clients among the seven are used. Others sites provide nodes to IPFS DHT, monitors to Rados and generates gossip traffic for Cassandra.

Concretely, the following operations are performed: one client creates the objects on its site. Then, caches are dropped and another client located on another site reads the objects. Read is performed twice in order to analyze the benefits of having the implicit creation of a copy on the local site for IPFS. We remind that for Rados and Cassandra, objects are not explicitly relocated on

Table 3. Mean time (seconds) to read twice one object stored on a remote site with Rados (a), Cassandra (b) and IPFS (c). The topology is composed of 7 sites but only one is used to read. Bold values are particularly discussed in the text.

Mean remote **reading** time (seconds) First read				Mean remote **reading** time (seconds) Second read			
Number \ Size	256 KB	1 MB	10 MB	Number \ Size	256 KB	1 MB	10 MB
1	1.80	3.34	**9.36**	1	1.84	3.42	9.21
10	1.80	3.31	**8.38**	10	1.83	3.29	8.10
100	1.72	3.09	**12.14**	100	1.72	3.09	11.66

(a) – Rados

Mean remote **reading** time (seconds) First read				Mean remote **reading** time (seconds) Second read			
Number \ Size	256 KB	1 MB	10 MB	Number \ Size	256 KB	1 MB	10 MB
1	1.46	3.01	**9.65**	1	1.41	3.06	9.43
10	1.53	3.97	12.43	10	1.53	3.75	12.52
100	3.77	8.26	**19.86**	100	3.87	8.14	21.43

(b) – Cassandra

Mean remote **reading** time (seconds) First read				Mean remote **reading** time (seconds) Second read			
Number \ Size	256 KB	1 MB	10 MB	Number \ Size	256 KB	1 MB	10 MB
1	0.99	1.24	3.03	1	0.18	0.43	**0.35**
10	0.70	1.15	5.23	10	0.16	0.36	0.31
100	1.28	**4.00**	38.85	100	0.21	0.61	2.96

(c) – IPFS

the site the user performs read (*i.e.* data placement constraints are not modified dynamically in Rados and in Cassandra). We just evaluate the time to perform a remote read. The goal is to show the need for data relocation.

Tables 3(a), (b) and (c) show the access times we get in this scenario for Rados, Cassandra and IPFS respectively. Writing times are the same as in the previous experimentation when data are written on only one site and thus we have not reported the results in Table 3. Regarding read accesses, for the first ones, Rados client contacts directly the remote OSD storing the requested object (with a network latency equal to $L_{Fog} + L_{Core}$). So the increase of access time in reading is only due to the transfer of objects over the link having a L_{Core} latency between the client and the remote storage node. It takes 9.36 s to read 1 object of 10 MB remotely. This is roughly five times the time we measured in the previous experiment (2.53 s in Table 2(a)). We observe the remote read is more efficient with Rados with small objects. With a lot of objects, the parallelism between the objects limits the increase of access times due to the network latency. As an example with only 10 objects of 10 MB it is approximately 4 times longer to read remotely than locally (8.38 vs 2.27 s) but with 100 objects it becomes only 2.08 times longer to read remotely (12.14 vs 5.83 s).

With IPFS and Cassandra, requests are sent to a local storage node that locates the object and retrieves it before forwarding it to the client (as shown by the sequences diagrams in the Figs. 5 and 6 on Pages 12 and 14 respectively). This mechanism increases the reading time. Moreover, only half of the requests (the ones that requested objects to the node which does not store them) was forwarded for local accesses. In this new experiment, because objects are stored remotely, the forward is performed for all requests.

For Cassandra, a remote read of 1×10 MB takes 9.65 s whereas it lasted only 1.78 s in the previous experiment to perform a local one (Table 2(b)). The metadata management does not imply an increasing of access time because with Cassandra, once the gossip has been propagated, every node can locate any object without any communication. Like in Rados, the increase of access time is only due to the object transfer using a high latency network link. We point out that Cassandra is the system that gets the highest increase of access times: a remote read of 100 objects of 10 MB takes 19.86 s per object whereas a local one in the previous experiment took 8.85 s.

For IPFS, when the read is done, the local node writes the object locally and updates the DHT asynchronously. The increase of access time for a remote read comes from the data transfer but also from the access to the DHT. In this scenario, each remote read requires a DHT request whereas some local read does not need it. We observe that access times for a remote read are 5 times more important than for a local access in all cases (as an example, 4.00 vs 1.23 s in Table 2(c) 100×1 MB), except for 100×10 MB.

The last columns of the Table 2(c) that, the access times for the second read in IPFS are in the same order of magnitude than in the previous experiment. Namely, IPFS spends 0.35 s to read 1 object of 10 MB (vs 0.57 s in the previous experiment). The small improvement of access times is due to the fact in this scenario, there is only one site solicited while the DHT is spread on 7 sites. When a request is sent to a node that does not store the object, this node downloads it from all the nodes storing a replica. In a second read, the replica stored locally (due to the first read) and the original replica stored remotely are requested in parallel. This strategy may degrade the performance and increase the amount of traffic sent between the sites. To conclude on IPFS, access times are low because the requested nodes serve a copy of objects they kept in the first read.

For Rados and Cassandra, access times are identical for the first and the second read. The mobility of data is not explicit and thus the second access generates a remote read again. Because access times are high in case of remote reading, we next evaluate what is the influence of the network latency on these values.

Impact of Inter-sites Latency (L_{Core}) in Case of Remote Access. The goal of this experiment is to show how the remote read is impacted by L_{Core},

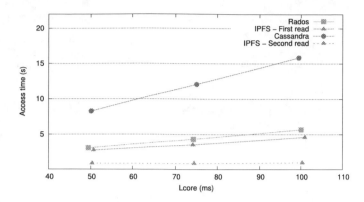

Fig. 13. Access time to read one object stored remotely when the value of L_{core} latency vary from 50 ms to 100 ms. A workload of 400×256 MB and a topology with 7 sites are used.

to show the need to relocate the objects on the local site. We performed the same test and varied the value of L_{Core} latency between 50 ms and 100 ms. But this time, we used the same scenario as in the second experiment, where a client reads data stored remotely.

Figure 13 shows the access times we got for reading. The increase of access times is as much important as in the case where L_{Fog} latency varied because data are sent using the inter-sites links. Rados and Cassandra behave like in Sect. 4.2, when the latency inside the sites were varying for a local access. As shown in the Fig. 10 on the impact of L_{Core} latency in a local access scenario, metadata sent asynchronously does not impact the access times, thus only the object transfers are impacted by the network latencies. For IPFS, the increase of latency also impacts the DHT to determine the location of the objects. The access times for the second read are lower for IPFS, because as said previously, objects are retrieved from the local nodes which stored a replica at the end of the first read. The small increasing of access time is due to the DHT that needs to be accessed when the request for the second read is sent to the node that does not store the object. We suppose with 1000 objects, the second read will be influenced by L_{Core} value as for the local read in Fig. 10: in this case, the DHT access will represent a large part of the access time. This additional experiment shows the latency L_{Core} has an important influence on access times for remote access. Objects should be relocated on the closest site instead of being reading remotely.

4.4   Summary of the Evaluation of the Three Systems

To conclude, completion times for local accesses depend essentially on four parameters: the number of sites, the latencies inside and between the sites and the number of objects accessed. Table 4 summarizes for each system what are the parameters which have an impact on the local access times.

Table 4. Stability of the access times when the following parameters are increasing.

	Rados	Cassandra	IPFS
Number of sites	☺☺	☺☺	☺
Latency L_{fog}	☺	☺☺	☺☺
Latency L_{core}	☺☺	☺	☺
Number of accessed objects	☺	☺☺	☺☺

Rados is sensible to the latency between the sites (L_{Core}) because with a high latency greater than 100 ms, it stops to work. The Paxos protocol as well as the number of pools needed in a Fog context makes it non scalable to a huge number of sites and a huge number of objects increases the amount of network traffic but this traffic has a low impact on the access times.

Cassandra is sensible to the latency to reach the site of Fog (L_{Fog}) as well as the inter-sites latency (L_{Core}). Adding sites generates more network traffic and higher access times. Nevertheless, it differs from the others systems because the workload characteristics (the number of accessed objects and their size) has no influence on the access times. Cassandra is scalable to a very important number of objects but may be limited in number of sites (time to get a the status and the range of keys the other nodes are responsible for may become long).

We showed IPFS provides low access times that are not so impacted when the L_{Fog} and L_{Core} latencies are increased (as the number of objects access is small). The second experiment showed the relocation of data is needed in a Fog context: IPFS is the only system that is able to place automatically and natively the data as close as the user as possible. For this reason, IPFS may be considered to be used in a Fog environment. Nevertheless, the amount of network traffic exchanged between the sites, highly correlated to the access times, depends on the number of accessed objects which is a scalability challenge when a huge number of objects is accessed. In the next section, we evaluate more precisely the impacts of the DHT on the access times when IPFS is used with more clients. We also propose a solution to mitigate the network traffic exchanges in case of local reads.

5   Coupling IPFS with a Scale-Out NAS System

In this section, we focus on IPFS. We first evaluate the impact of the DHT on the access times and then, we propose to couple IPFS with a Scale-Out NAS to mitigate the use of the DHT for local reads. We evaluate the benefit of this approach regarding the cost of accessing remote meta data.

5.1   Cost of Accessing a Global DHT Covering All the Sites

We now evaluate in IPFS how the DHT impacts the access times. We focus on the local access of one site, when a client reads and write objects stored locally.

These experiments are performed on a topology composed of 3 sites, each site containing 4 storage nodes. Only one site is associated to 10 clients in order to increase the number of objects accessed. The latency to reach the Fog site (L_{Fog}) is still equal to 10 ms but we increase the inter-sites latency (L_{Core}) to the extreme value of 200 ms. This value can correspond to the inter-sites latency of a mobile Fog site located in a train or in a bus (see Fig. 1). We now use a tmpfs as a low-level backend to reduce the impact of the storage mechanisms on the access times and to conduct a more fair comparison between IPFS and IPFS coupled with a Scale-Out NAS (*i.e.*, we would like to remove the possible bias that can be generated by ext4 file system). Finally, we implemented our own benchmark by imitating the YCSB one. The goal was to be able to easily measure the access time of each object individually. Each of the 10 clients writes and reads 100 objects on the site, for a total of 1000 objects accessed. Figure 14 shows for a given client, the reading time of each object while accessing 100 objects of 256 KB stored locally on the site. Values are given for IPFS used alone as well as for our solution labelled "IPFS+RozoFS" that will be detailed in the next section.

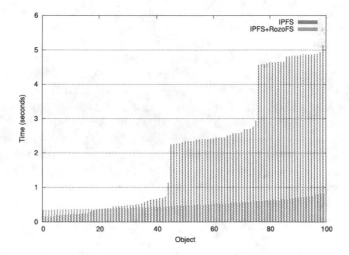

Fig. 14. Time to read every object for a given client and a given iteration with a workload of 100×256 KB.

The first thing we observe when IPFS is used alone is the big gap in access times between the first object read and the last one. We also observe 4 plateaux in the curve, delimiting set of objects that have a similar reading time. The first plateau can be seen for the first 25 objects. These objects are read quickly because there are 4 IPFS nodes on the site and with 100 requests, 25 requests in probability will be sent to a node that stores the requested object. Therefore, the DHT is not accessed to locate these objects. Then, the second plateau (objects 25 to 43) shows the objects that are a bit longer to read than the previous ones.

For these objects the DHT has to be accessed and the object relocated on the node the request is sent to. But the node storing the location of the object is located within the site, so there is no request sent outside the site, keeping a low access time. Finally, the longer objects to read (objects 43 to 100) are ones for which the location of the object is stored on a node located outside the site, reachable in one (objects 43 to 78) or several hops (objects 78 to 100).

This experiment shows that with a bigger latency between Fog sites and more clients, the DHT of IPFS increases significantly the access times. We now present how to fix this problem and how we obtain the result of the second histogram labelled "IPFS+RozoFS".

5.2   Coupling IPFS with a Scale-Out NAS

We propose to improve IPFS by adding a Scale-Out NAS deployed locally and independently on each site of Fog. Instead of storing the objects in the local storage device directly, IPFS nodes store the objects in the Scale-Out NAS deployed on the site. This enables all the nodes of a site to access all the objects stored on it without using the DHT to locate them.

In writing, clients send their objects to an IPFS node which stores them in the Scale-Out NAS system. The DHT is still updated asycnhronously to make the objects available for the other sites. In reading, when a locally stored object is requested, the IPFS node will find it in the Scale-Out NAS and thus will not request the DHT to locate it. The object will be sent directly to the client, lowering both the access times and the amount of network traffic exchanged between the sites of Fog. The DHT is only accessed to locate objects located on the other sites. We also point out the Scale-Out NAS system enables IPFS to work in case of network partitioning because clients can access objects stored locally without the need to contact the other sites to locate the objects.

We propose to evaluate this approach using IPFS on top a RozoFS [40], an open-source solution that is able to achieve high performance both for sequential and random access. RozoFS uses a metadata-server to locate data. It is not a problem to use such a metadata server because RozoFS cluster is limited to one site, IPFS nodes does not suffer from extra latency to reach it. RozoFS distributes (thanks to the Mojette erasure code) each object onto several storage nodes (here over 3 nodes). Just 2 nodes out of the 3 are necessary to decode and read the object. Any other Scale-Out NAS system could participate in theory to the demonstration of the interest of getting a storage backend under an Object Store system as IPFS. We compare the performance of our approach with the performance obtained using a traditional IPFS cluster.

The topology and the software architecture used is described in Fig. 15. There are only 3 sites and each site contains one client, 4 storage nodes and a metadata server for RozoFS. The storage nodes of RozoFS are colocated on the IPFS nodes. The coupling may be easily implemented because as explained in the Fig. 6 of the Sect. 3.3, an IPFS node does not access the DHT when it first finds the object locally. This coupling of IPFS with RozoFS consists to place the folder IPFS uses to store the objects in a RozoFS POSIX mountpoint. Nonetheless, we made a

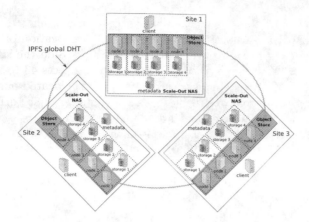

Fig. 15. Topology used to deploy an object store on top of a Scale-Out NAS local to each site.

small modification in IPFS. By default, each time an IPFS node wants to read an object stored remotely, it accesses the DHT and contacts the nodes storing it. However, it does not request only this object but all the previous requested objects for which the download is not finished yet. This increases the network traffic between sites because objects are received several times. Our modification consists to request only the object to the nodes specified in the DHT.

Table 5 shows the access times when IPFS is used natively and on top of RozoFS with 3 clients writing and reading on their site (for a L_{Core} latency

Table 5. Mean time (seconds) to write or read one object using IPFS alone (a) and IPFS on top of RozoFS (b).

		Mean **writing** time (seconds)			Mean **reading** time (seconds)			
	Number ╲ Size	256 KB	1 MB	10 MB	Number ╲ Size	256 KB	1 MB	10 MB
3 sites	1	0.17	0.22	0.34	1	0.25	0.28	0.54
	10	0.17	0.21	0.40	10	0.26	0.27	0.54
	100	0.33	1.07	3.92	100	0.29	0.50	1.98

(a) – Using the default approach of IPFS.

		Mean **writing** time (seconds)			Mean **reading** time (seconds)			
	Number ╲ Size	256 KB	1 MB	10 MB	Number ╲ Size	256 KB	1 MB	10 MB
3 sites	1	0.18	0.23	0.38	1	0.14	0.18	0.31
	10	0.17	0.22	0.43	10	0.14	0.18	0.36
	100	0.33	1.08	3.97	100	0.19	0.36	1.83

(b) – Using IPFS on top of a RozoFS cluster deployed in each site.

back 50 ms). The first thing we notice is the access times using IPFS alone are in the same order of magnitudes than the ones we got in the previous experiment (Table 2(c)). For example it takes 1.07 s to write one object in a 100 × 1 MB workload using 3 sites whereas it took 1.32 s in Table 2(c) using 7 sites. Only the scenario of 100 × 10 MB gets higher access times (11.54 s with 7 sites vs 3.92 with 3 sites). Using a `tmpfs` removes the need to flush data on a hard drive. The table also shows the writing access times are similar using RozoFS as a backend or IPFS alone. As an example, it takes 0.21 s to write one object with a 10 × 1 MB workload with IPFS used alone and 0.22 s when the coupling IPFS with RozoFS is used. Indeed in the both cases, the DHT is updated asynchronously. From these results we can say that RozoFS does not add an overhead in terms of access time. In reading, not to access the DHT reduces the access times. As an example 1.83 s are needed to read one object of 10 MB (in a 100 × 10 MB workload) using IPFS on top of RozoFS whereas 1.98 s are needed when IPFS is used alone. In average, reading time are 34% shorter when IPFS is used on top of RozoFS.

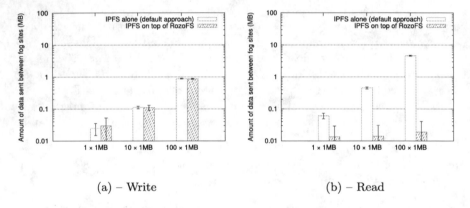

(a) – Write   (b) – Read

Fig. 16. Cumulative amount of network traffic exchanged between all the sites while clients write and read objects located on their sites.

Figure 16 shows the amount of network traffic sent between the sites. We observe in writing an equivalent amount of traffic because in the two cases, the DHT is updated asynchronously (0.89 MB with 100 objects). But in reading, the amount of network traffic has been dramatically reduced when RozoFS is used as a backend of IPFS. With 100 objects, the amount of network traffic is reduced from 4.62 MB when IPFS is used alone to 0.02 MB when we use our coupling. The explanation is the DHT is not accessed anymore for local accesses and the only network traffic between the sites is to maintain the routing table of the DHT. Finally, we observe in Fig. 14 using 10 clients and an important inter-sites latency ($L_{Core} = 200$ ms) that the coupling solution provides a low guarantee of access times because the time to access each object is approximately the same (approximately 0.50 s).

To conclude on this part, accessing the DHT increases the access times, even to read objects stored locally. To solve this problem, we proposed to add a Scale-Out NAS system on each site. This solution prevents the DHT to be accessed in a local read, reducing the reading times and the amount of network traffic exchanged between the sites. This preliminary result is encouraging and invite us to continue in this direction in the future.

6   Related Works

An important problem caused by the need of mobility is how to locate the objects. We can find simple analogies between network and Fog storage. A host on a network identified by its IP (Internet Protocol) address corresponds to an object on a site identified by its key. Mobility support is a problematic studied in network. The following approaches can be classified in two categories: either a centralized server establishes the relation between an address and the location of the node or the address contains some information about the location of the node. In this last case, the address has to change when the node moves. In a Fog storage the two approaches are difficult to use. The first one causes difficulties of scalability whereas the second one is not acceptable because it means that the key of an object changes according to the location of the object. The following paragraphs give some examples of these two approaches.

In a traditional IP network, IP address has two roles, the first role is to allow the packet to be routed in the correct network and to the correct machine. The second role is to identify each machine of the network. In case of mobility, the address of a user has to change in most of IP network because of this first usage for routing: the address describes the location of the user. In Mobile IP networks [28], a user keeps it IP address, no matter its geographical position. In the Fog, a user needs to keep a low access time to its data, no matter its geographical position. In a Mobile IP network, the IP of the user is announced from the base station it is connected to allowing routing mechanisms. A similar concept might be found for the Fog storage.

A similarity can also be found with the Locator/Identifier Separation Protocol (LISP) proposed by Farinacci et al. [21]. In this work, the authors propose to separate the two roles previously described. The IP address is only used an identifier and the location of the machine is determined thanks to a directory service. If we transpose this approach to the Fog: the key of an object could be the identifier of the object and a directory service is used to locate the object. The main problem of this approach is the scalability of the directory service. Contrary to LISP, Taroko [42], a protocol to route datagrams in a mobile ad-hoc network, knows the location of the destination node from its address. Transposing this approach to a fog storage system, means that the key of the object contains the location of the object. The drawback of this approach is the key of the object will change when data are moved from a site to another. Object's key, like address in Taroko will change in case of mobility.

We found similar concepts in 3GPP networks [1]. In these networks, a centralized home location register (HLR) is used to determine the base station each user is connected to. It is used to route the packets to the users. This centralized approach does not seem scalable to locate objects because it does not provide a disconnected mode. Also, when the user is not directly connected to the network of its operator (roaming), the HLR to use is found from the International Mobile Subscriber Identity (IMSI) provided by the user. If we transpose this strategy to the Fog, it means that the object identifier should contain the site the object is stored to or at least the site storing the location of the object. The approaches used in 3GPP transposed in the Fog context mean that the key of the object is used to determine the metadata server storing the location of the object. The drawback is the same as in 3GPP: you cannot change your operator without changing your IMSI number. In the Fog, it means we cannot change the metadata server used by an object without changing the key of this object. To summarize, the 3GPP approach mixes the both strategies: using a "centralized" metadata server and storing the location in the identifier. We can point out that the problematic of network containment was not addressed.

The following propositions are not specially focused on the Fog computing but it shows that network field faces with similar problems. Partial solutions have also been proposed for Cloudlets and Mobile Clouds. In Cloudlets [27], Jararweh *et al.* propose two approaches, a centralized approach where the system tracks the mobile devices and a decentralized approach where the mobile device is in charge of managing its movement. In a Fog context, it can be transposed in the fact the user store its own metadata and is responsible of its object's placement. The main drawback of this approach is that the data movement is only in charge of the user. Data cannot be moved by the system itself, for example to optimize the placement for energetic considerations because the clients will not found its objects anymore. It can be difficult to notify the client because it can be offline when data movement is performed. The main difference between Cloudlets and Mobile Cloud is a difference of scale. While Mobile Cloud considers large site with several servers, the Cloudlet approach considers a site as containing just a small server.

The previous approaches showed the most used technique are to specify the location of an object in its key (which is a problem in a mobility context) or to use a centralized metadata servers (which causes scalability problem). It also exists some P2P approaches to distribute this centralized metadata server. Clarke *et al.* [15] proposed in Freenet to look for resources using a preference list to direct the requests from one node to another. This epidemic approach is similar to some routing protocols such as PRoPHET [33], used more recently in a low connected environment. The drawback of a such protocol is that it cannot guarantee that an existing resource can be found. The same problem occurs in most of the non structured P2P network such as GNUtella [43].

Structured peer to peer network address this issue. A distributed hash table such as Kademlia DHT guarantee an existing key is found but it looses the locality of metadata. In the Pastry DHT [14], node's locality is exploited by placing close nodes at near locations in the DHT. In the Fog context, it could be used to avoid sending requests outside the site when requests are for objects stored locally. Recently, Wilkinson *et al.* [53] store the location of the objects in a blockchain. Vorik *et al.* [50] have a similar approach, users store the files of other users in exchange of virtual money. A blockchain keeps trace of what is stored on each node. Because the blockchain is replicated on every node in the network, it allows clients in a Fog context, to locate any object and to access data in case of network partitioning. But this approach have also some drawbacks, especially in case of mobility. The blockchain is an append-only data structure, data can only be added, not modified and not removed. Thus, if the location of an object is added each time it is moved, the size of the blockchain will increase a lot. Also, the time to complete a transaction can be a problem: if a client moves, it does not want the location of the data be updated several minutes later: the blockchain may not be scalable beyond 7 transactions per second [17]. Brand *et al.* [10] use a totally different approach by proposing different sites to use different storage system. It also uses a hierarchical namespace to avoid updating the metadata for each new object stored.

To summarize this part, the approaches for mobility support do not meet the property of data locality and network containment (there is no locality in a naive DHT) or do not work in case of network partitioning (if the address of the metadata server is found in the object key, the metadata server has to be on the same partition as the client). The coupling between an object store solution and a Scale-Out NAS system solves this problem in an original way.

7   Conclusion and Future Work

We presented a list of expected properties for Fog storage systems and evaluated three off-the-shelf object store solutions (namely Rados, Cassandra and IPFS) using the Yahoo Cloud System Benchmark (YCSB). Performance is measured in terms of access times and network traffic. We also evaluated the impact on the access times of the network latencies between the sites of Fog and also between the clients and their closest site.

The first experiments concerned the evaluation of the performance in a local access as well as in a remote access scenario. It showed that IPFS is the best candidate for the Fog context because of its ability to scale to a huge number of site and the low access times it provided. We also showed that IPFS is less sensible to the network latency between the clients and the sites of Fog (contrary to Cassandra). The major drawback of IPFS is the need to access the DHT each time an object read is not stored on the requested node. That leads to generate a huge amount of network traffic between the sites and to an increasing of access times while accessing object stored locally.

To deal with this problem, we proposed to add a Scale-Out NAS system on each site. The Scale-Out NAS shares the object stored on a site among all the IPFS nodes of the site and avoids to access the DHT when an object to read is locally stored. Experiments using RozoFS as a Scale-Out NAS showed that it reduces the local reading times by 34% in average and the amount of network traffic between the sites.

Even if these first results are encouraging, many problems are still open. We considered the clients always contact their closest site. This is a strong assumption because some sites may provide more resources than others (in terms of storage space for example). A mechanism to determine the site to contact is needed or to forward asynchronously. Nodes churn and replication between the sites were not considered in this paper but they need to be considered in a more realistic Fog networking environment.

A   Details of the Observed Network Traffic

Table 6 gives the details of the amount of network traffic exchanged between the sites in the scenario using the workload of 100 objects of 1 MB on 7 sites. Compared to the Figs. 8 and 9 (page 21), this Figure shows the amount of network sent between the sites but also the local overhead sent inside each site.

For Rados, it shows that one site sends more data than the others. Indeed, the site 1 sends 10 times more data because it is where the elected monitor is. It could lead to different performance on different sites because all the sites do not have the same role. The traffic is not well-balanced between the sites and some sites can have more important access times. With Cassandra, all the sites have the same role. There is no site sending more data than the others. We observe the impact of the forwarding mechanism described in the Sect. 3.2: inside each site, approximately 150 MB are exchanged whereas only 100 MB are stored (overhead about 50%). This overhead will be increased if we use more than two storage nodes per site because fewer requests will be sent directly to the node storing the object. Finally, we also observe the forward mechanism during the reading operation with IPFS: the amount of network traffic inside each site has an overhead of 50%. Table 6 shows for IPFS the forwarding mechanism we got for reading: 50% more network traffic is sent inside the sites in reading Indeed this overhead is produced, when the client sends the request to the node which does not store the object. To conclude on Table 6, we saw Rados has a site sending more traffic than the others while Cassandra and IPFS have an overhead of network traffic inside each site due to the forwarding mechanisms.

Table 6. Mean amount of data **in kilobytes** sent between the sites (source site in column and destination in row) for the scenario where **100 objects of 1 MB** are written and read on **7 sites** using Cassandra (a), Rados (b) and IPFS (c).

	Site 1	Site 2	Site 3	Site 4	Site 5	Site 6	Site 7
Amount of data sent while **writing** (KB)							
Site 1	**157924**	5	6	8	5	6	6
Site 2	7	**164507**	6	7	7	7	7
Site 3	7	7	**149175**	6	8	8	7
Site 4	10	9	8	**164313**	9	9	9
Site 5	10	9	10	10	**157726**	11	10
Site 6	10	10	11	11	12	**161713**	12
Site 7	12	12	12	10	12	13	**163908**
Amount of data sent while **reading** (KB)							
Site 1	**142719**	7	8	8	8	6	7
Site 2	8	**162345**	8	9	9	10	9
Site 3	10	10	**153008**	11	10	9	8
Site 4	13	12	11	**174439**	11	11	10
Site 5	12	11	13	12	**157729**	13	11
Site 6	12	13	12	13	14	**174799**	13
Site 7	14	14	12	13	13	14	**153007**

(a) – Cassandra

	Site 1	Site 2	Site 3	Site 4	Site 5	Site 6	Site 7
Amount of data sent while **writing** (KB)							
Site 1	108400	14	40	41	35	21	37
Site 2	551	108225	16	12	18	15	24
Site 3	617	18	108259	37	25	37	29
Site 4	632	46	27	108237	28	32	32
Site 5	639	28	33	33	108223	31	31
Site 6	640	26	38	42	35	108061	40
Site 7	657	45	46	46	38	44	108251
Amount of data sent while **reading** (KB)							
Site 1	108292	19	40	46	35	36	40
Site 2	632	108187	18	14	21	17	27
Site 3	668	21	108209	41	29	44	33
Site 4	683	50	31	108190	34	40	38
Site 5	691	33	39	39	108195	40	39
Site 6	693	31	46	50	44	108611	50
Site 7	710	55	56	55	49	56	108218

(b) – Rados

	Site 1	Site 2	Site 3	Site 4	Site 5	Site 6	Site 7
Amount of data sent while **writing** (KB)							
Site 1	**107418**	268	168	232	100	164	288
Site 2	268	**109655**	265	24	116	276	137
Site 3	178	253	**112605**	162	41	24	159
Site 4	235	23	167	**109538**	181	186	233
Site 5	140	114	41	168	**108142**	209	321
Site 6	164	282	206	206	211	**107658**	105
Site 7	299	134	167	243	331	104	**108627**
Amount of data sent while **reading** (KB)							
Site 1	**165595**	738	667	563	157	450	989
Site 2	722	**161474**	926	292	384	681	378
Site 3	656	963	**157808**	434	352	43	580
Site 4	561	248	452	**170178**	812	565	940
Site 5	143	402	290	788	**162622**	954	845
Site 6	449	686	214	602	941	**150680**	334
Site 7	1038	401	546	923	818	357	**177598**

(c) – IPFS

References

1. 3GPP: Network architecture. TS 23.002, 3rd Generation Partnership Project (3GPP), September 2008

2. Aazam, M., Huh, E.N.: Fog computing and smart gateway based communication for cloud of things. In: Proceedings of the 2014 International Conference on Future Internet of Things and Cloud. FICLOUD 2014, pp. 464–470. IEEE Computer Society, Washington, DC (2014)

3. Abramova, V., Bernardino, J.: NoSQL databases: MongoDB vs Cassandra. In: Proceedings of the International C* Conference on Computer Science and Software Engineering. C3S2E 2013, pp. 14–22. ACM, New York (2013)

4. Abramova, V., Bernardino, J., Furtado, P.: Evaluating Cassandra scalability with YCSB. In: Decker, H., Lhotská, L., Link, S., Spies, M., Wagner, R.R. (eds.) DEXA 2014. LNCS, vol. 8645, pp. 199–207. Springer, Cham (2014). doi:10.1007/978-3-319-10085-2_18

5. Anwar, A., Cheng, Y., Gupta, A., Butt, A.R.: MOS: workload-aware elasticity for cloud object stores. In: Proceedings of the 25th ACM International Symposium on High-Performance Parallel and Distributed Computing. HPDC 2016, pp. 177–188. ACM, New York (2016)

6. Balouek, D., et al.: Adding virtualization capabilities to the Grid'5000 testbed. In: Ivanov, I.I., Sinderen, M., Leymann, F., Shan, T. (eds.) CLOSER 2012. CCIS, vol. 367, pp. 3–20. Springer, Cham (2013). doi:10.1007/978-3-319-04519-1_1

7. Benet, J.: IPFS - Content Addressed, Versioned, P2P File System. Technical report, Protocol Labs, Inc. (2014)

8. Bonomi, F., Milito, R., Natarajan, P., Zhu, J.: Fog computing: a platform for Internet of Things and analytics. In: Bessis, N., Dobre, C. (eds.) Big Data and Internet of Things: A Roadmap for Smart Environments. SCI, vol. 546, pp. 169–186. Springer, Cham (2014). doi:10.1007/978-3-319-05029-4_7

9. Bonomi, F., Milito, R., Zhu, J., Addepalli, S.: Fog computing and its role in the Internet of Things. In: Proceedings of the First Edition of the MCC Workshop on Mobile cloud computing. MCC 2012, pp. 13–16 (2012)

10. Brand, G.B., Lebre, A.: GBFS: efficient data-sharing on hybrid platforms: towards adding WAN-wide elasticity to DFSes. In: 2014 International Symposium on Computer Architecture and High Performance Computing Workshop (SBAC-PADW), pp. 126–131, October 2014

11. Brewer, E.A.: Towards robust distributed systems (abstract). In: Proceedings of the Nineteenth Annual ACM Symposium on Principles of Distributed Computing. PODC 2000, p. 7. ACM, New York (2000)

12. Byers, C.C., Wetterwald, P.: Fog computing distributing data and intelligence for resiliency and scale necessary for IoT: the Internet of Things. In: Ubiquity, pp. 4:1–4:12, November 2015

13. Carns, P.H., Ligon L, W.B., Ross, R.B., Thakur, R.: PVFS: a parallel file system for Linux clusters. In: Proceedings of the 4th Annual Linux Showcase & Conference. ALS 2000, vol. 4, p. 28. USENIX Association, Berkeley (2000)

14. Castro, M., Druschel, P., Hu, Y.C.: Exploiting network proximity in distributed hash tables. In: International Workshop on Future Directions in Distributed Computing (FuDiCo), pp. 52–55 (2002)

15. Clarke, I., Sandberg, O., Wiley, B., Hong, T.W.: Freenet: a distributed anonymous information storage and retrieval system. In: Federrath, H. (ed.) Designing Privacy Enhancing Technologies. LNCS, vol. 2009, pp. 46–66. Springer, Heidelberg (2001). doi:10.1007/3-540-44702-4_4

16. Cooper, B.F., Silberstein, A., Tam, E., Ramakrishnan, R., Sears, R.: Benchmarking cloud serving systems with YCSB. In: Proceedings of the 1st ACM Symposium on Cloud Computing. SoCC 2010, pp. 143–154. ACM, New York (2010)

17. Croman, K., et al.: On scaling decentralized blockchains. In: Clark, J., Meiklejohn, S., Ryan, P.Y.A., Wallach, D., Brenner, M., Rohloff, K. (eds.) FC 2016. LNCS, vol. 9604, pp. 106–125. Springer, Heidelberg (2016). doi:10.1007/978-3-662-53357-4_8

18. Dabek, F., Cox, R., Kaashoek, F., Morris, R.: Vivaldi: a decentralized network coordinate system. SIGCOMM Comput. Commun. Rev. **34**(4), 15–26 (2004)

19. Donovan, S., Huizenga, G., Hutton, A., Ross, C., Petersen, M., Schwan, P.: Lustre: building a file system for 1000-node clusters. In: Proceedings of the Linux Symposium (2003)

20. Dubey, H., Yang, J., Constant, N., Amiri, A.M., Yang, Q., Makodiya, K.: Fog data: enhancing telehealth big data through fog computing. In: Proceedings of the ASE BigData & SocialInformatics. ASE BD&SI 2015, pp. 14:1–14:6 (2015)
21. Farinacci, D., Fuller, V., Meyer, D., Lewis, D.: The Locator/ID Separation Protocol (LISP). Technical report. Request for Comments 6830, Internet Engineering Task Force, October 2015
22. Firdhous, M., Ghazali, O., Hassan, S.: Fog computing: will it be the future of Cloud Computing? In: Third International Conference on Informatics & Applications, Kuala Terengganu, pp. 8–15 (2014)
23. Garcia, P.G., Montresor, A., Epema, D., Datta, A., Higashino, T., Iamnitchi, A., Barcellos, M., Felber, P., Riviere, E.: Edge-centric computing: vision and challenges. SIGCOMM Comput. Commun. Rev. 45(5), 37–42 (2015)
24. Gettys, J., Nichols, K.: Bufferbloat: dark buffers in the internet. Commun. ACM 55(1), 57–65 (2012)
25. Hong, K., Lillethun, D., Ramachandran, U., Ottenwälder, B., Koldehofe, B.: Mobile fog: a programming model for large-scale applications on the Internet of Things. In: Proceedings of the Second ACM SIGCOMM Workshop on Mobile Cloud Computing. MCC 2013, pp. 15–20. ACM, New York (2013)
26. Hupfeld, F., Cortes, T., Kolbeck, B., Stender, J., Focht, E., Hess, M., Malo, J., Marti, J., Cesario, E.: The XtreemFS architecture – a case for object-based file systems in grids. Concurr. Comput. Pract. Exp. 20(17), 2049–2060 (2008)
27. Jararweh, Y., Ababneh, F., Khreishah, A., Dosari, F., et al.: Scalable cloudlet-based mobile computing model. Procedia Comput. Sci. 34, 434–441 (2014)
28. Johnson, D.D.B., Arkko, J., Perkins, C.E.: Mobility Support in IPv6. Technical report. Request for Comments 6275, Internet Engineering Task Force, October 2015
29. Jorgensen, N.T.K., Rodriguez, I., Elling, J., Mogensen, P.: 3G Femto or 802.11g WiFi: which is the best indoor data solution today? In: 2014 IEEE 80th Vehicular Technology Conference (VTC2014-Fall), pp. 1–5, September 2014
30. Lakshman, A., Malik, P.: Cassandra: a decentralized structured storage system. SIGOPS Oper. Syst. Rev. 44(2), 35–40 (2010)
31. Lamport, L.: Paxos made simple, fast, and byzantine. In: Procedings of the 6th International Conference on Principles of Distributed Systems. OPODIS 2002, Reims, 11–13 December 2002, pp. 7–9 (2002)
32. Legout, A., Urvoy-Keller, G., Michiardi, P.: Understanding BitTorrent: an experimental perspective. Technical report, INRIA, Institut Eurecom (2005)
33. Lindgren, A., Doria, A., Davies, E.B., Grasic, S.: Probabilistic routing protocol for intermittently connected networks. Technical report. Request for Comments 6693, Internet Engineering Task Force, October 2015
34. Markopoulou, A., Tobagi, F., Karam, M.: Loss and delay measurements of internet backbones. Comput. Commun. 29(10), 1590–1604 (2006). Monitoring and Measurements of IP Networks
35. Maymounkov, P., Mazières, D.: Kademlia: a peer-to-peer information system based on the XOR metric. In: Druschel, P., Kaashoek, F., Rowstron, A. (eds.) IPTPS 2002. LNCS, vol. 2429, pp. 53–65. Springer, Heidelberg (2002). doi:10. 1007/3-540-45748-8_5
36. Nielsen, J.: Nielsen's law of internet bandwidth (1998)
37. Padhye, J., Firoiu, V., Towsley, D., Kurose, J.: Modeling TCP throughput: a simple model and its empirical validation. SIGCOMM Comput. Commun. Rev. 28(4), 303–314 (1998)

38. Palankar, M.R., Iamnitchi, A., Ripeanu, M., Garfinkel, S.: Amazon S3 for science grids: a viable solution? In: Proceedings of the 2008 International Workshop on Data-Aware Distributed Computing. DADC 2008, pp. 55–64. ACM, New York (2008)
39. Pallis, G., Vakali, A.: Insight and perspectives for content delivery networks. Commun. ACM **49**(1), 101–106 (2006)
40. Pertin, D., David, S., Évenou, P., Parrein, B., Normand, N.: Distributed file system based on erasure coding for I/O intensive applications. In: 4th International Conference on Cloud Computing and Service Science (CLOSER), Barcelone, April 2014
41. Qiu, D., Srikant, R.: Modeling and performance analysis of bittorrent-like peer-to-peer networks. SIGCOMM Comput. Commun. Rev. **34**(4), 367–378 (2004)
42. Ridoux, J., Kassar, M., Boc, M., Fladenmuller, A., Viniotis, Y.: Performance of Taroko: a cluster-based addressing and routing scheme for self-organized networks. In: Proceedings of the 2006 International Conference on Wireless Communications and Mobile Computing. IWCMC 2006, pp. 109–114. ACM, New York (2006)
43. Ripeanu, M.: Peer-to-Peer architecture case study: Gnutella network. In: Proceedings of the First International Conference on Peer-to-Peer Computing, pp. 99–100, August 2001
44. Shvachko, K., Kuang, H., Radia, S., Chansler, R.: The hadoop distributed file system. In: Proceedings of the 2010 IEEE 26th Symposium on Mass Storage Systems and Technologies (MSST). MSST 2010, pp. 1–10. IEEE Computer Society, Washington, DC (2010)
45. Couto Souza, R.D.S., Secci, S., Campista, M.E.M., Costa, L.H.M.K.: Network design requirements for disaster resilience in IaaS Clouds. IEEE Commun. Mag. **52**(10), 52–58 (2014) L.H. , : Network design requirements for disaster resilience in IaaS Clouds. IEEE Commun. Mag. **52**(10), 52–58 (2014)
46. Sui, K., Zhou, M., Liu, D., Ma, M., Pei, D., Zhao, Y., Li, Z., Moscibroda, T.: Characterizing and improving wifi latency in large-scale operational networks. In: Proceedings of the 14th Annual International Conference on Mobile Systems, Applications, and Services. MobiSys 2016, pp. 347–360. ACM, New York (2016)
47. Tang, B., Chen, Z., Hefferman, G., Wei, T., He, H., Yang, Q.: A hierarchical distributed fog computing architecture for big data analysis in smart cities. In: Proceedings of the ASE BigData & SocialInformatics. ASE BD&SI 2015, pp. 28:1–28:6. ACM, New York (2015)
48. Tatebe, O., Hiraga, K., Soda, N.: Gfarm grid file system. New Gener. Comput. **28**(3), 257–275 (2010)
49. Vaquero, L.M., Rodero-Merino, L.: Finding your way in the fog: towards a comprehensive definition of fog computing. SIGCOMM Comput. Commun. Rev. **44**(5), 27–32 (2014)
50. Vorick, D., Champine, L.: Sia: simple decentralized storage. Technical report, NebulousLabs, Boston (2014)
51. Weil, S.A., Brandt, S.A., Miller, E.L., Maltzahn, C.: CRUSH: controlled, scalable, decentralized placement of replicated data. In: Proceedings of the 2006 ACM/IEEE Conference on Supercomputing. SC 2006 (2006)
52. Weil, S.A., Leung, A.W., Brandt, S.A., Maltzahn, C.: RADOS: a scalable, reliable storage service for petabyte-scale storage clusters. In: Proceedings of the 2nd International Workshop on Petascale Data Storage: Held in Conjunction with Supercomputing 2007. PDSW 2007, pp. 35–44 (2007)
53. Wilkinson, S., Boshevski, T., Brandoff, J., Buterin, V.: Storj a peer-to-peer cloud storage network. Technical report, Storj Labs Inc. (2014)

54. Yannuzzi, M., Milito, R., Serral-Gracia, R., Montero, D., Nemirovsky, M.: Key ingredients in an IoT recipe: Fog Computing, Cloud Computing, and more Fog Computing. In: 2014 IEEE 19th International Workshop on Computer Aided Modeling and Design of Communication Links and Networks (CAMAD), pp. 325–329, December 2014
55. Yi, S., Hao, Z., Qin, Z., Li, Q.: Fog computing: platform and applications. In: Proceedings of the 2015 Third IEEE Workshop on Hot Topics in Web Systems and Technologies (HotWeb). HOTWEB 2015, pp. 73–78. IEEE Computer Society, Washington, DC (2015)
56. Yi, S., Li, C., Li, Q.: A survey of fog computing: concepts, applications and issues. In: Proceedings of the 2015 Workshop on Mobile Big Data. Mobidata 2015, pp. 37–42. ACM, New York (2015)
57. Yi, S., Qin, Z., Li, Q.: Security and privacy issues of fog computing: a survey. In: Xu, K., Zhu, H. (eds.) WASA 2015. LNCS, vol. 9204, pp. 685–695. Springer, Cham (2015). doi:10.1007/978-3-319-21837-3_67
58. Zao, J.K., Gan, T.T., You, C.K., Méndez, S.J.R., Chung, C.E., Wang, Y.T., Mullen, T., Jung, T.P.: Augmented brain computer interaction based on fog computing and linked data. In: 2014 International Conference on Intelligent Environments (IE), pp. 374–377, June 2014
59. Zhang, B., Mor, N., Kolb, J., Chan, D.S., Goyal, N., Lutz, K., Allman, E., Wawrzynek, J., Lee, E., Kubiatowicz, J.: The cloud is not enough: saving IoT from the cloud. In: Proceedings of the 7th USENIX Conference on Hot Topics in Cloud Computing. HotCloud 2015, p. 21. USENIX Association, Berkeley (2015)

Scientific Workflow Scheduling
with Provenance Data in a Multisite Cloud

Ji Liu[1($\boxtimes$)], Esther Pacitti[1], Patrick Valduriez[1], and Marta Mattoso[2]

[1] Inria, Microsoft-Inria Joint Centre, LIRMM and University of Montpellier,
Montpellier, France
{ji.liu,patrick.valduriez}@inria.fr, esther.pacitti@lirmm.fr
[2] COPPE, Federal University of Rio de Janeiro, Rio de Janeiro, Brazil
marta@cos.ufrj.br

Abstract. Recently, some Scientific Workflow Management Systems
(SWfMSs) with provenance support (*e.g.* Chiron) have been deployed in
the cloud. However, they typically use a single cloud site. In this paper,
we consider a multisite cloud, where the data and computing resources
are distributed at different sites (possibly in different regions). Based on
a multisite architecture of SWfMS, *i.e.* multisite Chiron, and its provenance model, we propose a multisite task scheduling algorithm that considers the time to generate provenance data. We performed an extensive
experimental evaluation of our algorithm using Microsoft Azure multisite cloud and two real-life scientific workflows (Buzz and Montage). The
results show that our scheduling algorithm is up to 49.6% better than
baseline algorithms in terms of total execution time.

Keywords: Scientific workflow · Scientific workflow management system · Scheduling · Parallel execution · Multisite cloud

1 Introduction

Many large-scale *in silico* scientific experiments take advantage of scientific workflows (SWfs) to model data operations such as loading input data, data processing, data analysis, and aggregating output data. SWfs enable scientists to model
the data processing of these experiments as a graph, in which vertices represent
data processing activities and edges represent dependencies between them. An
SWf is the assembly of scientific data processing activities with data dependencies between them [13]. An activity is a description of a piece of work that forms
a logical step within an SWf representation [23] and a task is the representation of an activity within a one-time execution of the activity to process a data
chunk. A data chunk is the smallest set of data that can be processed by a program in an activity. Since the tasks of the same activity process different data
chunks [23], they are independent. Within one activity, each task processes a
data chunk, which has no dependency with other tasks of this activity. Different
SWfs, *e.g.* Montage [4] and Buzz [16], can be represented this way since there

© Springer-Verlag GmbH Germany 2017
A. Hameurlain et al. (Eds.): TLDKS XXXIII, LNCS 10430, pp. 80–112, 2017.
DOI: 10.1007/978-3-662-55696-2_3

are many tasks that exploit the same program to process different data chunks. As it takes much time to execute a data-intensive SWf, efficient execution is an important issue.

A Scientific Workflow Management System (SWfMS) is a tool to execute SWfs [23]. Some implementations of SWfMSs are publicly available, *e.g.* Pegasus [15] and Chiron [29]. An SWfMS generally supports provenance data, which is the metadata that captures the derivation history of a dataset, including the original data sources, intermediate datasets, and the workflow computational steps that were applied to produce this dataset [23]. Provenance data, which is used for SWf analysis and SWf reproducibility, may be as important as the scientific experiment itself [23]. The provenance data is typically stored in a database to provide on-line provenance query [28], and contains the information regarding activities, tasks and files. During the execution of a task, there may be multiple exchanges of provenance data between the computing node and the provenance database.

In order to execute a data-intensive SWf within a reasonable time, SWfMSs generally exploit High Performance Computing (HPC) resources and parallel computing techniques. The HPC resources are generally obtained from a computer cluster, grid or cloud environment. Most of existing SWfMSs have been designed for a computer cluster.

Recently, some SWfMSs with provenance support (*e.g.* Chiron) have been deployed in the cloud. They typically focus on the execution of an SWf at a single cloud site or in even a single computing node [19,20]. Although there are some multisite solutions [17,32], they do not support provenance data, which is important for the analysis of SWf execution. However, the input data necessary to run an SWf may well be distributed at different sites (possibly in different regions), which may not be allowed to be transferred to other sites because of big amounts or proprietary. And it may not be always possible to move all the computing resources (including programs) to a single site for execution. In this paper, we consider a multisite cloud that is composed of several sites (or data centers) of the same cloud provider, each with its own resources and data. In addition, we also take into consideration of the influence of the functionality of provenance data on the SWf multisite execution. The difference between multisite cloud and the environment of single-site or supercomputer is that, in multisite cloud, the data or the computing resources are distributed at different sites and the network bandwidths among different sites are different. In addition, the SWf execution in a multisite cloud is different from the query execution in database and P2P environments because of the programs to execute, security, and diversity.

To enable SWf execution in a multisite cloud with distributed input data, the execution of the tasks of each activity should be scheduled to a corresponding cloud site (or site for short). Then, the scheduling problem is to decide at which sites to execute the tasks in order to achieve a given objective, *e.g.* reducing execution time. Since it may take much time to transfer data between two different sites, the multisite scheduling problem should take into account the resources at different sites, *e.g.* data stored at each site, and different bandwidths between different sties. This is different from the execution at a single site, where data can be shared among different computing nodes and the bandwidths are very big and almost the same for different nodes. In addition, the time to transfer the provenance data cannot be ignored in a multisite cloud environment, which is different from the execution without provenance data. Compared with the approach of scheduling activities in a multisite environment [25], the task scheduling is fine-grained, which enables the execution of the same activity at different sites to deal with distributed data and programs.

We focus on the task scheduling problem to reduce the makespan, *i.e.* the execution time, of executing an SWf in a multisite cloud. We use a distributed SWfMS architecture with a master site that coordinates the execution of each site and that stores all the provenance data of the SWf execution. In this architecture, the intersite transferred data can be intermediate data or provenance data produced by the SWf execution. The intermediate data is the data generated by executing activities and can also be the input data for the tasks of following activities. In the multisite cloud, the bandwidth between two different sites (of different regions) may be small. For data-intensive SWfs, there may be many data, *e.g.* intermediate data and provenance data, to transfer across different sites for the execution of a task while the time to execute the task can be very small, *e.g.* a few seconds or even less than one second. As a result, the time to transfer intermediate data and the time to generate the provenance data cannot be ignored in the scheduling process. Thus, we also consider the time to transfer both the intermediate data and the provenance data in the scheduling process in order to better reduce the overall execution time of SWf execution.

The difference between our work and others is multisite execution with provenance support. In the paper, we make the following contributions. First, we propose multisite Chiron, with a novel architecture to execute SWfs in a multisite cloud environment while generating provenance data. Second, an extended multisite provenance model and global provenance management of distributed provenance data in a multisite cloud. Third, we propose a novel multisite task scheduling algorithm, *i.e.* Data-Intensive Multisite task scheduling (DIM), for SWf execution with provenance support in multisite Chiron. Fourth, we carry out an extensive experimental evaluation, based on the implementation of multisite Chiron in Microsoft Azure, and using two real SWf use cases (Buzz and Montage). This paper is a major extension of [24], with more details on related work and problem definition and the adaptation of single site Chiron to multisite Chiron. The added value compared with [24] is about 40% and the main differences are in: the model to estimate the time to execute a bag of tasks (Sect. 5.2); the experiments of Montage and the improvement of the implementation of scheduling algorithms (Sect. 6.3); the complexity analysis (Sect. 5.3) and the convergence analysis of DIM algorithm (Appendix).

This paper is organized as follows. Section 2 introduces the related work. Section 3 presents the problems for task scheduling of SWf execution in a multisite cloud environment. Section 4 gives the design of a multisite SWfMS. Section 5 explains our proposed scheduling algorithm. Section 6 gives our experimental evaluation. Section 7 concludes the paper.

2   Related Work

Classic scheduling algorithms, *e.g.* Opportunistic Load Balancing (OLB) [26], Minimum Completion Time (MCT) [26], min-min [18], max-min [18] and Heterogeneous Earliest Finish Time (HEFT) [38], address the scheduling problem for the objective of reducing execution time within a single site. The OLB algorithm randomly assigns each task to an available computing node without considering the feature of the task or the computing node. The MCT algorithm schedules each task to the computing node that can finish the execution first. HEFT gives the priority to each task according to the dependencies of tasks and the workload of the task. Then, it schedules the tasks with the highest priority to the computing node that can finish the execution first. The min-min algorithm schedules the task, which takes the least time to execute, to the computing node that can finish the execution first. The max-min algorithm schedules the task, which takes the biggest time to execute, to the computing node that can finish the execution first. Since the size of each data chunk of the same activity is similar and that the tasks of the same activity exploit the same program, it is reasonable to assume that the tasks of the same activity have the same workload. We also assume that the tasks of the same activity are independent since each task processes a data chunk. Thus, the HEFT, min-min and max-min algorithms degrade to the MCT algorithm for this kind of tasks. Some other solutions [35,37,39] for SWf scheduling also focus on single site execution. These techniques do not consider the time to generate provenance data. Dean and Ghemawat [12] propose to schedule tasks to where the data is. Although this method focuses on single site, it considers the cost to transfer data among different computing nodes. However, this algorithm depends on the location of data. When the data is not evenly distributed at each computing node, this algorithm may lead to unbalanced load at some computing nodes and long execution time of tasks. De Oliveira *et al.* [11] propose a provenance based task scheduling algorithm for single site cloud environments. Some adaptation of SWfMSs [6,9] in the cloud environment can provide the parallelism in workflow level or activity level, which is coarse-grained, at a single site cloud. These methods cannot perform parallelism of the tasks of the same activities and they cannot handle the distributed input data at different sites.

A few multisite scheduling approaches are proposed, but they do not consider the distribution of input data at different sites and have no support for provenance data, which may incur much time for intersite data transfer. Duan *et al.* [17] propose a multisite multi-objective scheduling algorithm with consideration of different bandwidths in a multisite environment. However, they do not consider the input data distribution at different sites and do not provide provenance support, which may incur much time for intersite provenance data transfer. In previous work [21,25], we proposed solutions of multisite activity scheduling of SWfs. However, the activity scheduling method is coarse-grained:

it can schedule the entire execution of each activity to a site but cannot schedule different tasks of one activity to different sites. Thus, it cannot handle the distributed input data of an SWf in a multisite cloud environment. Luis *et al.* [32] propose caching metadata in the memory and replicating the metadata for SWf execution in a multisite cloud. The metadata is the description information of files at each site. In this method, data transfer is analyzed in multi-site SWf execution, stressing the importance of optimizing data provisioning. However, the metadata is not yet explored on task scheduling and, they just simulated the SWf execution in the experiments. Their method can be used to optimize the metadata management in our multisite Chiron in the future.

There is also some work in scheduling tasks for query optimization with the consideration of data distribution in databases [7, 8, 30]. However, the major difference between SWf scheduling and query optimization lies in the kind of programs used to process data. The programs used in a query are user-defined functions and typically run within the database system while the programs in SWfs are typically black box code managing their own data outside the scope of the SWfMS. Furthermore, the query execution generates data within the database while the programs in SWfs generate files, which are processed by I/O operations.

Compared with P2P [27, 31], a major difference is that multisite cloud does not have as many sites. Another difference is that the security issue in multisite cloud is more important than in P2P, *e.g.* some data cannot be moved to another site.

2.1 Single Site Chiron

Chiron [29] is an SWfMS for the execution of data-intensive SWfs at a single site, with provenance support. At a single site, Chiron takes one computing node as a master node and the other nodes as slave nodes, as shown in Fig. 1. In a cloud environment, a computing node is a Virtual Machine (VM). Designed for HPC environments, Chiron relies on a Shared File System[1], *e.g.* Network File System (NFS) [33], for managing data. All the computing nodes in the cluster can read or write the data stored in the shared file system. Chiron exploits a relational database, *i.e.* PosgreSQL, to store provenance data.

There are six modules, *i.e.* textual UI, activity manager, single site task scheduler, task executor, provenance data manager and shared file system, in the single site Chiron. The users can use a textual User Interface (UI) to interact with Chiron, in order to start an instance of Chiron at each computing node. During the execution of an SWf, each activity and its dependencies are analyzed by the activity manager to find executable activities, *i.e.* unexecuted activities, of which the input data is ready [29]. In order to execute an activity, the corresponding tasks are generated by the activity manager. Afterwards, the task scheduler schedules each task to a computing node. During SWf execution, the

---

[1] In a shared file system, all the computing nodes of the cluster share some data storage that are generally remotely located [22].

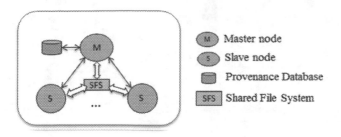

Fig. 1. Architecture of single site Chiron.

tasks of each activity are generated independently and the scheduling of the tasks of each activity is done independently. The scheduling process is performed at the beginning of the execution of each activity when the tasks are generated and to be scheduled at each site. At the beginning of each activity, the corresponding tasks of this activity are generated and scheduled without interaction with other activities. In single site Chiron, each time a slave node is available, it requests new tasks from the master node, which in turn searches for unexecuted tasks and dispatches them to the slave. This approach is efficient for single site implementations, where communication latency is negligible and there is a shared file system. Then, the task execution module at each computing node executes the corresponding scheduled tasks. When all the tasks of the executable activity are executed, the activity manager analyzes the activities to find new executable activities to execute. The process of activity analysis, task scheduling and task execution are repeated until all activities have been executed. Since the input data, intermediate data and output data of SWfs are stored in a shared file system, Chiron does not need to manage data transfer between different computing nodes. During SWf execution, the activity manager, the task scheduler and the task executor generate provenance data, which is gathered by the provenance data manager. The provenance data manager is located at the master node of the cluster.

The single site provenance model [29] is shown in Fig. 2. In this model, an SWf is composed of several activities. An activity has an operator, *i.e.* the program for this activity. The status of the activity can be ready, running or finished. The *activationCommand* of an activity is to execute the activity. The *extractorCommand* is to generate provenance data for the corresponding tasks. The time at which the activity execution starts is *executionStart* and the time at which it ends is *executionEnd*. One activity is related to several tasks, input relations and output relations. One relation is the input or output parameters for the activity. Each relation has its own attributes and tuples. The tasks of an activity are generated based on the input relation of the activity. A task processes the files associated with the corresponding activity. Each task has a status, *i.e.* ready, running or finished. In addition, the start time and end time of its execution is recorded as *ExecutionStart* and *ExecutionEnd*. During exe-

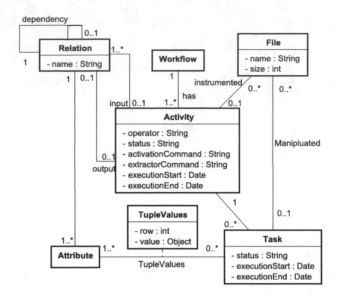

Fig. 2. Single site provenance model [29].

cution, the corresponding information of activities, files and tasks are stored as provenance data.

3   Problem Definition

This section introduces some important terms, *i.e.* SWf and multisite cloud, and formally defines the task scheduling problem we address.

An SWf is the assembly of activities and data dependencies where the activities are connected by data dependencies, *i.e* there is at least a path between every pair of activities. The path is a combination of data dependencies without the consideration of the direction between two activities. An SWf is generally represented as a Directed Acyclic Graph (DAG). Let us denote an SWf by $W(V, E)$. $V = \{v_1, v_2, ..., v_n\}$ represents a set of n vertices, which represent the scientific data processing activities. $E = \{e_{i,j}: v_i, v_j \in V$ and Activity v_j consumes the output data of Activity $v_i\}$ represents a set of edges that correspond to dependencies between activities in V. Activity v_i is the parent activity of Activity v_j and Activity v_j is the child activity of Activity v_i. If it has no parent activity, an activity is a start activity. If it has no child activity, an activity is an end activity. If it has both parent activity or child activity, an activity is an intermediate activity. Since an activity may process big amount of data, it corresponds to multiple tasks. Thus, as shown in Fig. 3, Activity A_k may have n tasks $\{t_1, t_2, ..., t_n\}$, each consuming a data chunk produced by the tasks of parent activities of Activity A_k, *i.e.* Activities A_i and A_j. For data-intensive SWfs, the time to transfer data cannot be ignored compared with the time to process data.

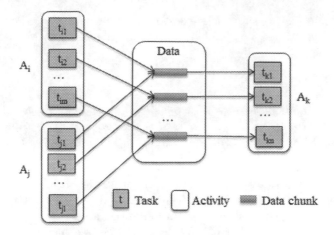

Fig. 3. Activity and tasks.

A multisite cloud $MS(S) = \{S, Conf\}$ is a cloud with multiple sites (data centers) of the same cloud provider, each being explicitly accessible to cloud users. $S = \{s_1, s_2, ..., s_m\}$ represents a set of sites while $Conf = \{c_1, c_2, ..., c_m\}$ represents the cloud configurations of each cloud site for the user. A cloud configuration c_i is a combination of parameters of diverse available resources allocated to the user at a site, which may contain information about quality, quantity, and types of the resources. A multisite cloud configuration defines the instances of VMs and storage resources for the users at a multisite cloud. In this paper, a cloud site corresponds to a combination of resources, *e.g.* a cluster of VMs, data and cloud services, which are physically located at a data center. The cloud services can be database or message queue service. In the cluster of VMs, each VM is a computing node.

We assume that the input data of an SWf is distributed at different sites and cannot be moved across different sites because of the proprietary and the security of the data stored at the site. In addition, some laws also restrict the movement of data among different regions. Thus, the tasks of the start activity should be scheduled at the site where the data is. Moreover, we assume that the intermediate data can be moved across different sites and that the time to transfer the input data of tasks between two different sites and the time to generate provenance data is non-negligible compared with the execution time of a task. During the execution, the input data of each activity can be distributed at different sites. Thus, the tasks of the intermediate activities or end activities can be scheduled at any site. In this paper, we focus on the task scheduling of intermediate and end activities.

Let T be a bag of tasks corresponding to the same activity. Then, the scheduling process of T is to choose the sites in S to execute the tasks in T, *i.e.* mapping each task to an execution site, while the input data of each task is distributed at different sites. A scheduling plan $(SP(T, S))$ is a mapping between tasks and sites, which specifies which task is executed at which site. Based on an estimation of execution time (see details in Sect. 5.2), the problem we address is the following [30]:

$min(\text{TotalTime}(SP(T, S)))$
subject to
distributed input data

The decision variable is $SP(T, S)$, which is defined as a hash table (key-value pairs): $SP(T, S) = \{(t_1, s_2), (t_2, s_1), ..., (t_n, s_m)\}$ where $t_i \in T$ and $s_j \in S$.

Thus, the task scheduling problem is how to generate a scheduling plan $SP(T, S)$ that reduces $\text{TotalTime}(SP(T, S))$ of all the tasks in T with consideration of distributed input data and provenance data. The distribution of the input data of each task can be also represented as a hash table, *e.g.* $\text{Dist}(t, S)$ $= \{(F_1, s_2), (F_2, s_3), ..., (F_k, s_m)\}$ (F_i is the name of a file and $s_j \in S$), which is known before execution. $\text{Dist}(t, S)$ represents the distribution of the input file of Task t in the multisite S. The key is the name of the corresponding file and the value is the name of the site where the data of the file is stored.

4   System Design

In this section, we present the distributed architecture of multisite Chiron, with the modifications to adapt the single site Chiron to a multisite Cloud. Multisite Chiron can manage the communication of Chiron instances at each site and automatically take advantage of resources distributed at each site to process the distributed input data.

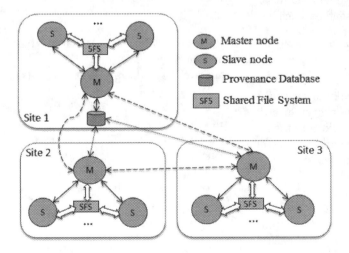

Fig. 4. Architecture of multisite Chiron.

In the execution environment of multisite Chiron, there is a master site (site 1 in Fig. 4) and several slave sites (Sites 2 and 3 in Fig. 4). The master site is similar to the execution environment of a single site Chiron with computing nodes, shared file system and a provenance database. Moreover, a queuing service (see Sect. 6.2) is deployed at the master site. A slave site is composed of a cluster of VMs with a deployed shared file system. In addition, the master node of each site is configured to enable the message communication and data transfer with other sites. Furthermore, the master node also schedules the tasks at each site and transfers the provenance data generated by each node to a centralized database.

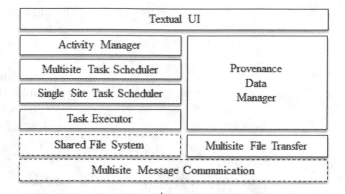

Fig. 5. Multisite layered architecture.

The layered architecture of multisite Chiron is depicted in Fig. 5. The textual UI is present at each node of each site to start an instance of Chiron. The activity manager is located at the master node of the master site to analyze the activities to find executable activities. The multisite task scheduler is located at the master node of the master site, which schedules the tasks to be executed. The provenance data manager works at the master node of each site to gather provenance data for the tasks executed at each site and updates the provenance data in the provenance database. The task executor is present at each node of each site to execute tasks. The shared file system is deployed at the master node of each site and is accessible to all the nodes of the same site. The multisite file transfer and multisite message communication work at the master node of each site to enable the communication of different sites. The other modules are the same as presented in Sect. 2.1.

In a multisite cloud, multisite Chiron analyzes the data dependencies of each activity. When the input data of an activity is ready [29], it generates tasks. Then, the tasks of each activity are independently scheduled to each site. All the previous processes are realized at the master node of the master site. Then, the data is transferred to the scheduled sites and the tasks are executed at the scheduled sites. Although the input data of an SWf cannot be moved, the

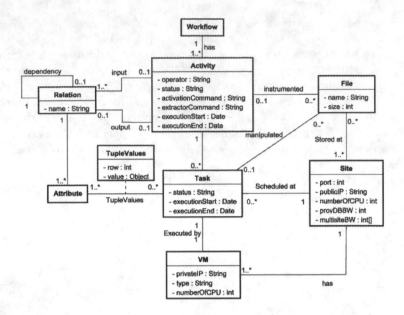

Fig. 6. Multisite provenance model.

intermediate data can be moved. After the execution of tasks, the provenance data [29] of each site are transferred to the provenance database. When the tasks of all the activities are executed, the execution of an SWf is finished.

In order to extend Chiron to a multisite environment, three key aspects, i.e. provenance model, multisite communication and multisite scheduling, must be considered. First, we adapt the provenance model to the multisite environment. As shown in Fig. 6, we add the information about site and computing node (VM) into the provenance model. A site has its own public IP address, public ports for the communication with other sites, number of virtual CPUs, bandwidth to transfer data to the provenance database and bandwidth to transfer data to other sites. A site can contain several VMs. Each VM has its private IP address (which can only be recognized by the devices deployed in the same Web domain), the type of VM, and the number of virtual CPUs. The type of a VM is configured by a cloud user. In a multisite environment, the provenance database is located at a master site while the provenance data is directly stored in the local file system of the master node, which is not the shared file system, because of good performance. Since one task is executed at one computing node of a specific site, a task is related to one computing node and one site. A file can be stored at several sites. Since the input data of a task may be stored at one site (Site s_1) and processed at another site (Site s_2), it is transferred from s_1 to s_2 before being processed. As a result, the data ends up being stored at the two sites. Thus, one file is related to several sites. In addition, the provenance data can provide data location information for the scheduling process. As a result, users can also get execution information, *i.e.* which task is executed at which site, from the provenance database. The other objects and relationships remain the same as in the single site provenance model as presented in Sect. 2.1.

In multisite environments, the provenance data is stored at each site first and then transferred to the centralized provenance database asynchronously with the execution of other tasks. In long running SWfs, provenance data needs to be queried at runtime for monitoring. Since it is convenient for the users to analyze the provenance data in a centralized database, we choose a centralized site, *i.e.* the master site, to store provenance data. In a multisite environment, the provenance data transfer may have a major influence on the data transfer of task scheduling. Latency hiding techniques can be used to hide the time to transfer data but it is difficult to hide the time to transfer the real-time provenance data generated during execution. Overall, the multisite scheduling problem should take into account the resources at different sites and intersite data transfer, including intermediate data to be processed by tasks and the provenance data.

Second, to support communication between different sites, we add two modules, *i.e.* multisite message communication module and multisite file transfer module. The multisite message communication module is responsible for the exchange of control messages among different sites. The control messages are generated for synchronizing the execution of each site and sharing information among different sites. The synchronization ensures that the activities are executed after their input is ready, *i.e.* after their parents activities are executed, at each site. The multisite file transfer module transfers files to be processed by a task from the site where the files are stored to the site where the task is executed. In fact, the architecture of Chiron is the combination of master-worker model and peer-to-peer model. The master-worker model is responsible for the synchronization among different sites by message communication while the peer-to-peer model is used to share data among sites through multisite file transfer module. The implementation techniques of the two modules are detailed in Sect. 6.2.

Third, we provide a multisite task scheduling module in multisite Chiron, which is detailed in Sect. 5.

5 Task Scheduling

In this section, we propose a multisite task scheduling algorithm, *i.e.* Data-Intensive Multisite task scheduling (DIM). Then, we present the method to estimate the total time of a bag of tasks at a single site cloud, which is used in the DIM algorithm. Finally, we analyze the complexity of the DIM algorithm.

5.1 Multisite Task Scheduling

Multisite task scheduling is done with a two Level (2L) approach (see Fig. 7) because of small complexity. The first level performs multisite scheduling, where each task is scheduled to a site. In this paper, we focus on this level and propose DIM, which is designed for this level. Then, the second level performs single site scheduling, where each task is scheduled to a computing node of the site by

the default scheduling strategy (dynamic FAF [29]) of Chiron. A task processes
an input data chunk within an activity. Different tasks process different data
chunks. When an activity has n input data chunks, n tasks are executed independently. Synchronization is based on data dependency between activities as
defined at the SWf specification. In the experiments we forced a synchronization so that the next activity only starts after all tasks of the previous activity
are executed. Compared with a one Level (1L) approach that schedules tasks
directly to computing nodes at different cloud sites, this 2L approach may well
reduce the multisite scheduling complexity (see Sect. 5.3). According to [34], 2L
scheduling also significantly outperforms 1L scheduling in terms of performance,
i.e. the speedup of execution. In addition, the 2L scheduling approach can exploit
the existing scheduling solutions of single site SWfMSs. In this paper, we focus
on the multisite scheduling part, since we use the default scheduling solutions of
Chiron for single site scheduling. However, even in the 2L scheduling approach,
the solution space of the multisite level scheduling is still very large and complex.

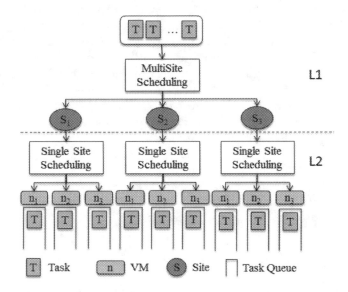

Fig. 7. Multisite scheduling. The master node at the master site schedules tasks to
each site. At each site, the master node schedules tasks to slave nodes.

In our layered architecture (see Sect. 4), the multisite scheduling is performed
at the master node of the master site. For the tasks of data-intensive SWfs, the
time to transfer task input data and the time to generate provenance data should
not be ignored, in particular in case of low bandwidth of intersite connection and
big amounts of data in the files to be transferred between different sites. This
is why we consider the time to transfer task input data and provenance data in
the scheduling process. The method to estimate the total time of a bag of tasks
at a single site is detailed in Sect. 5.2. In addition, during the scheduling, if the

---

Algorithm 1. Data-Intensive Multisite task scheduling (DIM)

Input: T: a bag of tasks to be scheduled; S: a set of cloud sites
Output: $SP(T, S)$: the scheduling plan for T in S
  1: $SP(T, S) \leftarrow \emptyset$
  2: **for each** $t \in T$ **do**
  3:    $s \leftarrow GetDataSite(\text{Dist}(t, S))$
  4:    $SP(T, S) \leftarrow SP(T, S) \cup \{(t, s)\}$
  5:    TotalTime($SP(T, S)$)
  6: **while** MaxunbalanceTime($SP(T, S)$) is reduced in the last loop **do**
  7:    $sMin \leftarrow MinTime(S)$
  8:    $sMax \leftarrow MaxTime(S)$
  9:    $SP(T, S) \leftarrow \text{TaskReschedule}(sMin, sMax, SP(T, S))$
end

---

data cannot be moved, the associated tasks are scheduled at the site where the data is stored. As explained in Sect. 2.1, the tasks of each activity are generated and scheduled independently.

The DIM algorithm schedules a bag of tasks onto multiple sites (see Algorithm 1). Since it takes much time to transfer data among different sites, we first schedule the tasks to where their input data is stored in DIM. However, after this first step, when the data is evenly distributed, workload at each site may be unbalanced, which leads to bigger execution. Thus, at the second step, we adjust the scheduling of tasks until load balance is achieved among different sites so as to reduce the execution time. The details are explained as follow. First, the tasks are scheduled according to the location of input data, *i.e.* the site that stores the biggest amount of input data (Lines 2–5), which is similar to the scheduling algorithm of MapReduce [12]. Line 3 searches the site that stores the biggest part of input data corresponding to Task t. Line 4 schedules Task t at Site s. The scheduling order (the same for Algorithm 2) is based on the *id* of each task. Line 5 estimates the total time of all the tasks scheduled at Site s with consideration of generating provenance data and intersite data transfer according to Formula 3. Then, the total time at each site is balanced by adjusting the whole bag of tasks scheduled at that site (lines 6–9). Line 6 checks if the maximum difference of the estimated total time of tasks at each site can be reduced by verifying if the difference is reduced in the previous loop or if this is the first loop. While the maximum difference of total time can be reduced, the tasks of the two sites are rescheduled as described in Lines 7–9. Lines 7 and 8 choose the site that has the minimal total time and the site that has the maximum total time, respectively. Then, the scheduler calls the function $TaskReschedule$ to reschedule the tasks scheduled at the two selected sites to reduce the maximum difference of total time.

In order to achieve load balancing of two sites, we propose $TaskReschedule$ algorithm. Let us assume that there are two sites, *i.e.* Sites s_i and s_j. For the tasks scheduled at each site, we assume that the total time of Site s_i is bigger than Site s_j. In order to balance the total time at Sites s_i and s_j, some of the

---

Algorithm 2. Tasks Rescheduling

Input: s_i: a site that has bigger total time for its scheduled tasks; s_j: a site that has smaller total time for its scheduled tasks; $SP(T, S)$: original scheduling plan for a bag of tasks T in multisite S

Output: $SP(T, S)$: modified scheduling plan
1: $Diff \leftarrow CalculateExecTimeDiff(s_i, s_j, SP(T, S))$ ▷ Absolute value
2: $T_i \leftarrow GetScheduledTasks(s_i, SP(T, S))$
3: **for each** $t \in T_i$ **do**
4:      $SP'(T, S) \leftarrow ModifySchedule(SP(T, S), \{(t, s_j)\})$
5:      $Diff' \leftarrow CalculateExecTimeDiff(s_i, s_j, SP'(T, S))$ ▷ Absolute value
6:      **if** $Diff' < Diff$ **then**
7:          $SP(T, S) \leftarrow SP'(T, S)$
8:          $Diff \leftarrow Diff'$

end

---

tasks scheduled at Site s_i should be rescheduled at Site s_j. Algorithm 2 gives the method to reschedule a bag of tasks from Site s_i to Site s_j in order to balance the load between the two sites. Line 1 calculates the difference of the total time of two sites according to Formula 3 with a scheduling plan. In the function $CalculateExecTimeDiff(s_i, s_j, SP(T, S))$, based on the scheduling plan ($SP(T, S)$) and the method to estimate the total execution of tasks at a single site (see Sect. 5.2), the total execution time of Site s_i and s_j can be calculated. Then, the difference ($Diff$) of the total execution between the two sites can also be calculated. Line 2 gets all the tasks scheduled at Site s_i. For each Task t in T_i (line 3), it is rescheduled at Site s_j if the difference of total time of the two sites can be reduced (lines 4–8). The task that has no input data at Site s_j is rescheduled first. Line 4 reschedules Task t at Site s_j. Line 5 calculates the total time at Sites s_i and s_j. Lines 6–7 updates the scheduling plan if it can reduce the difference of total time of the two sites by rescheduling Task t and if the total time of Site s_i is still bigger than or equal to that of Site s_j.

5.2 Estimation of Execution Time

In this section, we propose the model to estimate the time to execute a bag of tasks in multiple sites and the time to execute the scheduled tasks at each site. The time to execute a bag of tasks in multiple sites can be expressed as the maximum time to execute all the tasks scheduled among each site as shown in Formula 1.

$$TotalTime(SP(T, S)) = \max_{T_i \subset T, s_i \subset S, 0 \leq i \leq m} TotalTime(T_i, s_i) \tag{1}$$

T_i represents the bag of tasks scheduled at Site s_i according to the scheduling plan $SP(T, S)$ and m represents the number of sites.

We now give the method to estimate the total time to execute a bag of tasks at a single site, which is used in both the DIM algorithm and the MCT algorithm to achieve load balancing of different sites. Formula 2 gives the estimation of total time without considering the time to generate provenance data, which is used in the MCT algorithm.

$$TotalTime(T, s) = ExecTime(T, s) \\ + InputTransTime(T, s) \tag{2}$$

T represents the bag of tasks scheduled at Site s. $ExecTime$ is the time to execute the bag of Tasks T at Site s, *i.e.* the time to run the corresponding programs. $InputTransTime$ is the time to transfer the input data of the tasks from other sites to Site s. In the DIM algorithm, we use Formula 3 to estimate the total time with consideration of the time to generate provenance data.

$$TotalTime(T, s) = ExecTime(T, s) \\ + InputTransTime(T, s) \\ + ProvTransTime(T, s) \tag{3}$$

$ProvTransTime$ is the time to generate provenance data in the provenance database.

We assume that the workload of each task of the same activity is similar. The average workload (in GFLOP) of the tasks of each activity and the computing capacity of each VM at Site s is known to the system. The computing capacity (in GFLOPS) indicates the workload that can be realized per second. Then, the time to execute the tasks can be estimated by dividing the total workload by the total computing capacity of site s, as shown in Formula 4.

$$ExecTime(T, s) = \frac{|T| * AvgWorkload(T)}{\sum_{VM_i \in s} ComputingCapacity(VM_i)} \tag{4}$$

$|T|$ represents the number of tasks in Bag T. $AvgWorkload$ is the average workload of the bag of tasks.

The time to transfer input data can be estimated as the sum of the time to transfer the input data from other sites to Site s of each task as in Formula 5.

$$InTransTime(T, s) = \sum_{t_i \in T} \sum_{s_i \in S} \frac{InDataSize(t_i, s_i)}{DataRate(s_i, s)} \tag{5}$$

$InDataSize(t_i, s_i)$ represents the size of input data of Task t_i, which is stored at Site s_i. The size can be measured at runtime. $DataRate(s_i, s)$ represents the data transfer rate, which can be configured by users. S represents the set of sites.

Finally, the time to generate provenance data is estimated by Formula 6.

$$ProvTransTime(T, s) = |T| * TransactionTimes(T) \\ * AvgTransactionTime(s) \tag{6}$$

$|T|$ represents the number of tasks in Bag T. We can estimate $AvgTransaction-Time$ by counting the time to perform a transaction to update the provenance data of a task at the provenance database from Site s. $TransactionTimes(T)$ represents the number of transactions to perform for generating the provenance data of each task in Bag T. It can be configured according to the features of the SWfMS.

5.3   Method Analysis

In this section, we analyze the complexity of the 2L scheduling and the DIM algorithm. Let us assume that N $(N \gg 2)$ tasks are scheduled to M $(M > 2)$ sites, each of which has K $(K > 2)$ computing nodes. The complexity of the 2L approach is $M^N + K^N$, where M^N is the complexity of the multisite level and K^N is the complexity of the single site level. Assume that there are N_i tasks scheduled at site s_i while $\sum_{i=1}^{M} N_i = N$. Thus, the complexity of single site scheduling is:

$$\prod_{i=1}^{M} K^{N_i} = K^{\sum_{i=1}^{M} N_i}$$

$$= K^N \tag{7}$$

Thus, the complexity of the single site scheduling of the 2L approach is K^N. However, the complexity of the 1L approach is $(M * K)^N$. Let us assume that $N > 2, M > 2$ and $K > 2$.

$$M^N + K^N < (\frac{1}{2} * M * K)^N + (\frac{1}{2} * M * K)^N$$

$$< (\frac{1}{2})^{(N-1)} * (M * K)^N \tag{8}$$

$$< (M * K)^N$$

From Formula 8, we can conclude that $N^M + N^K < N^{M*K}$, i.e. the complexity of the 2L scheduling approach is smaller than that of the 1L scheduling approach.

Let us assume that we have n tasks to be scheduled at m sites and $n \gg m$. The complexity of the first loop (lines 2–5) of the DIM algorithm is $\mathcal{O}(n)$. The complexity of the $TaskReschedule$ algorithm is $\mathcal{O}(n)$, since there may be n tasks scheduled at a site in the first loop (lines 2–5) of the DIM algorithm. The complexity of $MinTime(S)$ and $MaxTime(S)$ is $\mathcal{O}(m)$, which is much smaller than $\mathcal{O}(n)$. Thus, the complexity of Lines 7–9 is $\mathcal{O}(n)$. Assume that the difference between the maximum total time and the minimum total time is T_{diff}. The maximum value of T_{diff} can be $n * avg(T)$ when all the tasks are scheduled at one site while there is no task scheduled at other sites. $avg(T)$ represents the average execution time of each task, which is a constant value. After m (m^2) times[2] of rescheduling tasks between the site of maximum total time and the site of minimum total time, the maximum difference of total time of any two sites should be reduced to less than $\frac{T_{diff}}{\sqrt{2}}$ (see Appendix). Thus, the complexity of the second loop (lines 6–9) of the DIM algorithm is $\mathcal{O}(m \cdot n \cdot \log n)$ $(\mathcal{O}(m^2 \cdot n \cdot \log n))$. Therefore, the complexity of the DIM algorithm is $\mathcal{O}(m \cdot n \cdot \log n)$ $(\mathcal{O}(m^2 \cdot n \cdot \log n))$. The complexity indicates that when the number of tasks or sites are small, the scheduling problem is simple. Since m is much smaller than n, it is only a little bit higher than those of OLB and MCT, which is $\mathcal{O}(m \cdot n)$, but yields high reduction in SWf execution (see Sect. 6.3).

---

[2] When each site has the same computing capacity, this is m. But when not all the sites have the same computing capacity, this should be m^2.

6   Experimental Evaluation

In this section, we present an experimental evaluation of our DIM scheduling algorithm using Microsoft Azure multisite cloud [3]. First, we present two real-life SWfs, *i.e.* Buzz and Montage, as use cases. Then, we explain the techniques for the implementation of intersite communication of multisite Chiron in Azure. Afterwards, we show the experimental results of executing the two SWfs in Azure with different multisite scheduling algorithms.

6.1   SWf Use Cases

In this section, we present two SWfs, *i.e.* Buzz and Montage, to evaluate our proposed algorithms. The two SWfs have different structures, which can show that our proposed algorithm is suitable for different SWfs.

Buzz Workflow. Buzz workflow is a data-intensive SWf that searches for trends and measures correlations in scientific publications. It analyses data collected from bibliography databases such as the DBLP Computer Science Bibliography (DBLP) [2] or the U.S. National Institutes of Health's National Library of Medicine (PubMed) during the last 20 years. Buzz workflow is composed of thirteen activities, which are shown in Fig. 8. Boxes in the figure represent SWf activities and arrows represent the data dependencies. The FileSplit activity gathers the information of scientific publications from a bibliography databases. The Buzz activity uses the gathered information to identify buzzwords, *i.e.* a word or phrase that can become popular for a specific period of time. The WordReduce activity organizes these publications according to buzzword and publication year, and it also computes occurrences of the buzzwords. Furthermore, the YearFilter activity selects buzzwords that appeared in the publications after a specific time. The BuzzHistory activity creates a history for each buzzword. The FrequencySort activity computes the frequency of each buzzword. With this information, the HistogramCreator activity generates some histograms with word frequency varying the year. On the other hand, the Top10 activity selects ten of the most frequent words in recent years, whilst the ZipfFilter activity selects terms according to a Zipf curve that is specified by word frequency values [36]. In addition, the CrossJoin activity merges results from the Top10 activity and the ZipfFilter activity. The Correlate activity computes correlations between the words from the Top10 activity and buzzwords from the ZipfFilter activity. Using these correlations, the TopCorrelations activity takes the terms that have a correlation greater than a threshold. Finally, the GatherResults activity presents these selected words with the histograms.

There are five activities, *i.e.* FileSplit, Buzz, BuzzHistory, HistogramCreator and Correlate, which correspond to multiple tasks. In our experiment, the tasks of the five activities are scheduled by the multisite scheduling algorithm. The other activities exploit a database management system to process data at the master site.

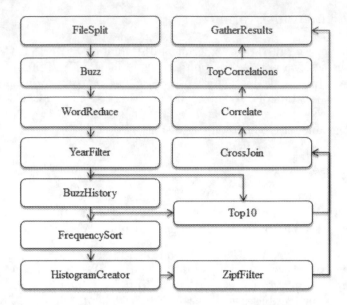

Fig. 8. Buzz workflow.

Montage Workflow. Montage is a data-intensive SWf for computing mosaics of input images [14]. The input data and the intermediate data are of considerable size and require significant storage resources. However, the execution time of each task is relatively small, which can be at most a few minutes. The structure of the Montage SWf is shown in Fig. 9. Activity 1, mProjectPP, reprojects single images to a specific scale. The mDiffFit activity performs a simple image difference between a single pair of overlapping images, which is generate by the mProjectPP activity. Then, the mConcatFit activity merges multiple parameter files into one file. Afterwards, mBgModel uses the image-to-image difference parameter table to interactively determine a set of corrections to apply to each image to achieve a "best" global fit. The mBackground activity removes a background from a single image. This activity takes the output data of the mProjectPP activity and that of the mBgModel activity. The mImgTbl activity prepares the information for putting the images together. The mAdd activity generates an output mosaic and the binning of the mosaic is changed by the mShrink activity. Finally, the mJPEG activity creates a JPEG image from the mosaic. In addition, Montage can correspond to different square degrees [14] (or degree for short), which represents the size of the mosaics image. Each degree represents a certain configuration of the input data and the parameters and the lower degree corresponds to fewer input data.

There are three activities, *i.e.* mProjectPP, mDiffFit, mBackground, which correspond to multiple tasks in the Montage SWf of 0.5, 1 and 2°. Montage has fewer activities of multiple tasks than Buzz. However, DIM is designed for

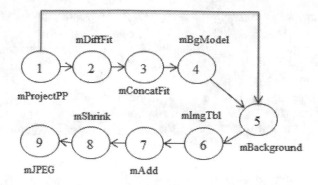

Fig. 9. Montage workflow.

scheduling a bag of multiple tasks. Thus, the advantage of DIM is less obvious in executing Montage than Buzz, which is shown in Sect. 6.3.

6.2   Intersite Communication

In this section, we present the detailed techniques for the multisite file transfer module and multisite message communication module. We choose Azure Service Bus [1] to realize the functionality of message communication module. Azure Service Bus is a generic, cloud-based messaging system for the communication among different devices. The communication can be based on the HTTP protocol, which does not need to maintain connection information (HTTP is stateless). Although this may bring more overhead for each message, the amount of control messages is low and this cost is negligible. The file transfer module is realized by Java TCP connections between two master nodes of two different sites. Since the idle intersite TCP connections may be cut down by the cloud operator, *e.g.* every 5–10 min. in Azure, the connections are maintained by sending *keepalive* messages. For instance, two messages per time period. Before execution, a task is scheduled at a site by the multisite task scheduler. If they are not stored at the scheduled site, the input files of the task are transferred to the scheduled site by the multisite file transfer module.

6.3   Experiments

This section gives our experimental evaluation of the DIM algorithm, within Microsoft Azure. Azure [3] has multiple cloud sites, *e.g.* Central US (CUS), West Europe (WEU) and North Europe (NEU). We instantiated three A4 [5] (8 CPU cores) VMs at each of the three site, *i.e.* CUS, WEU and NEU. We take WEU as master site. We deploy an A2 (2 CPU cores) VM at WEU and install PostgreSQL database as provenance data. We assume that the input data of the SWfs are distributed at the three sites. We compare our proposed algorithm with two representative baseline scheduling algorithms, *i.e.* Opportunistic Load Balancing

(OLB) and Minimum Completion Time (MCT). In the experiment, we assume the input data of SWfs cannot be moved. Thus, we schedule the tasks of start activities, e.g. FileSplit and mProjectPP, to where the data is while exploiting DIM, OLB or MCT to schedule tasks of the other activities. In the multisite environment, OLB randomly selects a site for a task while MCT schedules a task to the site that can finish the execution first. In the following figures, the execution time is the absolute time for SWf execution and the data-transfer size refers to the input data of tasks, *i.e.* the intermediate data transferred across different sites, which does not include the provenance data. In addition, since the resource utilization also depends on the programs used in different SWfs and that each SWf exploits various programs, we did not measure it.

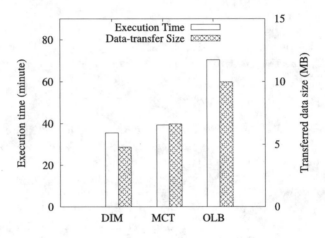

Fig. 10. Buzz execution time. The amount of data is 60 MB.

First, we used a DBLP 2013 XML file of 60 MB as input data for Buzz SWf in our experiments. The input data is evenly partitioned into three parts, which have almost the same amount of data. Each part is distributed and stored at a site while configuration files of Buzz SWf are present at all the three sites. We take WE as a master site to execute the Buzz workflow. The provenance database and Azure Service Bus are also located at the WE site. The execution result corresponding to each scheduling algorithm is shown in Fig. 10. The execution time in Figs. 10, 11, 12 and 13 represents the total execution time including data transfer and scheduling time. Table 1 shows the execution time, the time to transfer input data and the time to generate provenance data in one task of Buzz activity. This table shows that the time to transfer input data and provenance data should not be ignored compared with the time to execute the task.

Figure 10 shows that DIM is much better than MCT and OLB in terms of both execution time and transferred data size. The execution time of DIM is 9.6% smaller than that of MCT and 49.6% smaller than that of OLB. The size of the data transferred between different sites with MCT is 38.7% bigger

Table 1. Various time. The unit of data is KB and the unit of time is second. "Input" and "Provenance" represent the corresponding data. The task is executed at the CUS site.

Execution time	Input size	Input transfer time	Provenance transfer time
1.12	40	1.945	0.78

than that with DIM and the size of OLB is 108.6% bigger than that with DIM. Although OLB is a random algorithm, it distributes the tasks to each site with the same probability and the transferred data remains the same for the same configuration of the SWf and cloud environment. As a result, the size of intersite transferred data can represent the average results, i.e. which are calculated from the execution of multiple tasks.

Second, we performed an experiment using a DBLP 2013 XML file of 1.29 GB as input data for Buzz SWf while configuration files of Buzz SWf are present at all the three sites. The other configuration is the same as the first one. The execution result corresponding to each scheduling algorithm is shown in Fig. 11.

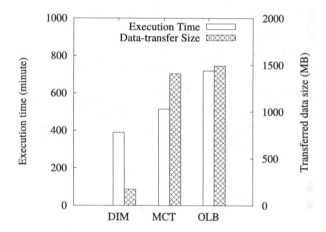

Fig. 11. Buzz SWf execution time. The amount of data is 1.29 GB.

Figure 11 shows that the advantage of DIM in terms of both execution time and transferred data size compared with MCT and OLB increases with bigger amounts of input data. The execution time corresponding to DIM is 24.3% smaller than that with MCT and 45.9% smaller than that with OLB. The size of the data transferred between different sites with MCT is 7.19 times bigger than that with DIM and the size with OLB is 7.67 times bigger than that with DIM.

Since the DIM algorithm considers the time to transfer intersite provenance data and makes optimization for a bag of tasks, i.e. global optimization, it can reduce the total time. Since DIM schedules the tasks to where the input data is located at the beginning, DIM can reduce the amount of intersite transferred data compared with other algorithms. MCT only optimizes the load balancing for each individual task, *i.e.* local optimization, among different sites without consideration of the time to transfer intersite provenance data. It is a greedy algorithm that can reduce the execution time by balancing the total time of each site while scheduling each task. However, it cannot optimize the scheduling for the whole execution of all the tasks of an activity. In addition, compared with OLB, MCT cannot reduce much the transferred data among different sites. Since OLB simply tries to keep all the sites working on arbitrary tasks, it has the worst performance.

Furthermore, we executed the Montage SWf with 0.5° with three sites, *i.e.* CUS, WEU and NEU. The size of input data is 5.5 GB. The input data is evenly partitioned to three parts stored at the corresponding sites with configuration files stored at all the three sites. The execution time and amount of intersite transferred data corresponding to each scheduling algorithm are shown in Fig. 12.

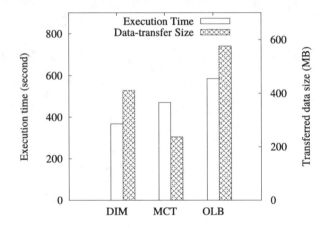

Fig. 12. Montage SWf execution time. 0.5°.

The execution results of Montage with 0.5° reveals that the execution time of DIM is 21.7% smaller than that of MCT and 37.1% smaller than that of OLB. This is expected since DIM makes optimization for a bag of tasks in order to reduce intersite transferred data with consideration of the time to transfer intersite intermediate data and provenance data. MCT is optimized for load balancing only with consideration of intermediate data. OLB has no optimization for load balancing. In addition, the intersite transferred data of DIM is 42.3% bigger than that of MCT. Since DIM is designed to achieve load balancing of each site to reduce total time, it may yield more intersite transferred data in order to achieve load balance. However, the amount of intersite transferred data of DIM is 28.6% smaller than that of OLB. This shows the efficiency of the optimization for the data transfer of DIM. Moreover, when the degree (0.5) is low, there is less data to be processed by Montage, and the number of tasks to schedule is small. Since DIM is designed for high numbers of tasks, the amounts of intersite transferred data are not reduced very much in this situation.

In addition, we executed Montage SWf of 1° in the multisite cloud. We used the same input data as in the previous experiment, *i.e.* 5.5 GB input data evenly distributed at three sites. The execution time and the amount of intersite transferred data corresponding to each scheduling algorithm are shown in Fig. 13.

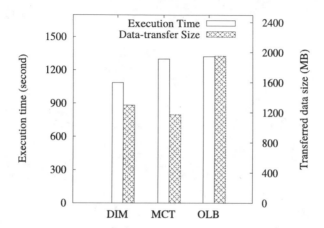

Fig. 13. Montage SWf execution time. 1°.

The execution results of Montage with 1° reveals that the execution time of DIM is 16.4% smaller than that of MCT and 17.8% smaller than that of OLB. As explained before, this is expected since DIM can reduce the execution time by balancing the load among different sites compared with MCT and OLB. In addition, the intersite transferred data of DIM is 10.7% bigger than that of MCT. This is much smaller than the value for 0.5° (42.3%), since there are more tasks to schedule when the degree is 1 and DIM reduces intersite transferred data for a big amount of tasks. However, the amount of intersite transferred data is bigger than that of MCT. This happens since the main objective of DIM is to reduce execution time instead of reducing intersite transferred data. In addition, the amount of intersite transferred data of DIM is 33.4% smaller than that of OLB, which shows the efficiency of the optimization for the data transfer of DIM.

We also executed the Montage SWf of 2° in the multisite cloud. The configuration is the same as in the previous execution of Montage. The results in Fig. 14 show that, although the total execution time of DIM is higher than those of MCT and OLB, the execution time without scheduling time is still smaller than those of MCT (7.0%) and OLB (12.8%). The amount of intersite transferred data of DIM is 29.2% and 61.8% smaller than those of MCT and OLB, which shows that DIM can greatly reduce intersite transferred data for scheduling big numbers of tasks. Since the cost to get information from the provenance database is expensive, the scheduling time is high when the SWf has many tasks. However, we

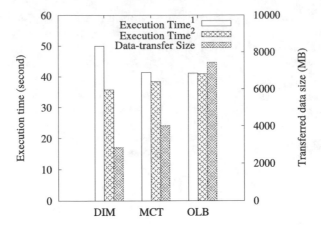

Fig. 14. Montage execution time. $2°$. Execution time[1] represents the total execution including the scheduling time and data transfer. Execution time[1] represents the execution time without scheduling time.

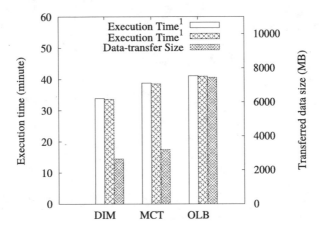

Fig. 15. Montage execution time. $2°$. Execution time[1] represents the total execution including the scheduling time and data transfer. Execution time[1] represents the execution time without scheduling time.

could simply load the provenance data once in memory for scheduling and use the in-memory data to run the scheduling algorithms, which largely reduces the scheduling time. We improved the implementation of the scheduling algorithms based on this method, and executed the Montage SWf of $2°$ with the optimized version of multisite Chiron. The results are shown in Fig. 15. The total execution time of DIM is 12.7% and 17.6% smaller than those of MCT and OLB.

We also measured the time to execute the scheduling algorithms to generate scheduling plans while executing Buzz and Montage. The scheduling time is shown in Table 2. The complexity of MCT is the same as that of OLB, which

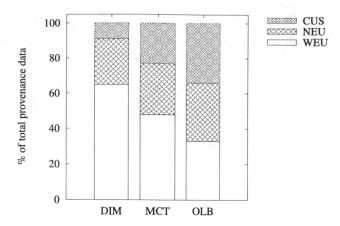

Fig. 16. Distribution of provenance during the execution of Buzz workflow. The size of input data is 1.2 GB.

Table 2. Scheduling time. The time unit is second. The size of the input data of Buzz^{60} SWf is 60 MB and that of Buzz$^{1.29}$ is 1.29 GB. The degree of Montage$^{0.5}$ is 0.5, that of Montage^{1} is 1 and that of Montage^{2} is 2. "(O)" represents the scheduling time corresponding to the optimized implementation of scheduling algorithms.

Algorithm	DIM	MCT	OLB
Buzz^{60}	71.4	9.8	1.3
Buzz$^{1.29}$	633	109	17
Montage$^{0.5}$	8.4	3.7	1.1
Montage^{1}	29.2	28.8	1.5
Montage^{2}	855.4	178.7	10.9
Montage^{2}(O)	15.5	15.1	10.9

is $\mathcal{O}(m \cdot n)$. However, the scheduling time of MCT is much bigger than OLB (without the optimization of the implementation of scheduling algorithms). The reason is that MCT needs to interact with the provenance database to get the information of the files in order to estimate the time to transfer the files among different sites. The table shows that the time to execute DIM is much higher than OLB for both Buzz and Montage (without the optimization of the implementation of scheduling algorithms) since the complexity of DIM is higher than that of OLB and that DIM has more interactions with the provenance database in order to estimate the total time to execute the tasks at a site. When there is significant number of tasks to schedule (for the Buzz$^{1.29}$ SWf), the time to execute DIM is much bigger than that of MCT because of higher complexity and the frequent interaction with the provenance database. However, when the number of tasks is not very big, the time to execute DIM is similar to that of MCT, both of which are much bigger than that of OLB, since it takes much time to communicate with the provenance database to get the data location information for the estimation of the total time to execute tasks at each site. This overhead can be calculated according to Formula 9, where $|T|$ represents the number of tasks and $AvgTransactionTime$ is the average time for one transaction (see Formula 6). We improved the implementation of the scheduling algorithms by loading the provenance data into the memory once and using the in-memory provenance data for the scheduling algorithms. We measured the scheduling time for executing Montage of $2°$. The results show a major improvement, *i.e.* the scheduling time of DIM is almost the same as those of MCT and OLB. The scheduling time of the three scheduling algorithms is always small compared with the total execution time, which is acceptable for task scheduling during SWf execution time. In addition, based on the measured scheduling time, we estimate that when the number of tasks is less than one million, the scheduling time of DIM with the improved implementation is less than 10% of the total execution time, which is acceptable. According to [10], an SWf of a million tasks is already much bigger than a very large SWf (1000 tasks). Although the scheduling time of DIM may be higher than those of MCT and OLB, the execution time of SWfs corresponds to DIM is much smaller than those of MCT and OLB as explained in the experiments. This means that DIM generates better scheduling plans compared with MCT and OLB.

$$EstimationOverHead(T) = |T| * AvgTransactionTime \qquad (9)$$

Table 3. Size of provenance data. The unit of the data is MB. The size of the input data of Buzz SWf is 1.2 GB and the degree of Montage is 1.

Algorithm	DIM	MCT	OLB
Buzz	301	280	279
Montage	10	10	10

Furthermore, we measured the size of provenance data and the distribution of the provenance data. As shown in Table 3, the amount of the provenance data corresponding to the three scheduling algorithms are similar (the difference is less than 8%). However, the distribution of the provenance data is different. In fact, the bandwidth between the provenance database and the site is in the following order: WEU > NEU > CUS[3]. As shown in Figs. 16 and 17, the provenance data generated at the CUS site is much bigger than those generated at the NEU site and the WEU site for the DIM algorithm. In addition, the percentage of provenance data at WEU corresponding to DIM is much bigger than MCT (up to 95% bigger) and OLB (up to 97% bigger). This indicates that DIM can schedule

---

[3] For instance, the time to execute "SELECT count(*) from eactivity" at the provenance database from each site: 0.0027s from the WEU site, 0.0253s from the NEU site and 0.1117s from the CUS site.

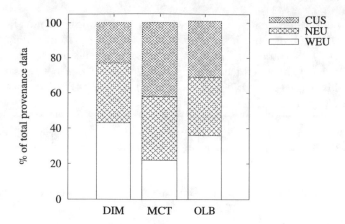

Fig. 17. Distribution of provenance during the execution of Montage workflow. The degree is 1.

tasks to the site (WEU) that has bigger bandwidth with the provenance database (the database is at the WEU site), which yields bigger percentage of provenance data generated at the site. This can reduce the time to generate provenance data in order to reduce the overall multisite execution time of SWfs. However, MCT and OLB are not aware of the provenance data transfer costs, which correspond to bigger multisite execution time. In the algorithm, we used the predefined bandwidth and execution time, which depends largely on if the user is familiar with the environment and the SWf. We leave study of the preciseness of the cost estimation as future work.

From the experiments, we can see that DIM performs better than MCT (up to 24.3%) and OLB (up to 49.6%) in terms of execution time although it takes more time to generate scheduling plans. DIM can reduce the intersite transferred data compared with MCT (up to 719%) and OLB (up to 767%). As the amount of input data increases, the advantage of DIM becomes more important.

7   Conclusion

In this paper, we proposed a solution based on multisite Chiron to execute a SWf using provenance data and process distributed data in a multisite cloud.

Multisite Chiron is able to execute SWfs in a multisite cloud with geographically distributed input data. We proposed the architecture of multisite Chiron, defined a new provenance model for multisite SWf execution and a global method to gather the distributed provenance data in a centralized database. Based on this architecture, we proposed a new scheduling algorithm, *i.e.* DIM, which considers the latency to transfer data and to generate provenance data in multisite cloud. We analyzed the complexity of DIM ($\mathcal{O}(m \cdot n \cdot \log n)$), which is quite acceptable for scheduling bags of tasks. We used two real-life SWfs, *i.e.* Buzz and Montage to evaluate the DIM algorithm in Microsoft Azure with three sites.

The experiments show that although its complexity is higher than those of OLB and MCT, DIM is much better than two representative baseline algorithms, *i.e.* MCT (up to 24.3%) and OLB (up to 49.6%), in terms of execution time. In addition, DIM can also reduce significantly data transfer between sites, compared with MCT (up to 719%) and OLB (up to 767%). The advantage of DIM becomes important with high numbers of tasks.

Acknowledgment. Work partially funded by EU H2020 Programme and MCTI/ RNP-Brazil (HPC4E grant agreement number 689772), CNPq, FAPERJ, and INRIA (SciDISC project), Microsoft (ZcloudFlow project) and performed in the context of the Computational Biology Institute (www.ibc-montpellier.fr). We would like to thank Weiwei Chen and the Pegasus project for their help in modeling and executing the Montage SWf.

Appendix

In this section, we analyze the convergence of the DIM algorithm. Since there are finite tasks in the bag of tasks scheduled at Site s_i, Algorithm 2 always converges. Next, let us analyze the convergence of Algorithm 1. In order to make the problem simple, we assume that the total time at the two sites are the same after executing Algorithm 2 and we denote the time to transfer data, including input data and provenance data, as $\alpha * ExecTime(T, s)$ in Formula 3. Thus, we have:

$$TotalTime(T, s) = (1 + \alpha) * ExecTime(T, s) = C * \frac{|T|}{CC(s)}$$

$$C = (1 + \alpha) * AvgWorkload(T) \tag{10}$$

$$CC(s) = \sum_{VM_i \in s} ComputingCapacity(VM_i)$$

$TotalTime(T, s)$, $|T|$, $AvgWorkload(T)$ and $ComputingCapacity(VM_i)$ represent the same values as those in Formula 3. $CC(s)$ represents the computing capacity at each site. C and $CC(s)$ are constant values. We denote the total execution time at each site by T_{opt} when all the sites are in the optimal situation, *i.e.* each site has the same total execution time. We denote a cost function in Formula 11 to measure the distance of current scheduling plan (SP) and the optimal scheduling plan.

$$J(SP) = \sum_{i=1}^{m} (J(s_i)) = \sum_{i=1}^{m} (TotalTime(T_i, s_i) - T_{opt})^2 \tag{11}$$

where $J(s_i)$ represents the cost function of Site s_i. T_i and s_i are defined by the scheduling plan SP.

First, let us analyze the situation when all the sites have the same computing capacity. In each iteration of Algorithm 1, we choose two sites (s_i, s_j) with the maximum total execution time and minimum total execution time. That means that we choose at least one site s_i, which has the biggest distance between the current situation and the optimal situation among all the sites as shown in Formula 12. In addition, the total execution time of the maximum total execution time should be bigger than or equal to T_{opt} and the total execution time of the minimum total execution time should be smaller than or equal to $Topt$ as shown in Formula 13.

$$J(s_i) = \max_{j=1}^{m}(TotalTime(T_j, s_j) - T_{opt})^2 \tag{12}$$

$$(TotalTime(T_i, s_i) - T_{opt}) * (T_{opt} - TotalTime(T_j, s_j)) \geq 0 \tag{13}$$

We denote the other site by s_j. Since the two sites have the same computing capacity, we denote the total execution time of each site by $TotalTime'(T, s_{ij})$ after executing Algorithm 2. Since the two sites have the same execution time, according to Formula 10, they should have the same number of tasks, which is denoted by T. Thus, we have Formula 14.

$$TotalTime(T_i, s_i) = C * \frac{|T_i|}{CC(s)}$$

$$TotalTime(T_j, s_j) = C * \frac{|T_j|}{CC(s)}$$

$$TotalTime'(T, s_{ij}) = C * \frac{|T|}{CC(s)} \tag{14}$$

$$2 * |T| = |T_i| + |T_j|$$

According this formula, we can get Formula 15.

$$TotalTime'(T, s_{ij}) = \frac{TotalTime(T_i, s_i) + TotalTime(T_j, s_j)}{2} \tag{15}$$

Thus, the cost function of the two selected sites after one iteration can be expressed as Formula 16.

$$
\begin{aligned}
J'(SP', s_i, s_j) &= (TotalTime'(T, s_i) - T_{opt})^2 + (TotalTime'(T, s_j) - T_{opt})^2 \\
&= 2 * (TotalTime'(T, s_{ij}) - T_{opt})^2 \\
&= 2 * (\frac{TotalTime(T_i, s_i) + TotalTime(T_j, s_j)}{2} - T_{opt})^2 \\
&= 2 * (\frac{(TotalTime(T_i, s_i) - T_{opt}) - (T_{opt} - TotalTime(T_j, s_j))}{2}))^2 \\
&= \frac{(TotalTime(T_i, s_i) - T_{opt})^2 + (T_{opt} - TotalTime(T_j, s_j)^2}{2} \\
&\quad - (TotalTime(T_i, s_i) - T_{opt}) * (T_{opt} - TotalTime(T_j, s_j)) \\
&= \frac{J(SP, s_i, s_j)}{2} \\
&\quad - (TotalTime(T_i, s_i) - T_{opt}) * (T_{opt} - TotalTime(T_j, s_j))
\end{aligned}
\tag{16}
$$

where we denote the scheduling plan after the iteration by SP'. We denote the cost function of the two selected sites before the iteration as $J(SP, s_i, s_j)$.

According to Formula 13, we get the Formula 17.

$$J'(SP', s_i, s_j) < \frac{J(SP, s_i, s_j)}{2} \tag{17}$$

Thus, after m iterations, $J(SP)$ becomes less than $\frac{J(SP)}{2}$. The minimum modification in one iteration should be bigger than $\frac{C}{CC(s)}$. Thus, after at most $m * \log_2(J(SP) - \frac{C}{CC(s)})$ iterations, Algorithm 1 terminates.

Then, let us consider a situation where some sites ($\rho m,\ > 1 \rho > 0$) have much bigger computing capacity than other sites (($1 - \rho)m$). We assume that after executing Algorithm 2 between two sites of different computing capacity, the total execution time of the two sites becomes the original total execution time of the site, which has bigger computing capacity. In this situation, in order to reduce $J(SP)$ to $\frac{J(SP)}{2}$, we need at most $\rho * (1 - \rho) * m^2$. Thus, after at most $\rho * (1 - \rho) * m^2 * \log_2(J(SP) - \frac{C}{CC(s)})$ iterations, Algorithm 1 terminates. Furthermore, the other situations are between the first situation where all the sites have the same computing capacity and this situation.

References

1. Azure service bus. http://azure.microsoft.com/en-us/services/service-bus/
2. DBLP Computer Science Bibliography. http://dblp.uni-trier.de/
3. Microsoft Azure. http://azure.microsoft.com
4. Montage. http://montage.ipac.caltech.edu/docs/gridtools.html
5. Parameters of different types of VMS in microsoft Azure. https://azure.microsoft.com/en-us/pricing/details/virtual-machines/
6. Bhuvaneshwar, K., Sulakhe, D., Gauba, R., Rodriguez, A., Madduri, R., Dave, U., Lacinski, L., Foster, I., Gusev, Y., Madhavan, S.: A case study for cloud based high throughput analysis of NGS data using the globus genomics system. Comput. Struct. Biotechnol. J. **13**, 64–74 (2015)
7. Bouganim, L., Fabret, F., Mohan, C., Valduriez, P.: Dynamic query scheduling in data integration systems. In: Proceedings of the 16th International Conference on Data Engineering, pp. 425–434 (2000)
8. Bouganim, L., Kapitskaia, O., Valduriez, P.: Memory-adaptive scheduling for large query execution. In: Proceedings of the 1998 ACM CIKM International Conference on Information and Knowledge Management, pp. 105–115 (1998)
9. Cala, J., Xu, Y., Wijaya, E.A., Missier, P.: From scripted HPC-based NGS pipelines to workflows on the cloud. In: 14th IEEE/ACM International Symposium on Cluster, Cloud and Grid Computing (CCGrid), pp. 694–700 (2014)
10. Calheiros, R.N., Buyya, R.: Meeting deadlines of scientific workflows in public clouds with tasks replication. IEEE Trans. Parallel Distrib. Syst. **25**(7), 1787–1796 (2014)
11. de Oliveira, D., Ocaña, K.A.C.S., Baião, F., Mattoso, M.: A provenance-based adaptive scheduling heuristic for parallel scientific workflows in clouds. J. Grid Comput. **10**(3), 521–552 (2012)
12. Dean, J., Ghemawat, S.: Mapreduce: simplified data processing on large clusters. In: 6th Symposium on Operating System Design and Implementation (OSDI), pp. 137–150 (2004)

13. Deelman, E., Gannon, D., Shields, M., Taylor, I.: Workflows and e-science: an overview of workflow system features and capabilities. Future Gener. Comput. Syst. **25**(5), 528–540 (2009)
14. Deelman, E., Singh, G., Livny, M., Berriman, B., Good, J.: The cost of doing science on the cloud: the montage example. In: International Conference for High Performance Computing, Networking, Storage and Analysis, pp. 1–12 (2008)
15. Deelman, E., Singh, G., Su, M.-H., Blythe, J., Gil, Y., Kesselman, C., Mehta, G., Vahi, K., Berriman, G.B., Good, J., Laity, A., Jacob, J.C., Katz, D.S.: Pegasus: a framework for mapping complex scientific workflows onto distributed systems. Sci. Program. **13**(3), 219–237 (2005)
16. Dias, J., Ogasawara, E.S., de Oliveira, D., Porto, F., Valduriez, P., Mattoso, M.: Algebraic dataflows for big data analysis. In: IEEE International Conference on Big Data, pp. 150–155 (2013)
17. Duan, R., Prodan, R., Li, X.: Multi-objective game theoretic scheduling of bag-of-tasks workflows on hybrid clouds. IEEE Trans. Cloud Comput. **2**(1), 29–42 (2014)
18. Etminani, K., Naghibzadeh, M.: A min-min max-min selective algorithm for grid task scheduling. In: The Third IEEE/IFIP International Conference in Central Asia on Internet (ICI 2007), pp. 1–7 (2007)
19. Hiden, H., Watson, P., Woodman, S., Leahy, D.: E-science central: cloud-based e-science and its application to chemical property modelling. Technical report CS-TR-1227 (2010)
20. Hiden, H., Woodman, S., Watson, P., Cala, J.: Developing cloud applications using the e-science central platform. Philos. Trans. R. Soc. London A Math. Phys. Eng. Sci. **371**, 2012 (1983)
21. Liu, J., Pacitti, E., Valduriez, P., de Oliveira, D., Mattoso, M.: Multi-objective scheduling of scientific workflows in multisite clouds. Future Gener. Comput. Syst. **63**, 76–95 (2016)
22. Liu, J., Pacitti, E., Valduriez, P., Mattoso, M.: Parallelization of scientific workflows in the cloud. Research report RR-8565 (2014)
23. Liu, J., Pacitti, E., Valduriez, P., Mattoso, M.: A survey of data-intensive scientific workflow management. J. Grid Comput. **13**, 457–493 (2015)
24. Liu, J., Pacitti, E., Valduriez, P., Mattoso, M.: Scientific workflow scheduling with provenance support in multisite cloud. In: 12th International Meeting on High Performance Computing for Computational Science VECPAR, p. 8 (2016)
25. Liu, J., Silva, V., Pacitti, E., Valduriez, P., Mattoso, M.: Scientific workflow partitioning in multisite cloud. In: Lopes, L., et al. (eds.) Euro-Par 2014. LNCS, vol. 8805, pp. 105–116. Springer, Cham (2014). doi:10.1007/978-3-319-14325-5_10
26. Maheswaran, M., Ali, S., Siegel, H.J., Hensgen, D., Freund, R.F.: Dynamic matching and scheduling of a class of independent tasks onto heterogeneous computing systems. In: 8th Heterogeneous Computing Workshop, p. 30 (1999)
27. Martins, V., Pacitti, E., Dick, M.E., Jiménez-Peris, R.: Scalable and topology-aware reconciliation on P2P networks. Distrib. Parallel Databases **24**(1–3), 1–43 (2008)
28. Mattoso, M., Dias, J., Ocana, K.A., Ogasawara, E., Costa, F., Horta, F., Silva, V., de Oliveira, D.: Dynamic steering of HPC scientific workflows: a survey. Future Gener. Comput. Syst. **46**, 100–113 (2014)
29. Ogasawara, E.S., Dias, J., Silva, V., Chirigati, F.S., de Oliveira, D., Porto, F., Valduriez, P., Mattoso, M.: Chiron: a parallel engine for algebraic scientific workflows. Concurr. Comput. Pract. Exp. **25**(16), 2327–2341 (2013)
30. Özsu, M.T., Valduriez, P.: Principles of Distributed Database Systems. Springer, New York (2011). doi:10.1007/978-1-4419-8834-8

31. Pacitti, E., Akbarinia, R., Dick, M.E.: P2P Techniques for Decentralized Applications. Synthesis Lectures on Data Management. Morgan & Claypool Publishers, San Rafael (2012)
32. Pineda-Morales, L., Costan, A., Antoniu, G.: Towards multi-site metadata management for geographically distributed cloud workflows. In: 2015 IEEE International Conference on Cluster Computing, CLUSTER, pp. 294–303 (2015)
33. Sandberg, R., Golgberg, D., Kleiman, S., Walsh, D., Lyon, B.: Design and implementation of the sun network filesystem. In: Innovations in Internetworking, pp. 379–390 (1988)
34. Schenk, O., Gärtner, K.: Two-level dynamic scheduling in PARDISO: improved scalability on shared memory multiprocessing systems. Parallel Comput. **28**(2), 187–197 (2002)
35. Smanchat, S., Indrawan, M., Ling, S., Enticott, C., Abramson, D.: Scheduling multiple parameter sweep workflow instances on the grid. In: 5th IEEE International Conference on E-Science, pp. 300–306 (2009)
36. Tarapanoff, K., Quoniam, L., de Araújo Júnior, R.H., Alvares, L.: Intelligence obtained by applying data mining to a database of french theses on the subject of brazil. Inf. Res. **7**(1), 41–53 (2001)
37. Topcuouglu, H., Hariri, S., Wu, M.: Performance-effective and low-complexity task scheduling for heterogeneous computing. IEEE Trans. Parallel Distrib. Syst. **13**(3), 260–274 (2002)
38. Wieczorek, M., Prodan, R., Fahringer, T.: Scheduling of scientific workflows in the askalon grid environment. SIGMOD Rec. **34**(3), 56–62 (2005)
39. Yu, Z., Shi, W.: An adaptive rescheduling strategy for grid workflow applications. In: IEEE International Parallel and Distributed Processing Symposium (IPDPS), pp. 1–8 (2007)

Cost Optimization of Data Flows
Based on Task Re-ordering

Georgia Kougka[(✉)] and Anastasios Gounaris

Department of Informatics, Aristotle University of Thessaloniki,
Thessaloniki, Greece
{georkoug,gounaria}@csd.auth.gr

Abstract. Analyzing big data with the help of automated data flows
attracts a lot of attention because of the growing need for end-to-end
processing of this data. Modern data flows may consist of a high number
of tasks and it is difficult for flow designers to define an efficient execution order of the tasks manually given that, typically, there is significant
freedom in the valid positioning for some of the tasks. Several automated
execution plan enumeration techniques have been proposed. These solutions can be broadly classified into three categories, each having significant limitations: (i) the optimizations are based on rewrite rules similar
to those used in databases, such as filter and projection push-down, but
these rules cover only the flow tasks that correspond to extended relational algebra operators. To cover arbitrary tasks, the solutions (ii) either
rely on simple heuristics, or (iii) they exhaustively check all orderings,
and thus cannot scale. We target the second category and we propose an
efficient and polynomial cost-based task ordering solution for flows with
arbitrary tasks seen as black boxes. We evaluated our proposals using
both real runs and simulations, and the results show that we can achieve
speed-ups of orders of magnitude, especially for flows with a high number
of tasks even for relatively low flexibility in task positioning.

1 Introduction

Complex data analysis becomes more and more critical in order to extract high-
quality information from raw data that is nowadays produced at an extreme scale.
The ultimate goal is to derive actionable information in a timely manner. To this
end, the usual practice is to employ fully automated data-centric flows (or simply
called data flows) both for business intelligence [6] and scientific purposes [21]. The
fact that data flows are typically data and/or computation intensive, combined
with the volatile nature of the environment and the data, gives rise to the need
for efficient optimization techniques tailored to data flows.

Data flows define the processing of large data volumes as a sequence of
data manipulation tasks. An example of a real-world, analytic flow is one that
processes free-form text data retrieved from Twitter (tweets) that comment on
products in order to compose a dynamic report considering sales, advertisement
campaigns and user feedback after performing a dozen of steps [26]. Example

© Springer-Verlag GmbH Germany 2017
A. Hameurlain et al. (Eds.): TLDKS XXXIII, LNCS 10430, pp. 113–145, 2017.
DOI: 10.1007/978-3-662-55696-2_4

steps include the extraction of date information, quantifying the user sentiment through text analysis, filtering, grouping and expanding the information contained in the tweets through lookups in (static) data sources. Another example is to process newspaper articles, perform linguistic analysis, extract named entities and then establish relationships between companies and persons [24]. The tasks in a flow can either have a direct correspondence to operators of the extended relational algebra, such as filters, grouping, aggregates and joins, or encapsulate arbitrary data transformations, text analytics, machine learning algorithms and so on.

One of the most important steps in the data flow design is the specification of the execution order of the constituent tasks [13,22,26]. In practice, this can be the result of a manual procedure, which may result in non-optimal flow execution plans with regards to the sequence of tasks. Furthermore, even if a data flow execution plan is optimal for a specific input data set, it may prove significantly suboptimal for another data set with different statistical characteristics [11].

Automated plan enumeration solutions can be broadly classified into three categories. The first category is exemplified by the approaches followed by systems such as Pig [23] and JAQL, which utilize a rich set of rules to enhance an initial flow execution plan. These rules constitute a direct knowledge transfer from database query optimization, e.g., filter and projection push-down [10], but can cover only the tasks that have counterparts in the extended relational algebra. In general, data flow optimization is different from traditional query optimization in that the tasks do not necessarily belong to an algebra with clear semantics, and as such, are treated as black box, e.g., like user-defined functions (UDFs).

The second category consists of heuristics, e.g., [25,34], and simple extensions of optimization techniques initially proposed for database queries with UDFs [7,12]. A strong point of these plan enumeration solutions is that they can handle arbitrary tasks. Their weakest point is that they leave significant room for further improvements as proved in this work. The third category covers exhaustive solutions that are optimal for small flows but inapplicable to large flows because they do not scale with the size of the flow, e.g. [13].

In this work, we target the second category and we advance the state-of-the-art through the proposal of novel optimization algorithms that define the execution order of the tasks in a data flow in an efficient manner thus relieving the flow designers from the burden of selecting the task ordering on their own. The proposed solutions are applicable to large flows containing arbitrary data manipulation tasks and attain significantly better performance, i.e., they offer average speed-up of several factors, whereas in stand-alone cases, the speed-up can be up to two orders of magnitude. Our proposal refers to the logical level and is orthogonal to physical execution details; as such, it is applicable to both centralized and parallel execution environments.

The proposed optimization solutions were validated, as a proof of concept, in a real environment, namely Pentaho Data Integration (*PDI*), which is a widespread data flow tool [1]. Additionally, we performed thorough evaluations using synthetic data flows. The summary of our contributions is as follows:[1]

1. We introduce novel approximate low complexity algorithms that can be used for task reordering in data flows that have the form of a chain (Sect. 4). We show how we can further improve performance using optimizations that produce non-linear flow execution plans, where a task sends its output to several downstream tasks in parallel (Sect. 5).
2. We generalize the above results for flows with arbitrary number of sources and sinks thus covering any type of flow plans that are represented as directed acyclic graphs (DAGs) (Sect. 6).
3. We conduct thorough experiments using both real runs and simulations (Sect. 7). The evaluation results prove that the approaches introduced here significantly and consistently outperform the current state-of-the-art in all our experiments.

The remainder of this paper is structured as follows. A motivation case study is presented in Sect. 2. In Sect. 3, we formally introduce the main concepts, the problem, and its complexity. In Sects. 4 and 5, our solutions for optimizing chain flows are analyzed. Optimization of more generic flows is discussed in Sect. 6. Section 7 presents the experimental analysis and finally, the discussion of the related work and the conclusions are presented in Sects. 8 and 9, respectively.

2   Motivational Case Study

The purpose of this section is to demonstrate the inadequacy of existing approaches. We have implemented and executed a simple real-world chain (also referred to as *L-SISO*) flow in PDI, which consists of 13 tasks overall (configuration details are in Sect. 7). This flow retrieves tweets, extracts and analyzes tags referring to products, filters data and accesses static data sources in order to compose a dynamic report that associates sales with marketing campaigns (a full description can be obtained from [17]). Figure 1 presents the dependency constraints, which hold between tasks; the *DoF* in this case is 0.62, which is a representative value given that several real-world flows, as presented in [24], have *DoF* around 0.6. The dependency constraints and the *DoF* value are formally defined in the next section. Note that the four underlying static data sources are hidden behind the look-up tasks, and as such, the flow is treated as a chain.

In Fig. 2(top), a straight-forward implementation is presented, along with the cost and selectivity values of each task. These values are extracted through profiling. In a setting similar to the one used in the evaluation (see Sect. 7), this flow is

---

[1] An extended abstract of some of the ideas in Sect. 4 has appeared in [16]. Also, in an earlier technical report [17], we have presented additional algorithmic descriptions and examples of most of the solutions in Sects. 4 and 5 presented here. The material presented in this work and not appearing in [17] includes a thorough discussion of extensions to optimization techniques for database queries with UDF predicates, new techniques for multi-sink/source data flows, evaluation in a real system and fully revised synthetic experiments.

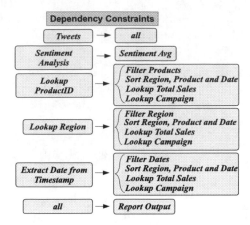

Fig. 1. The precedence constraints of the data flow in Fig. 2.

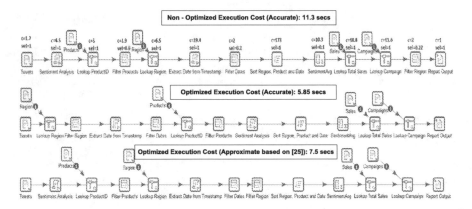

Fig. 2. Three alternative execution plans for our example data flow: the initial flow (top), the optimal one (middle) and the one produced by the technique in [25] (bottom)

capable of processing 1 million tweets in 11.3 s. Note that all constraints in Fig. 1 are satisfied. In the middle of this figure, the optimal execution plan is presented, which can drop the execution cost approximately to the half. The optimal plan is generated through exhaustive enumeration of alternatives with the constrain that tasks on the left part of Fig. 1 must precede those on the right part.

A question arises as to whether existing solutions of the first two categories in the introduction are capable of producing such a plan. Although, the plan is very simple, the answer is negative. First, due to the fact that the flow contains tasks not belonging to the extended relational algebra (e.g., extracting date with text processing, sentiment analysis, and so on), the solutions of the first category cannot perform any changes in the task ordering. The best performing scalable heuristics of the second category, according to the evidence of the evaluation in this work, has been proposed in [25]. This heuristic is based on greedy swaps of adjacent activities, if this plan transformation yields lower cost. The optimized plan is illustrated in Fig. 2 (bottom). In that case, the performance improvement is significant, but there is a clear gap between its plan and the optimal one.

The optimal execution plan for this scenario should move the filtering task *Filter Region*, which is initially the end, at the very beginning. Using methods as presented in [25], the region filter cannot move earlier unless the *campaign lookup* task is moved earlier as well due to the precedence constraints, an action that the greedy algorithm cannot cover. A less obvious optimization is to move the pair of date extraction and filtering tasks upstream although the former is expensive and not filtering. In the next section, we propose solutions that are capable of producing the optimal plan in this specific scenario and, further, they can scale to flows with hundreds of tasks.

Finally, exhaustive solutions cannot apply to flows with more than 20–25 tasks [17].

3   Preliminaries

In this paper, we deal with the problem of re-ordering the tasks of a data flow without violating possible precedence constraints between tasks, while the sum of the execution time for all tasks is minimized. The data flow is represented as a directed acyclic graph (DAG), where each task corresponds to a node in the graph and the edges between nodes represent intermediate data shipping among tasks.

3.1   Notation, Terminology and Assumptions

The main notation, terminology and assumptions are described as follows:

- Let $G = (T, E)$ be a DAG, where T denotes the nodes of the graph (that correspond to flow tasks) and E represents the edges (that correspond to the flow of data among the tasks). G corresponds to the execution plan of a data flow, defining one valid execution order of the tasks.
- $T = \{t_1, ..., t_n\}$ is a set of tasks[2] of size n. Each flow task is responsible for one or both of the following: (i) reading or retrieving or storing data, and (ii) manipulating data.
- Let $E = \{edge_1, ..., edge_m\}$ be a set of edges of size m. Each edge $edge_i, 1 \leq i \leq m$ equals to an ordered pair (t_j, t_k) denoting that task t_j sends data to task t_k, while m is less than or equal to $\frac{n(n-1)}{2}$; otherwise G cannot be acyclic.
- Let $PC = (T, D)$ be another DAG. D defines the precedence constraints (dependencies) that might exist between pairs of tasks in T. More formally, $D = \{d_1, ..., d_l\}$ is a set of l ordered pairs: $d_i = (t_j, t_k), 1 \leq i \leq l, 1 \leq j <$

---

[2] In the remainder of the paper, we will use the terms tasks, services and activities interchangeably.

$k \leq n$, where each such pair denotes that t_j must precede t_k in any valid G. In other words, G should contain a path from t_j to t_k. Essentially, the PC graph defines constraints on the valid edges of the G graph. This also implies that if D contains (t_a, t_b) and (t_b, t_c), it must also contain (t_a, t_c).

The PC and G graphs are semantically different, as the PC graph corresponds to a higher-level, non-executable view of a data flow, where the exact ordering of tasks is not defined; only a partial ordering is defined instead. To avoid confusion, we use dotted arrows for PC edges.

- A *single-input single-output* (*SISO*) data flow is defined as a flow G that contains only one task with no incoming edges, termed as *source*, from another task and only one task with no outgoing edges, termed as *sink*. In a *SISO* flow, there is a dependency edge d from the source task to any other non-sink task, and from all non-source tasks to the sink task.

- A *L-SISO* flow is a specific form of a *SISO* data flow, where the tasks can form a chain of tasks. More specifically, each node of the G graph has exactly only one incoming and outgoing edge, while *source* and *sink* tasks have only one outgoing and incoming edge, respectively. In Fig. 3, two examples of *SISO* flows are presented, where only the right one is a *L-SISO* flow.

  A *L-SISO* flow can be executed both as a linear and as a non-linear (parallel) flow, as Fig. 4 shows. In linear flows, G has the form of a chain, and each non-source and non-sink task has exactly one incoming and one outgoing edge. In non-linear flows, the output of a single task can be fed to multiple tasks in parallel. In the non-linear examples in the figures, the tasks that receive more than one input have been augmented to include a merge function. In the rightmost example in Fig. 4, the merge is a natural join on the outputs of tasks 2 and 3, whereas task 4 remains a unary task. More details on this are provided in Sect. 5.

- We define the *Degree-of-Freedom* quantity DoF for *L-SISO* flows as follows: $DoF = 1 - \frac{2l}{n(n-1)}$, where l is the size of set of dependencies as defined above and $DoF \in [0, 1]$. In the case that $DoF = 0$ then $l = \frac{n(n-1)}{2}$, which implies that the flow is fully constrained and there is absolutely no flexibility in the ordering of flow tasks (i.e., there is only one valid flow execution plan). Additionally, when $DoF = 1$ denotes that flow tasks can be ordered in an arbitrary manner. In general, the higher the DoF value, the higher the need for efficient optimization. [3]

- In general, data flows are *multiple-input multiple-output MIMO* data flows, as shown in Fig. 5. Each *MIMO* comprises a set of *L-SISOs*. In the example of the figure, there are multiple *L-SISOs*, e.g., $1 \rightarrow 2 \rightarrow 3 \rightarrow 7$, $4 \rightarrow 5 \rightarrow 6 \rightarrow 7$, $7 \rightarrow 8$, and $7 \rightarrow 9$. Also, generic *SISOs* consist of multiple *L-SISOs*, e.g., like the one in Fig. 3(left).

---

[3] Note that when $DoF = 1$, which is rarely the case in data flows, standard database query optimization solutions become applicable, because then each task can be treated in the same way a filter is treated with the simple extension that selectivity can be higher than that.

Fig. 3. Two examples of *SISO* data flows.

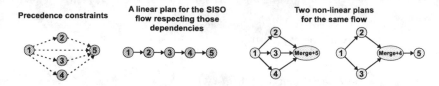

Fig. 4. Examples of three execution plans of a *L-SISO* data flow.

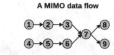

Fig. 5. A *MIMO* data flow.

In a data flow, we assume that each task receives some data items as an input and outputs some other data items as a result. Following the database terminology, each data item is referred to as a *tuple*. The task metadata that our optimization techniques require are:

- *Cost* (c_i): we use c_i, $1 \leq i \leq n$ as a metric of the time cost of each task per data item processed. This cost can also encapsulate the data transmission cost to the next tasks downstream.
- *Selectivity* (sel_i): it denotes the average number of returned data items per source tuple for the i-th service. For filtering operators, $sel_i < 1$, for data sources and operators that just manipulate the input $sel = 1$, whereas, for operators that may produce more output records for each input record, $sel_i > 1$. An example of a task with $sel_i < 1$ is a bank application that processes customers in order to report those with inactive accounts, while, an example of a task with $sel_i > 1$ is a bank procedure that outputs all the connected credit cards for a given account (assuming that each customer has more than one credit card on average).
- *Input* (inp_i): it denotes the size of the input of the i-th task t_i in number of tuples per input data tuple. It depends on the product of the selectivities of the preceding tasks in the execution plan G.[4] More formally, if T_i^{prec} is the set of all preceding tasks of t_i in G, $inp_i = \prod_{j=1}^{|T_i^{prec}|} sel_j$.

---

[4] Here, there is an implicit assumption that the selectivities are independent; if this is not the case, the product will be an arbitrarily erroneous approximation of the actual selectivity of the subplan before each task.

- *Output* (out_i): The size of the output of the i-th task per source tuple can be easily derived from the above quantities, as it is equal to $inp_i sel_i$.

Based on the above, each task is described as a triple $t_i = <c_i, sel_i, inp_i>$. Assuming that selectivities are independent, we can infer that inp_i is the only task characteristic that depends on the position of t_i in G; the cost and the selectivity of each task is independent of the exact G that may include t_i.

3.2   Problem Statement, Complexity, Optimality and Approach Overview

Problem Statement: Given an initial G graph, a set of tasks T with known cost and selectivity values, and a corresponding precedence constraint graph PC, we aim to find a valid G that minimizes the *sum cost metric (SCM)* per source tuple, defined as follows: $SCM(G) = inp_1 c_1 + inp_2 c_2 + ... + inp_n c_n$. The optimized plan is denoted as P. ☐

SCM's rationale is to provide a good approximation of the resource consumption during the flow execution regardless of physical execution details. Furthermore, in the specific case where all tasks are executed sequentially, it provides a good approximation of the execution time. Also, it is a common metric in query optimization as well [10]. Typically the user is capable of providing an initial G and a set of precedence constraints, possibly with the help of techniques, such as those in [24]. From the initial set of these constraints, the full PC graph can be easily derived through the computation of its transitive closure.

Note that more sophisticated cost models can be considered, e.g., models that define the cost of a task as a function of the input bytes and consider in the selectivity the number of attributes added or removed. The issue of a data flow cost model is largely orthogonal to our optimization solutions and we leave the investigation of cost modelling approaches to future work.

Problem Complexity and Optimality: In [5], where query operators with precedence constraints that are equivalent to our tasks are considered, it is proved that finding the optimal ordering of tasks is an NP-hard problem when (i) each flow task is characterized by its cost per input record and selectivity; (ii) the cost of each task is a linear function of the number of records processed and that number of records depends on the product of the selectivities of all preceding tasks (assuming independence of selectivities for simplicity); and (iii) the optimization criterion is the minimization of the sum of the costs of all tasks. All the above conditions hold for our case, so our problem is intractable. Moreover, in [5] it is discussed that *"it is unlikely that any polynomial time algorithm can approximate the optimal plan to within a factor of $O(n^\theta)$"*, where θ is some positive constant. As such, in this work, we do not make any formal claim as to how close the optimized plans derived by our solutions are to the optimal plans in the generic case. Note that if we modify the optimization criterion, e.g., to optimize the bottleneck cost metric or the critical path renders the problem tractable [2,28].

Algorithm 1. Rank ordering based high-level algorithm

Require: A set of n tasks, T={t_1, ..., t_n} and the PC graph
Ensure: A directed acyclic graph P representing the optimal plan
 1: Pre-processing phase: modify PC
 2: Apply KBZ algorithm, so that a G is produced.
 3: Post-processing phase: enhance G
 4: Set P← final G

Our approach in a nutshell: To cope with the problem complexity, we adopt a divide-and-conquer technique. From the initial G, which is either a *MIMO* or a generic *SISO*, we extract *L-SISO* segments. Then, we optimize *L-SISOs* in polynomial time independently.

4   Optimization of *L-SISO* flows

To tackle the limitations of existing solutions, exemplified in Sect. 2, we aim to develop approximate solutions that will be scalable for medium and large data flows while improving the performance. In the first subsection, we present solutions that are essentially extensions of existing UDF query optimization proposals so that they become applicable to our problem. Then, we present our main novelty with regards to approximate optimization of linear data flows.

The main rationale for optimizing linear plans for *L-SISO* data flows is described, as follows. Firstly, we employ the join ordering algorithm proposed in [14,19] as a core building block, which will be referred to as *KBZ*. The reason we choose *KBZ* is to avoid re-inventing the wheel and benefit from the existing proposals in query optimization to the largest possible extent. *KBZ* leverages the rank value of each task defined as $\frac{1-sel_i}{c_i}$, and also considers the dependencies among tasks. When there are no dependencies, it is known from database optimization research that ordering the tasks by their rank value yields the optimal execution plan [14,19]. The main approach of *KBZ* to handling the cases where such ordering is not possible because a task with a lower rank should precede a task with a higher rank is to merge these tasks. For example, assume that we merge t_i and t_j. Then, the cost of the merged task becomes $c_{ij} = c_i + sel_i c_j$ and the new selectivity is $sel_{ij} = sel_i sel_j$. The rank value of the merged task equals to $\frac{1-sel_{ij}}{c_{ij}}$. By successively merging tasks if needed, we ensure that all the remaining tasks are ordered by rank. This allows re-orderings of sets of tasks rather than individual tasks, and thus is capable of producing the optimal execution plan for the example shown in Fig. 2. The time complexity of *KBZ* algorithm is $O(n^2)$.

Our solutions can be described at a high-level as shown in Algorithm 1. The main challenge is to devise an efficient preprocessing technique, so that *KBZ* becomes applicable, since *KBZ* does not account for arbitrary dependencies between tasks. This step applies to the *PC* graph. A trivial step in that preprocessing phase is to remove all edges that can be inferred through the transitive closure. In addition, we need to post-process the result of the *KBZ* algorithm in order either to guarantee validity or to further improve the intermediate results. There are many options regarding how these two phases can be performed and in this section, we present three concrete suggestions, which constitute the novelty of this section.

Also note that the input does not require an initial G graph. This is because, for each *L-SISO*, respecting the precedence constraints is a necessary and sufficient validity condition for producing valid flows.[5]

4.1 Extending Solutions for Queries with UDFs

Approximate optimization solutions have been proposed for queries containing UDFs in [7,12], which leverage the task rank values as well. These techniques cannot be applied to the data flow optimization problem in their original form because the dependency constraints that they consider refer to pairs of a join and a UDF, rather than between UDFs. However, it is straightforward to apply extensions so that constraints between UDFs are taken into account; then we can treat flow tasks as UDFs.

The rationale of the technique in [7] is to order the tasks in descending order of their rank values provided that the dependencies are respected. Our proposed extension adopts this rationale as well, through applying a greedy algorithm. Specifically, the greedy extension starts from a plan containing only the source task and in each step, adds the task with the maximum rank, as defined above, without violating the precedence constraints. The extension of the technique in [7] is essentially the same as the greedy optimization solution, called *GreedyI*, which is thoroughly presented and evaluated in [17], where it is shown that *GreedyI* is outperformed by *Swap* [25].

Similarly, we extend the predicate migration algorithm [12], denoted as *PM-based*, in order to optimize data flows considering dependency constraints between tasks. The proposal in [12] states that tasks should be ordered by their rank values, and if a task with a lower rank is prerequisite of a task with a higher rank value, the former should be placed just before the latter. In order to apply this rationale to data flows, initially, we sort the tasks based on their rank values without taking into account the precedence constraints. In the post-processing phase, we detect possible constraint violations and resolve them by transposing the prerequisite tasks just before the task that they must precede. If the tasks that violate the existing constraints are more than one, they are transposed in the exact order they are initially positioned. This technique is proved less efficient than the rank ordering heuristics that we propose below, as shown in the evaluation in Sect. 7.

---

[5] Respecting the precedence constraints is not sufficient for generic flows. For example, for the left flow in Fig. 3, the precedence constraints as defined in this work cannot capture the requirement that tasks 2,3 and 4 should be placed in different branches than tasks 5 and 6.

4.2   Our First Rank Ordering-Based Algorithm RO-I

Our main proposals do not merely extend UDF-query optimization but build upon the *KBZ* algorithm. In its original form, *KBZ* algorithm considers only a specific form of precedence constraints, namely those representable as a rooted tree. The fact that *KBZ* algorithm allows only tree-shaped precedence constraint graphs implies that there should be no task with more than one independent prerequisite activity, and in such data flow scenarios, the *DoF* is very high and increases more with the number of tasks (e.g., more than $DoF = 0.9$ for a 100-node flow). Both of these cases do not occur frequently in practice.

In our first proposal, called *RO-I* (standing for *Rank Ordering-based I*), the pre-processing phase ensures the transformation of the precedence constraint graph into a tree-shaped one. This is done by maintaining the incoming edge with the highest rank and removing the other edges, if a task has more than one incoming edge. This process allows *KBZ* to run but may produce invalid flow orderings, due to the removal of dependencies during pre-processing. To fix that, we employ a post-processing phase where any resulting precedence constraint violations are resolved by moving tasks upstream if needed as prerequisites for other tasks placed earlier.

The worst case complexity of the pre-processing phase is $O(n^2)$ because we remove up to $n - 1$ incoming edges from each task and we repeat this for $n - 1$ tasks of the flow. Additionally, in the post-processing step, we check, for each of the n tasks, if any of the preceding tasks violates the precedence constraints. There can be up to $n - 1$ preceding tasks in a flow ordering. So, in the worst case, the complexity is $O(n^2)$.

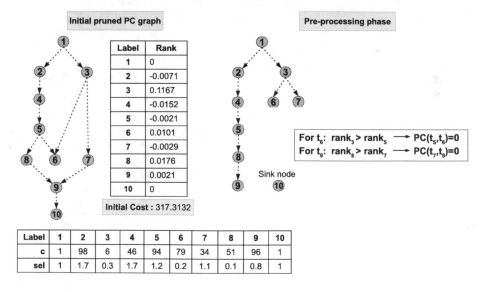

Fig. 6. An example of *RO-I* pre-processing phase.

An illustrative example of applying *RO-I* is depicted in Fig. 6. In that figure, we present the initial metadata and the pre-processing phase, in order to transform the precedence constraint graph into tree-shaped graph. The initial precedence constraint graph is pruned in the sense that all edges implied by the transitive closure are removed. The graph on the right side of the figure shows the final result after removing the edges (t_5, t_6), (t_7, t_9) (as shown in the figure, it is convenient to temporarily leave the sink task out, and after optimization, to attach it to the last task). Then, we apply the *KBZ* algorithm and finally, we apply the validity post-process phase of *RO-I* to ensure that the optimized execution flow plan does not violate the dependency constraints. In the transformed graph, KBZ has no knowledge for example, that t_6 should not be placed before t_5, and indeed it initially places t_6 in a way that violated the constraints. Figure 7 shows the complete way in which the output of *KBZ* on the top is transformed to a valid plan.

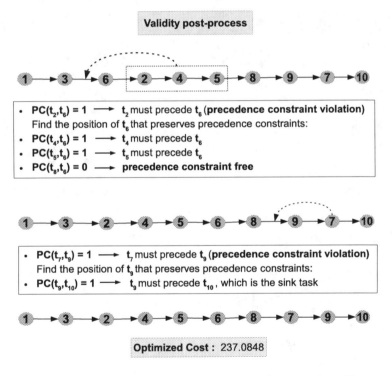

Fig. 7. The post-processing phase of *RO-I* for the example in Fig. 6.

4.3   RO-II

The *RO-II* algorithm follows a different approach in order to render *KBZ* applicable, that is to transform the *PC* graph to a tree. In the pre-processing

phase, this approximate algorithm first detects paths in the precedence constraint graph that share an intermediate source and sink. Then it merges them
to a single path based on their rank values. When there are multiple such paths,
we start merging from the most upstream ones and when there are nested paths,
we start merging from the innermost ones. In that way, all precedence constraints
are preserved at the expense of implicitly examining fewer re-orderings. Figure 8
illustrates in detail the steps of the application of *RO-II* in the flow of Fig. 6.
The steps 1–3 describe the pre-processing phase of *RO-II*, where we merge two
sub-segments into a linear sub-flow, because they create cycles by sharing the
same intermediate source and sink. In that example, after the merging procedure we enforce more precedence constraints than the original ones, so that the
task t_3 must precede not only task t_6 and t_7 but also tasks t_2, t_4, t_5 and t_8.
In other words, the merging process imposes more restrictions on the possible
re-orderings. As such, these local optimizations may still deviate from a globally
optimal solution significantly in the average case. *RO-II* does not require any
post-processing because its result is always valid.

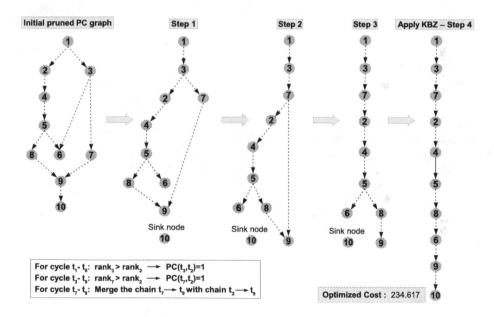

Fig. 8. An application example of *RO-II* with the metadata of Fig. 6.

In the case of *RO-II*, the time complexity remains $O(n^2)$ because, for each
merge process, we consider at most $O(n)$ flow tasks and we repeat this for all
the possible merge processes that can be up to n.

4.4   RO-III: An Enhancement to RO-II

After the evaluation of the proposed *RO-I* and *RO-II* algorithms, we isolated data flows where optimization yielded not near-optimal plans. A typical problem with *RO-II* is that it cannot move a filtering task to an earlier stage of the flow, even if this is not constrained by operator precedences, due to the additional restrictions that are implicitly incorporated as explained earlier. To address this problem, we propose RO-III, which tackles the limitations of *RO-II* with the help of a post-processing phase that we introduce (see Algorithm 2). We first apply the *RO-II* algorithm in order to produce an intermediate execution plan, and then we examine several transpositions. More specifically, we check all the possible re-orderings of each sub-flow of size from 1 to k tasks in the plan. The checks are applied from the left to the right. In this way, we address the problem of a task being "trapped" in a suboptimal place upstream in the flow execution due to the additional implicit constraints introduced by *RO-II*. This process is described by the three nested *for* loops in Algorithm 2 and is repeated until there are no changes in the flow plan. The reason we repeat it is because each applied transposition may enable further valid transpositions that were not initially possible.

Algorithm 2. RO-III post-processing phase

Require: A set of n tasks, T={t_1, ..., t_n}
    A directed acyclic graph with precedence constraints
    Optimized plan G as a directed acyclic graph returned by RO-II
Ensure: A directed acyclic graph P representing the optimal plan
1: **repeat**
2:    {k is the maximum subplan size considered}
3:    **for** i=1:k **do**
4:      **for** s=1:n-i **do**
5:        **for** t=s+i:n **do**
6:          consider moving subplan of size i starting from the sth task after the tth task in G
7:        **end for**
8:      **end for**
9:    **end for**
10: **until** no changes applied
11: P ← G

The post-processing phase of the *RO-III* algorithm has $O(kn^2)$ complexity, which is derived by the maximum number each of the three inner loops can execute. The *repeat* process in theory can execute up to n times, but according to our observations during experiments, we see that even for large flows, there is no change after 3 times. In all experiments, we set k to 5.

In Fig. 9, the result of the post-processing phase of algorithm *RO-III* is described. In this phase the optimized flow plan occurred by moving t_7 to a later stage.

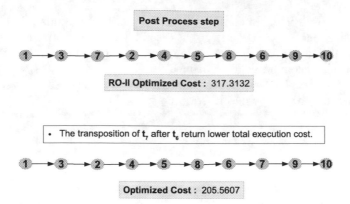

Fig. 9. The post-process phase of the *RO-III* algorithm taking as input the generated optimized execution plan of *RO-II*, as depicted in 8.

4.5 Discussion

The above algorithms explore a different and overlapping search space. There is no clear winner between *RO-I* and *RO-II*, but, in general, both of them outperform the solutions in Sect. 4.1, as will also be discussed in Sect. 7. By design, *RO-III* explores the largest search space and always outperforms *RO-II* (since *RO-III* is an extension to *RO-II*), as *RO-II* may fail to reorder a filtering task to an earlier stage of the flow. But there might be cases where *RO-III* is inferior to *RO-I* or even *Swap*, as a consequent of the fact that different plans are indirectly and directly evaluated by each technique. However, as elaborated in the evaluation section, such cases are relatively rare.

5 Producing Non-linear Plans for *L-SISO* flows

This section focuses on the advantages of non-linear (or parallel) execution plans for *L-SISO* flows. As we have explained in Sect. 3, in a parallel flow, each single task can have multiple outgoing edges, which implies that the output of such a task is fed, as input, to multiple tasks. In the right part of Fig. 4, we observe that a single task may have not only multiple outgoing edges, but also multiple ingoing edges. In this case, a single task receive as input data the output of multiple tasks, and merges them back into a single input. This is in line with the *AND-Join* workflow pattern as presented in [31], where the outgoing edge of multiple tasks that are executed in parallel converge into a single task.

In software tools, such as PDI, the merge process can be implemented by incorporating a common *sort merge self-join* on the record ids. A similar approach is followed also in flows consisting of calls to Web Services [28]. As such, merging multiple input streams incurs an extra execution cost. To assess this cost, we evaluated parallel data flows that were executed with the PDI tool. The conclusion was that the merge task cost has a small effect on the total flow execution cost due to the fact that the inputs are typically already ordered by their IDs; in other words, the merge task is similar to an additional lightweight activity. Additionally, the size of the input (inp_i) of a task t_i, which receives more than one incoming edge is defined similarly to the tasks with only one incoming edge, i.e., by computing the product of the selectivity values of the preceding tasks as we have described in Sect. 3.

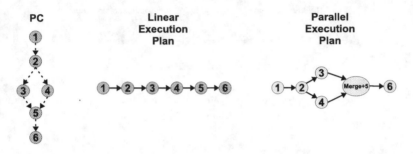

Fig. 10. Example of linear and non-linear execution plans for the same flow.

We now analyze the benefits of parallel flow execution by means of a theoretical example that considers two subsequent tasks t_3 and t_4 illustrated in Fig. 10, which are not in a precedence relation and an extra cost of the merge process that will be denoted as mc. In this figure, we show two alternative plans, a linear one (in the middle) and a parallel one (on the right). The SCM values of the two alternatives vary only with respect to activities t_4 and t_5. We distinguish between the following four cases (using a superscript to differentiate the inputs in the two cases):

- Case I: $sel_3 \leq 1$ and $sel_4 \leq 1$. The linear execution cost is lower than the parallel execution cost, because (i) $inp_4^{linear}c_4 < inp_4^{parallel}c_4$ as $inp_4^{linear} = sel_3 inp_4^{parallel}$ and $sel_3 < 1$, and (ii) $inp_5^{linear}c_5 < inp_5^{parallel}(c_5 + mc)$ due to the extra merge cost of the parallel version and given that $inp_5^{linear} = inp_5^{parallel}$. So, in that case, parallelism is not beneficial.
- Case II: $sel_3 \leq 1$ and $sel_4 > 1$. Similar with the Case I, the linear execution of the flow is more beneficial than the parallel; note that the selectivity value sel_4 does not affect the previous statements.
- Case III: $sel_3 > 1$ and $sel_4 > 1$. If $mc = 0$, the parallel execution results in better performance than the linear execution. In that case $inp_5^{linear}c_5 = inp_5^{parallel}(c_5 + mc)$. Because of the fact that $sel_3 > 1$, we deduce that $inp_4^{linear}c_4 > inp_4^{parallel}c_4$. In the generic case where $mc > 0$, we need to compute the estimated costs in order to verify which option is more beneficial, but we expect that, for small mc values, the parallel execution to outperform.

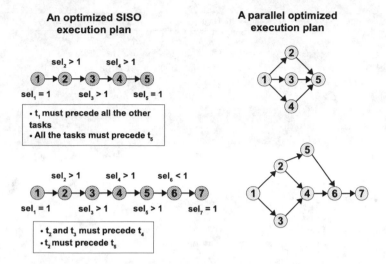

Fig. 11. Example of executing *L-SISO* flows in parallel.

- Case IV: $sel_3 > 1$ and $sel_4 \leq 1$. Following the rationale of the previous case, there is no clear winner between the two executions shown in Fig. 10. However, an optimized linear plan will place t_4 before t_3 thus corresponding to Case II, where the (new) linear plan is better than the parallel one.

In order to exploit the advantages of the optimization opportunities of Case III, we introduce a post-process phase in the solutions of Sect. 4 (see Algorithm 3). After the generation of an optimized linear execution plan, we apply a post-process step that restructures the flow in a way that subsequent tasks having selectivity greater than 1 are executed in parallel if this does not incur violations of the precedence constraints. This post-process step can be applied to any optimization algorithm that produces a linear ordering.

Two examples are presented in Fig. 11, where, in the upper flow scenario, we choose to parallelize t_2, t_3 and t_4, while in the flow case that is depicted in the bottom of the figure, we execute parallel only t_2 and t_3 and not t_4, because of the precedence constraints. Then, t_5 is appended after t_2 because of the constraints and is executed in parallel with t_4. As t_6 has selectivity value < 1, it is not executed in parallel with any other task.

The complexity is $O(n^2)$. The parallelization of each task is examined at most once, and for each such case, the preceding tasks need to be checked, the number of which cannot exceed n.

As a final note, in the previous discussion, we have silently assumed that sending the output to more than one task downstream does not incur an extra cost. This is common to centralized and share-memory parallel systems where the results of a task are kept in memory and are accessible to any subsequent task at no extra cost. In distributed settings where tasks are at distinct places,

---

Algorithm 3. Post-process step for parallel *L-SISO* flows

Require: An optimized linear plan P={$t_1 \rightarrow ... \rightarrow t_n$}
          A directed acyclic graph with precedence constraints
Ensure: A directed acyclic graph P representing the optimal parallel plan
1: i=1
2: **while** $i < n$ **do**
3:    j=i+1
4:    **while** $sel_{P(j)} > 1$ **do**
5:       Delete the edge between the tasks $t_{P(j-1)} \rightarrow t_{P(j)}$ from P
6:       **if** $t_{P(j)}$ is not predecessor in precedence constraint graph for no task in
        $t_{i+1} \ldots t_{j-1}$ **then**
7:          Connect the edge between the tasks (i) $t_{P(i)}$ and (ii) $t_{P(j)}$, i.e., create the
          edge $t_{P(i)} \rightarrow t_{P(j)}$ in P
8:       **else**
9:          Connect in P the edge between (i) all the preceding tasks in precedence
          constraint graph with no outgoing edges in P and (ii) $t_{P(j)}$
10:     **end if**
11:     $j = j + 1$
12:    **end while**
13:   Connect in P the edge between (i) all the tasks $t_{P(i+1)} \ldots t_{P(j-1)}$ with no out-
     going edges in P and (ii) $t_{P(j)}$
14:   i=j
15: **end while**

---

having multiple outgoing edges incurs extra cost, which however can be treated exactly as *mc*.

6   Optimizing *MIMO* Flows: The Complete Approach

So far we have discussed the case of chains with single-source and a single-sink task, but arbitrary *multiple-input multiple-output (MIMO)* flows can benefit from the solutions presented in the previous sections. The generic types of *MIMO* flows are described in [32], two of which are shown in Fig. 12. A main difference between *L-SISO* and *MIMO* flows is that apart from re-ordering tasks, additional optimization operations can apply. As explained in [25], the *factorize* and *distribute* operations can move an activity appearing in both input subflows of a binary activity to its output and the other way around, respectively.[6] This allows for example a filtering operation initially placed after a merge task to be pushed down to the merge inputs (provided that the filtering condition refers to both inputs), which is known to yield better performance.

Figure 12 displays exemplary MIMO data flows of types butterfly (top) and fork (bottom). In these cases, the optimization of *L-SISO* data flows can play an important role in optimizing *MIMO* flows as *MIMO* flows consist of a set of *L-SISO* flows. Algorithm 4 describes a divide-and-conquer proposal for optimizing

---

[6] [25] additionally considers the case that an activity can be further split in several sub-activities, which is not considered here.

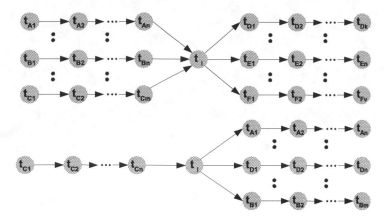

Fig. 12. Example *MIMO* data flows of type butterfly (top) and fork (bottom).

Algorithm 4. Optimization of *MIMO* flows

1: **repeat**
2:     Extract *L-SISO* segments
3:     **for** all *L-SISO* segments **do**
4:         Optimize *L-SISO* segments
5:     **end for**
6:     Apply factorize/distribute optimization thus modifying the *L-SISO* segments
7: **until** no changes

MIMO flows, which is based on the extraction of these linear segments of the flow and apply optimization algorithms only on the *L-SISO* sub-flows. Remember that in the generic case, we start from an initial valid plan rather than from the *PC* graph.

The extraction of the linear segments of a MIMO flow in line 2 of the algorithm can be performed in a simple manner with linear complexity. Traversing a path from a source, we stop when a task with multiple incoming edges is encountered (e.g., t_i in Fig. 12). The latter task plays the role of the sink for that segment. It also plays the role of the source for each segment starting from it. We iteratively repeat this process until all tasks are visited.

In lines 3–5, we exploit the optimization solutions that we proposed for *L-SISO* flows and use them as the main building block to optimize *MIMO* flows. Then, we check whether we can apply the factorize/distribute operations, which modify the linear segments. This process is repeated until it converges. In this work, we focus solely on task re-ordering (which corresponds to optimize the linear segments individually) and the investigation of further techniques that combine task re-orderings with additional operations is left for future work.

The complexity of Algorithm 4 is quadratic in the number of tasks of the largest *L-SISO* segment and also quadratic in the number of *L-SISO* segments, given that the *factorize* and *distribute* operations can occur an amount of times that is proportional to the number of segments.

6.1   The Special Case of SIMO and MISO Flows

The *single-input multiple-output (SIMO)* and *multiple-input single-output (MISO)* are two special structures of *MIMO* data flows. In the following, we introduce two techniques for optimizing such data flow cases, when no *factorize* and *distribute* operations are required, e.g., there are no cases where a filter after a binary join should be moved to both input branches upstream. To perform the optimizations below, we relax the definition of *L-SISOs* to include any chain of operators so that larger segments in the flow are optimized using the *RO-III* algorithm (Sect. 4).

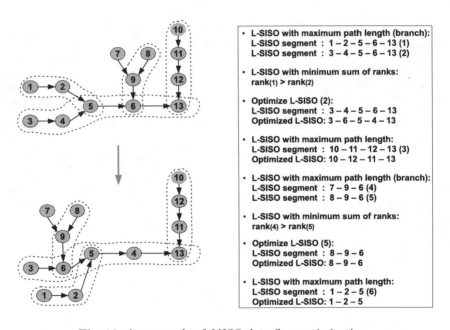

Fig. 13. An example of *MISO* data flow optimization.

In the case of the *MISO* data flows, like the one in Fig. 13, the first step is to find the *L-SISO* flow segment with the maximum length of path defined from the source to the sink task. In the case that we find two *L-SISO* segments with the same path length, we choose to optimize the sub-flow with the minimum sum of the rank values of the tasks that it consist of. This implies that we choose the *L-SISO* sub-flow with the most expensive tasks with high selectivity values.

A detailed example of our technique is described in Fig. 13. In the figure, the *L-SISO* segments are in dotted boundaries, omitting the trivial ones that consist of a source and a sink task only. In this example, the *L-SISO* segment

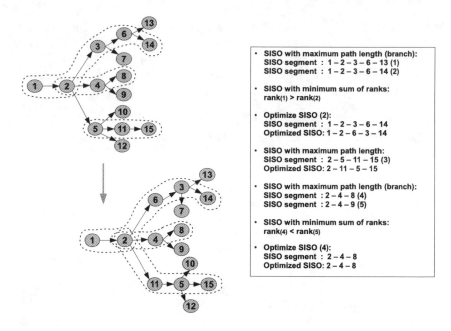

Fig. 14. An example of *SIMO* optimization.

$t_1 \to t_2 \to t_5 \to t_6 \to t_{13}$ **(1)** and $t_3 \to t_4 \to t_5 \to t_6 \to t_{13}$ **(2)** have equal length of path from their source tasks to their common sink task. So, we estimate the sum of the rank values of sub-flow *(1)* and *(2)* showing that the minimum sum of ranks corresponds to the *L-SISO* segment $t_3 \to t_4 \to t_5 \to t_6 \to t_{13}$ **(2)**. Then, we apply the *RO-III* algorithm to optimize this sub-flow by re-ordering its tasks, as shown in the bottom part of the figure.

After this optimization, the incoming edges of each of the tasks in the optimized subflow become immutable even when they come from external tasks, for example the edges $t_2 \to t_5$ and $t_9 \to t_6$ remain fixed. The corresponding tasks (t_5 and t_6) play the role of temporary sinks for the non-optimized branches. The next step is to isolate all the *L-SISO* segments that their tasks are not part of the already optimized *L-SISO* segment *(2)*, except for their temporary sinks that are tasks of the segment *(2)* in the example, e.g. $t_1 \to t_2 \to t_5$. For each of these, we follow the same procedure described earlier. Specifically, we find the maximum path length from each source task to its corresponding temporary sink. So, in the example, we optimize the *L-SISO* $t_{10} \to t_{11} \to t_{12} \to t_{13}$ **(3)**. Then, for equivalent *L-SISO* segments, such as $t_7 \to t_9 \to t_6$ and $t_8 \to t_9 \to t_6$, we follow the same approach until we finish with all branches.

For this technique to be correct, the precedence constraints need to be defined carefully. For instance, in the example of the figure, t_4 should be allowed to move downstream regarding the input of not only t_3 but t_1, t_7 and t_8, too.

Another special structure of *MIMO* flows is the *SIMO* one, where their optimization is based on the same rationale of the technique that we have just described. Figure 14 shows an example of the proposed technique. In this case, the main difference is that we initially consider one *L-SISO* segment for each sink. For example, the *L-SISO* segment $t_1 \rightarrow t_2 \rightarrow t_3 \rightarrow t_6 \rightarrow t_{13}$ and $t_1 \rightarrow t_2 \rightarrow t_3 \rightarrow t_6 \rightarrow t_{14}$ or $t_1 \rightarrow t_2 \rightarrow t_4 \rightarrow t_8$ and $t_1 \rightarrow t_2 \rightarrow t_4 \rightarrow t_9$, and so on. Then, we follow the same optimization procedure as for *MISO* data flows.

The main difference between these two techniques is that each segment reordering, like the reordering of the $t_1 \rightarrow t_2 \rightarrow t_3 \rightarrow t_6 \rightarrow t_{14}$ segment, may force the temporary source to change in order to avoid constraint violations for the remainder segments; the temporary source of the non optimized segment s belonging to the optimized segment s', is the most downstream vertex of s', which is connected to any vertex of s with a precedence constraint. For example, in Fig. 14, t_{13} is connected to t_3 in the optimized plan, assuming that, initially, there is a precedence constraint between both (i) t_3 and t_{13} and (ii) t_6 and t_{13}. Further in this example, we assume that moving t_{11} before t_5 does not compromise the validity of the output in t_{10} and t_{12}; otherwise, a precedence constraint between t_{11} and t_5 would exist.

7   Experimental Analysis

We split the evaluation part in three parts. The first one considers synthetic flows in a real environment. We use synthetic flows in order to thoroughly compare the techniques in a wide and configurable range of settings. In the second part, we focus on the computed cost of the resulting execution plans, which can be safely performed offline. The last part deals with the time overhead of the optimization techniques. According to [27], large flows are those that comprise 100 tasks, thus most of our experiments consider flows up to this size.

7.1   Data Flows in a Real System

In this set of experiments, we present running times when executing synthetic flows in Pentaho Data Integration - Kettle (*PDI*, v. 5.2). PDI supports two execution modes, pipelined execution (default) and sequential. We chose the latter so that the measured running time corresponds to the sum cost metric (*SCM*) targeted in our algorithms. The machine we used is equipped with an Intel Core i5 660 CPU and 6 GB of RAM.

The main purpose is to evaluate the performance optimization, which corresponds to the minimization of the estimated flow execution cost *SCM*. The performance improvements of our algorithms are measured as either the decrease in running time or the speed-up achieved. The speed-up of a faster algorithm A with respect to a slower one B is defined as follows: $Speed - up = \frac{SCM(B)}{SCM(A)}$.

We construct synthetic flows so that we thoroughly evaluate the algorithms in a wide range of parameter combinations and we are in a position to derive unbiased and generically applicable lessons for the behaviour of each algorithm. The main configurable parameters are two: (i) the cost and selectivity values of the flow tasks, which are distributed in the range of $[1, 100]$ and $(0, 2]$, respectively; and (ii) the values of *DoF*, where we considered *DoF* = *0.2, 0.4, 0.6, 0.8*; the smaller the *DoF* value, the less the opportunities for optimization exist. In this experiment, the size of the flows (i.e., the number of the tasks) is fixed to 30 and they process 100 K records. In order to conduct the experiments, we randomly generate precedence constraint DAGs and task characteristics in a simulation environment. In PDI, all the tasks were dummy ones, i.e., they did not perform any actual processing, but they repeated a processes a number of iterations proportional to their cost and produced an output record according to their assigned selectivity.

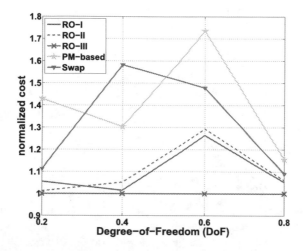

Fig. 15. Median normalized running times of a data flow with 30 tasks (the values are in normalized time units).

For every *DoF* value, we generate 10 test PC DAGs, and each individual DAG instantiation is executed 5 times. Unless otherwise mentioned, median values are presented. The medians better represent the practical value, and in general are lower than the average values, which are affected by outliers.

Figure 15 shows the behavior of the rank ordering-based optimization techniques proposed in Sect. 4. In the figure, the running times are normalized according to the lowest ones achieved by RO-III, so that improvements are more clearly presented. We see that the highest median improvements over the best performing between *Swap* and *PM-based* are for *DoF* values 0.4 and 0.6. More specifically, *Swap* exhibits higher times by 47.8% and 58.2% for *DoF* values of 0.4 and 0.6, respectively. *PM-based* exhibits higher times by 30.3% and 73.6% for *DoF* values of 0.4 and 0.6, respectively. The improvements are lower for flows with *DoF* of 0.2 or 0.8. However, both these cases are more rare in practice: when *DoF* = 0.8, simply ranking by the rank value as in filter ordering in database queries is sufficient, whereas, when *DoF* − 0.2, there is relatively small space for improvements. In other words, when *DoF* is low there is small space for re-orderings, whereas, for high DoF values, the need for sophisticated constraint-aware algorithms is ameliorated.

Regarding the behavior of our algorithms, RO-I outperforms RO-II by a small factor, for DoF values greater than 0.2. Also, the supremacy of RO-III is more evident for $DoF = 0.6$.

The numbers thus far discussed are median values. However, in individual DAGs, we observed significantly larger improvements due to RO-III. The maximum improvements of RO-III are presented in Table 1, and as shown, for these 30-task flows executed in PDI, RO-III can run up to more than 4 times faster.

Table 1. Maximum observed times RO-III is faster

alg	DoF			
	0.2	0.4	0.6	0.8
PM-based	1.84	2.41	4.77	2.06
Swap	1.84	3.30	3.62	1.39

7.2 Synthetic Scenarios

In this section we present a more extensive set of experiments, where the size of flows n ranges from 10 to 100 (without including the source and sink tasks). Each combination of DoF, costs, selectivities and flow size is instantiated 100 times. In Sect. 2, we presented the clear gap between the best heuristic to date, namely $Swap$, and the accurate solution for a real small flow. We aim to show how the rank ordering-based solutions are capable to significantly improve the performance of the data flow execution and how the parallelism of L-$SISO$ flows can be beneficial. Finally, we evaluate the proposals for $MIMO$ flows.

Performance of Rank Ordering-Based Solutions. Our first experiment compares the techniques for L-$SISO$ flows, and extends the evaluation rationale of the previous section in the sense that we include the performance of an initial non-optimized flow, derived by simple topological ordering of the constraints. Figure 16 presents the median speed-up achieved by the optimization solutions compared to the non-optimized case.

Several observations can be drawn. First, RO-III is a clear winner and its median performance is better in all cases without a single exception. Second, PM-$based$ solutions achieve significantly lower speed-ups than the other optimization algorithms. This supports our observation that using rank values only is not sufficient. Third, the median improvements of RO-III over the best heuristic of the state-of-the-art $Swap$ and PM-$based$ can be significant, as the RO-III can have 3 times better performance than these heuristics; this difference is observed for $n = 90$ and $DoF = 0.8$ and for $n = 100$ and $DoF = 0.8, 0.4$. We compare RO-III against $Swap$ and PM-$based$ more thoroughly later. Fourth,

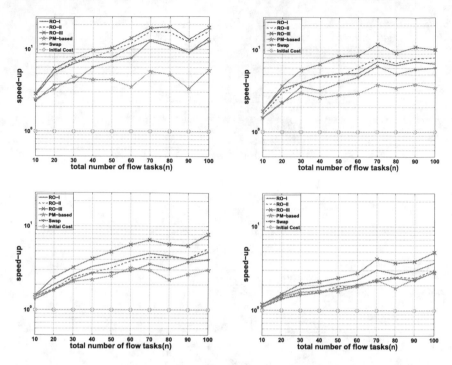

Fig. 16. Speed-ups with regards to the non-optimized flow for $DoF = 0.8$ (top-left), for $DoF = 0.6$ (top-right), for $DoF = 0.4$ (bottom-left) and for $DoF = 0.2$ (bottom-right).

RO-I outperforms RO-II for $DoF = 0.2$ on average, while RO-II outperforms RO-I for $DoF = 0.8$. For $DoF = 0.6, 0.4$, there is not a clear winner between RO-I and RO-II. Finally, we see that RO-II behaves worse than RO-III, which implies that the extensions of the latter are effective.

When considering average instead of median execution times, the average speed-ups for RO-III reach three orders of magnitude. This can be explained with isolated runs, where the speed-ups are five or six orders of magnitude. In other words, the plots in Fig. 16 are rather conservative in terms of potential of our proposals for improving on the SCM.

The numbers mentioned above refer to all the 100 flows for each combination of parameters. In Table 2, we present the speed-up that RO-III yields with regards to the best performing technique between *PM-based* or *Swap* on a more detailed basis (in each flow, a different technique may yield the highest performance). The table shows both the number of occurrences that one algorithm outperforms the others in each set of 100 random flows. For small flows of 10 tasks, there is a probability that all solutions yield the same execution plan. This probability ranges from 16% to 59% for flows with DoF equal to 0.8 and 0.2, respectively. For larger flows, it is extremely rare *PM-based* or *Swap* to find the same or a better plan (less than 1% of the cases).

Table 2. Detailed comparison of *RO-III* against the best performing between *Swap* and *PM-based*: number of cases, average and median speed-ups.

DoF = 0.8

n	RO-III better			same	RO-III worse		
	♯times	avg	median	♯times	♯times	avg	median
10	84	1.2895	1.1238	16	0	-	-
20	99	1.6539	1.3200	0	1	1.0656	1.0656
40	100	2.2130	1.3243	0	0	-	-
60	100	2.7779	1.4920	0	0	-	-
80	100	2.2587	1.2209	0	0	-	-
100	100	3.0435	1.1691	0	0	-	-

DoF = 0.6

n	RO-III better			same	RO-III worse		
	♯times	avg	median	♯times	♯times	avg	median
10	82	1.2981	1.1431	18	0	-	-
20	100	1.6657	1.2537	0	0	-	-
40	100	3.0637	1.4808	0	0	-	-
60	99	2.2811	1.4993	0	1	1.0103	1.0103
80	100	2.7548	1.8658	0	0	-	-
100	99	2.1876	1.3618	1	0	-	-

DoF = 0.4

n	RO-III better			same	RO-III worse		
	♯times	avg	median	♯times	♯times	avg	median
10	47	1.1993	1.1081	53	0	-	-
20	96	1.4283	1.2477	1	3	1.2489	1.0817
40	100	1.8940	1.3474	0	0	-	-
60	99	2.0278	1.4952	0	1	1.0909	1.0909
80	100	2.2472	1.5798	0	0	-	-
100	99	3.5996	1.5130	0	1	1.0793	1.0793

DoF = 0.2

n	RO-III better			same	RO-III worse		
	♯times	avg	median	♯times	♯times	avg	median
10	41	1.1375	1.0520	59	0	-	-
20	81	1.1495	1.0431	17	2	1.0471	1.0471
40	99	1.3974	1.1899	0	1	1.004	1.0471
60	100	1.5893	1.3329	0	0	-	-
80	99	1.6200	1.3645	0	1	1.0047	1.0471
100	100	1.9962	1.4778	0	0	-	-

The table also shows the average and median speed-ups. For flows with 100 tasks, the SCM drops to the half on average, if not more. For example, when $n = 100$ and $DoF = 0.4$, *PM-based* (resp. *Swap*) runs 11.35 (resp. 3.6) times slower than *RO-III* on average. In isolated runs, the performance improvements are more impressive and reach two orders of magnitude. For example, we have observed speed-ups of up to 645 (resp. 98) times with regards to *PM-based* (resp.

Swap) for $n = 100$. For smaller flows of $n = 50$, the maximum observed speed-up is 76 (resp. 41) times.

We conclude this part of the discussion with a comment on *RO-III* vs. *RO-I*. In average, *RO-III* is more efficient than *RO-I*, but in 1–6% of the cases, it produces costlier plans than *RO-I* by up to 44%. Also, in some combinations of parameters, the plans may be the same. By design, *RO-III* is never worse than *RO-II*.

Performance of Parallel Optimization Solutions This set of experiments is conducted in order to evaluate the performance of data flows when they are executed in parallel according to the techniques discussed in Sect. 5. To this end, we compare the parallel version of *Swap*, named as *PSwap*, against the parallel proposed rank ordering-based algorithms, denoted as *PRO-I,PRO-II,PRO-III*, respectively. We also compare against *PPM-based*. Initially, we assume that the merge cost mc is 0 and then, we repeat the experiments considering with non-zero merge cost. The value of the extra merge cost was defined after experiments in real data flows with the PDI tool. So, we set the $mc = 10$, that is an order of magnitude higher than the less expensive tasks and an order of magnitude lower than the most expensive ones. We examine data flows consisting of 50 and 100 tasks.

The comparisons are presented in Table 3, where it is shown that the parallelized version of *RO-III*, *PRO-III*, strengthens its position as the best performing technique. When the merge cost is considered, the names of the algorithms are coupled with the prime symbol (e.g., *PSwap′*); for the moment we do not focus on those table rows.

The aim of this evaluation is to show how often and to what extend parallelization is beneficial. The observed speed-ups are strongly correlated with the *DoF*. For low *DoF = 0.2*, we observe that *PRO-III* has at least 19% lower execution cost than *PSwap* when the flow consists of 50 tasks. The performance improvement increases as the size of the flow and/or *DoF* increases. For example, when we optimize flows with 100 tasks for the same *DoF* the observed improvement is 84% and 86% against *Swap* and *PM-based*, respectively. Additionally, for flows with 100 tasks but higher *DoF = 0.6*, we observe speed-ups up to 4 times.

The key observation after analyzing the individual runs is that, in the majority of the cases, parallel execution is beneficial. In the worst case, there is no performance improvement, producing non-linear plans can never lead to performance degradation. Table 4 shows the number of cases in each set of 100 examples, where the improvement was over 10%. We can see that *PSwap* is the algorithm that benefits the most from non-linear plans, whereas there are small benefits for *PRO-III*. This is partially due to the fact that *RO-III* already produces efficient plan what are harder to further improve upon.

We conclude that further refining the linear orderings with our proposed light-weight post-processing step can yield tangible performance improvements. The results after the application of the extra merge cost prove that its impact is not significant (see bottom part in Table 3) and the above observations still hold.

Table 3. Normalized SCM for data flows with n = 50,100 tasks.

alg	DoF			
	0.8	0.6	0.4	0.2
n = 100				
Initial	14.8634	10.6080	6.0250	2.6482
PSwap	1.3871	1.7109	1.4704	1.1854
PSwap′	1.4139	1.7389	1.5841	1.2188
PPM-based	2.5108	2.1285	1.6159	1.2030
PPM-based′	2.5813	2.2108	1.6600	1.2215
PRO-I	1.0985	1.2902	1.1688	1.0571
PRO-I′	1.1082	1.3011	1.1876	1.0748
PRO-II	1.0488	1.1814	1.3028	1.1930
PRO-II′	1.0538	1.1984	1.3251	1.2368
PRO-III	1.0000	1.0000	1.0000	1.0000
PRO-III′	1.0000	1.0002	1.0015	1.0037
n = 100				
Initial	37.8602	25.3375	18.3169	7.2005
PSwap	1.7214	2.1954	2.1684	1.8378
PSwap′	1.7778	2.2805	2.2565	1.9894
PPM-based	4.8242	4.4072	2.6290	1.8643
PPM-based′	4.8421	4.5622	2.7421	1.9683
PRO-I	1.5256	1.6575	1.4910	1.4188
PRO-I′	1.5410	1.7268	1.5312	1.5068
PRO-II	1.1097	1.5330	1.9290	1.9040
PRO-II′	1.1146	1.5670	2.0122	1.9817
PRO-III	1.0000	1.0000	1.0000	1.0000
PRO-III′	1.0000	1.0001	1.0009	1.0181

Table 4. Times per 100 runs where non-linear plans improve >10%

algo	DoF							
	n = 50				n = 100			
	0.2	0.4	0.6	0.8	0.2	0.4	0.6	0.8
PM-based	7	11	11	10	17	23	25	21
Swap	13	19	20	15	31	37	35	33
RO-I	9	6	10	10	15	17	19	12
RO-III	0	0	2	5	0	3	1	2

Performance of *MIMO* flows. This set of experiments considers the evaluation of the methodology that is analyzed in Sect. 6 for *MIMO* data flow optimization. We consider two cases of butterfly flows (see Fig. 12 (left)). In each case we consider 10 linear segments with 10 and 20 tasks, respectively; thus the overall number of tasks is 100 and 200. The *DoF* of each linear segment is 0.6.

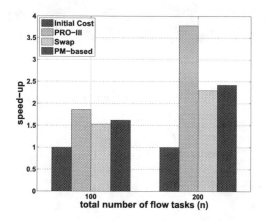

Fig. 17. *MIMO* optimization for n = 100, 200 and *DoF = 0.6* for its linear segments.

Figure 17 presents the median speed-ups of the *PRO-III*, *Swap* and *PM-based* algorithms over the non-optimized initial data flow. In the case where the linear segments are very small (10 tasks) the improvements are up to 86% (*PRO-III*). When the linear segment size increases to 20, *PRO-III* has median speed-up 3.8 times and 62% and 55% better performance improvement than *Swap* and *PM-based*, respectively. Overall, the results of the previous sections focusing on *L-SISO* flows generalize to *MIMO* flows as well.

7.3   Time Overhead

We also conduct an evaluation of the time overhead of the *RO-III*, *PRO-III* and *Swap* optimization algorithms. The purpose of this set of experiment is to show how these techniques scale as the size of data flow increases from 10 to 100 tasks for *DoF = 0.6*. The findings show that the optimization time of *RO-III* and *PRO-III* algorithms is similar and their differences are negligible. In Fig. 18, the key conclusion is that even for large flows, our proposals are capable of optimize a data flow in less than a second despite the fact that *Swap* algorithm scales better than rank ordering algorithms. The overhead of *RO-I* and *RO-II* lies in between the overhead of *RO-III* and *Swap* (not shown in the figure). Overall, our proposal seems to trade a very small time overhead for significant improvements in SCM.

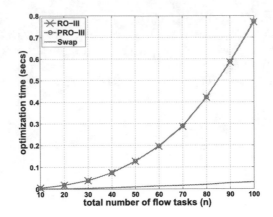

Fig. 18. The optimization time of *RO-III*, *PRO-III* and *Swap* for *DoF=0.6*.

8   Related Work

In this section, we take a deeper look at the proposals that optimize the flow execution plan through changes in the structure of the flow graph including task re-ordering.

For completeness, we start from flow optimization solutions that are inspired by query processing techniques, which are inferior to those already discussed in the beginning of Sect. 4. In [9], an optimization algorithm for query plans with dependency constraints between algebraic operators is presented. The adaptation of this algorithm in our *L-SISO* problem setting is reduced to optimization algorithms that are less efficient than *Swap* [17]. In [15], ad-hoc query optimization methodologies are employed in order to perform structure reformations, such as re-ordering and introducing new services in an existing workflow; in this work we investigate more systematic approaches.

Optimizations of Extract Transform Loading (ETL) flows are analyzed in [25]. In this proposal, ETL execution plans are considered as states and transitions, such as swap, merge, split, distribute and so on, are used to generate new states in order to navigate through the state space, which corresponds to the execution plan alternatives. However, the complete proposal for reducing the ETL workflow has exponential complexity. In our work, where we deal with task re-orderings only, the relevant part of the proposal in [25] corresponds to the *Swap* algorithm, which is explicitly considered in our evaluation. Additional simple heuristics proposed for minimizing the SCM have appeared in [20,34]; those heuristics are also reported to be inferior to *Swap* [17].

Another interesting approach to flow optimization is presented in [13], where the optimizations are based on the analysis of the properties of user-defined functions that implement the data processing logic. This work focuses mostly on techniques that infer the dependency constraints between tasks through examination of their internal semantics rather than on task re-ordering algorithms per se. An extension has appeared in [24], but this solution is not scalable.

In addition, there is a significant portion of proposals on flow optimization that proceed to flow structure optimizations but do not perform task re-ordering, as we do. As such, they are orthogonal to our work. For example, the proposals in [30,33] fall into this category. Several optimizations in workflows are also discussed in [4], but the techniques are limited to straightforward application of query optimization techniques, such as join re-ordering and pushing down selections. Additionally, there are optimization proposals for the parallel execution of online Web-Services represented as queries, such as the proposal in [28], which however aims to minimize the bottleneck cost rather than the sum of the task costs. The optimization techniques that have been proposed in [2,29] also aim to minimize the bottleneck cost. Another optimization proposal that targets a different optimization metric, namely throughput maximization in a parallel setting, is presented in [8]; the distinctive feature of this proposal is that it provides a set of concurrent execution plans. Finally, numerous proposals target efficient resource allocation. Contrary to our work, they assume an execution setting with multiple execution engines and do not deal with optimization of the flow task ordering, e.g., [18,26]. [21] discusses methodologies about how to execute and dispatch task activities in parallel computers, while some other proposals deal with task scheduling, e.g., [3].

9   Conclusions

In this work, we deal with the problem of specifying the optimal execution order of constituent tasks of a data flow in order to minimize the sum of the task execution costs. We are motivated by the significant limitations of fully-automated optimization solutions for data flows with arbitrary tasks, as, nowadays, the optimization of complex data flows is either left to the flow designers and is a manual procedure or relies on solutions that have limited efficiency or scalability. To fill the gap of efficient optimization techniques, we initially focus on flows with a single data source and sink, and propose a set of approximate algorithms that can yield improvements of several factors on average, and several orders of magnitude in isolated cases. We then introduce a post-process optimization phase for parallel execution of the flow tasks to further improve the performance of a data flow. Finally, we show that we can extend these solutions to more complex data flow scenarios that deal with arbitrary number of sources and sinks.

There are several avenues for further research, including deeper investigation of optimizing arbitrary *MIMO* flows, and consideration of other types of constraints, e.g., not allowing two tasks to be placed in the same branch. A more ambitious goal is to provide more holistic flow optimization algorithms, which combine task ordering with aspects, such as task implementation and scheduling.

References

1. Pentaho - Data Integration (Kettle) (2014). http://kettle.pentaho.com
2. Agrawal, K., Benoit, A., Dufossé, F., Robert, Y.: Mapping filtering streaming applications. Algorithmica **62**(1–2), 258–308 (2012)
3. Agrawal, K., Benoit, A., Magnan, L., Robert, Y.: Scheduling algorithms for linear workflow optimization. In: IPDPS (2010)
4. Böhm, M.: Cost-based optimization of integration flows. Ph.D. thesis (2011)
5. Burge, J., Munagala, K., Srivastava, U.: Ordering pipelined query operators with precedence constraints. Technical report 2005–40, Stanford InfoLab (2005)
6. Chaudhuri, S., Dayal, U., Narasayya, V.: An overview of business intelligence technology. Commun. ACM **54**, 88–98 (2011)
7. Chaudhuri, S., Shim, K.: Optimization of queries with user-defined predicates. ACM Trans. Database Syst. **24**(2), 177–228 (1999)
8. Deshpande, A., Hellerstein, L.: Parallel pipelined filter ordering with precedence constraints. ACM Trans. Algorithms **8**(4), 41:1–41:38 (2012)
9. Florescu, D., Levy, A., Manolescu, I., Suciu, D.: Query optimization in the presence of limited access patterns. In: ACM SIGMOD, pp. 311–322
10. Garcia-Molina, H., Ullman, J.D., Widom, J.: Database Systems - The Complete Book, 2nd edn. Pearson Education (2009)
11. Halasipuram, R., Deshpande, P.M., Padmanabhan, S.: Determining essential statistics for cost based optimization of an ETL workflow. In: EDBT, pp. 307–318 (2014)
12. Hellerstein, J.M.: Optimization techniques for queries with expensive methods. ACM Trans. Database Syst. **23**(2), 113–157 (1998)
13. Hueske, F., Peters, M., Sax, M., Rheinländer, A., Bergmann, R., Krettek, A., Tzoumas, K.: Opening the black boxes in data flow optimization. PVLDB **5**(11), 1256–1267 (2012)
14. Ibaraki, T., Kameda, T.: On the optimal nesting order for computing N-relational joins. ACM Trans. Database Syst. **9**(3), 482–502 (1984)
15. Kougka, G., Gounaris, A.: On optimizing workflows using query processing techniques. In: Ailamaki, A., Bowers, S. (eds.) SSDBM 2012. LNCS, vol. 7338, pp. 601–606. Springer, Heidelberg (2012). doi:10.1007/978-3-642-31235-9_43
16. Kougka, G., Gounaris, A.: Optimization of data-intensive flows: is it needed? is it solved? In: DOLAP, pp. 95–98 (2014)
17. Kougka, G., Gounaris, A.: Cost optimization of data flows based on task reordering. CoRR abs/1507.08492 (2015)
18. Kougka, G., Gounaris, A., Tsichlas, K.: Practical algorithms for execution engine selection in data flows. Future Gener. Comput. Syst. **45**, 133–148 (2015)
19. Krishnamurthy, R., Boral, H., Zaniolo, C.: Optimization of nonrecursive queries. In: VLDB, pp. 128–137 (1986)
20. Kumar, N., Kumar, P.S.: An efficient heuristic for logical optimization of ETL workflows. In: Castellanos, M., Dayal, U., Markl, V. (eds.) BIRTE 2010. LNBIP, vol. 84, pp. 68–83. Springer, Heidelberg (2011). doi:10.1007/978-3-642-22970-1_6
21. Ogasawara, E.S., de Oliveira, D., Valduriez, P., Dias, J., Porto, F., Mattoso, M.: An algebraic approach for data-centric scientific workflows. PVLDB **4**, 1328–1339 (2011)
22. Olston, C., Chopra, S., Srivastava, U.: Generating example data for dataflow programs. In: ACM SIGMOD

23. Olston, C., Reed, B., Srivastava, U., Kumar, R., Tomkins, A.: Pig Latin: a not-so-foreign language for data processing. In: SIGMOD Conference, pp. 1099–1110 (2008)
24. Rheinländer, A., Heise, A., Hueske, F., Leser, U., Naumann, F.: SOFA: an extensible logical optimizer for UDF-heavy data flows. Inf. Syst. **52**, 96–125 (2015)
25. Simitsis, A., Vassiliadis, P., Sellis, T.K.: State-space optimization of ETL workflows. IEEE TKDE **17**(10), 1404–1419 (2005)
26. Simitsis, A., Wilkinson, K., Castellanos, M., Dayal, U.: Optimizing analytic data flows for multiple execution engines. In: ACM SIGMOD. pp. 829–840 (2012)
27. Simitsis, A., Wilkinson, K., Dayal, U., Castellanos, M.: Optimizing ETL workflows for fault-tolerance. In: ICDE, pp. 385–396 (2010)
28. Srivastava, U., Munagala, K., Widom, J., Motwani, R.: Query optimization over web services. In: Proceeding of the 32nd Int. Conference on Very Large Data Bases VLDB, pp. 355–366 (2006)
29. Tsamoura, E., Gounaris, A., Manolopoulos, Y.: Decentralized execution of linear workflows over web services. Future Gener. Comput. Syst. **27**(3), 341–347 (2011)
30. Tziovara, V., Vassiliadis, P., Simitsis, A.: Deciding the physical implementation of ETL workflows. In: DOLAP, pp. 49–56 (2007)
31. Van Der Aalst, W.M.P., Ter Hofstede, A.H.M., Kiepuszewski, B., Barros, A.P.: Workflow patterns. Distrib. Parallel Databases **14**(1), 5–51 (2003)
32. Vassiliadis, P., Karagiannis, A., Tziovara, V., Simitsis, A.: Towards a benchmark for ETL workflows. In: International Workshop on Quality in Databases, QDB, pp. 49–60 (2007)
33. Vrhovnik, M., Schwarz, H., Suhre, O., Mitschang, B., Markl, V., Maier, A., Kraft, T.: An approach to optimize data processing in business processes. In: VLDB, pp. 615–626 (2007)
34. Yerneni, R., Li, C., Ullman, J., Garcia-Molina, H.: Optimizing large join queries in mediation systems. In: Beeri, C., Buneman, P. (eds.) ICDT 1999. LNCS, vol. 1540, pp. 348–364. Springer, Heidelberg (1999). doi:10.1007/3-540-49257-7_22

Fusion Strategies for Large-Scale Multi-modal Image Retrieval

Petra Budikova, Michal Batko[✉], and Pavel Zezula

Masaryk University, Brno, Czech Republic
{budikova,batko,zezula}@fi.muni.cz

Abstract. Large-scale data management and retrieval in complex domains such as images, videos, or biometrical data remains one of the most important and challenging information processing tasks. Even after two decades of intensive research, many questions still remain to be answered before working tools become available for everyday use. In this work, we focus on the practical applicability of different multi-modal retrieval techniques. Multi-modal searching, which combines several complementary views on complex data objects, follows the human thinking process and represents a very promising retrieval paradigm. However, a rapid development of modality fusion techniques in several diverse directions and a lack of comparisons between individual approaches have resulted in a confusing situation when the applicability of individual solutions is unclear. Aiming at improving the research community's comprehension of this topic, we analyze and systematically categorize existing multi-modal search techniques, identify their strengths, and describe selected representatives. In the second part of the paper, we focus on the specific problem of large-scale multi-modal image retrieval on the web. We analyze the requirements of such task, implement several applicable fusion methods, and experimentally evaluate their performance in terms of both efficiency and effectiveness. The extensive experiments provide a unique comparison of diverse approaches to modality fusion in equal settings on two large real-world datasets.

1 Introduction

Efficient management of multimedia data is quickly becoming a necessity in the current era of digital cameras, smart phones, and many other devices that allow people to produce and store enormous amounts of complex digital data. On one hand, the volumes of data currently available and the speed of its growth offer unprecedented resources for information mining and AI tasks. On the other hand, they also call for novel approaches to data organization that would be capable of dealing with large amounts of complex, heterogeneous content.

Although a number of multimedia search systems, both academic and commercial, have been created in recent years, the problem of effective and efficient retrieval still remains unsolved for many applications. Apart from the overall difficulty of the task, the multimedia retrieval field has also long suffered from a lack of suitable evaluation platforms and experimental data which made it difficult for researchers to

ⓒ Springer-Verlag GmbH Germany 2017
A. Hameurlain et al. (Eds.): TLDKS XXXIII, LNCS 10430, pp. 146–184, 2017.
DOI: 10.1007/978-3-662-55696-2_5

analyze the strengths and weaknesses of individual solutions, especially in the context of large-scale retrieval. Recently, several large multimedia datasets have been made available for research purposes; however, the organization and evaluation of realistic benchmarking tasks still remains a demanding process and the existing comparisons only cover a limited scope of problems and techniques.

This work presents a comparative analysis of a set of state-of-the-art data management techniques that employ the multi-modal retrieval paradigm. Specifically, we focus on approaches that can be used in interactive large-scale multimedia searching. The selected class of methods is first studied on a theoretical level and then examined experimentally. The experimental evaluation is targeted on image data processing, but the principles described in the theoretical sections also apply to many other domains.

1.1 Evolution of Image Retrieval

Historically, the evolution of complex data retrieval can be traced from early attribute- and text-based solutions [6] to more recent content-based search strategies [26,51] and finally the latest trends that combine multiple complementary techniques to obtain even better retrieval results [5]. The earlier approaches exhibit some very strong features but also significant drawbacks that prevented them from becoming a universal solution for complex data management. In particular, attribute-based and text-based searching can profit from mature database and text-retrieval technologies, but their usability is limited by the availability of descriptive metadata associated with the complex data objects. Content-based searching, on the other hand, exploits salient features that can be automatically extracted from data objects (e.g. a color histogram descriptor in case of image data). These are subjected to a suitable function that evaluates the similarity between pairs of objects, and the objects most similar to a given reference object are returned as the query result. A major advantage of this approach is the fact that no manually created metadata are necessary for supporting the data management; however, the content-based processing is often costly and approximate search strategies need to be applied to achieve online response times. Moreover, content-based searching often suffers from the *semantic gap* problem, i.e. the lack of correspondence between the information contained in the automatically extracted features and the human-perceived semantics of objects [83].

The most recent paradigm, termed *multi-modal (image) retrieval*, tries to overcome the limitations of the previous solutions by combining multiple complementary views on object relevance. This approach is very natural, as it follows the principles of human cognition processes [98]. Multi-modal retrieval techniques attempt to exploit as many information sources as possible, combining various content descriptors (e.g. color or shape descriptors in case of images) with context information available in different automatically captured metadata (e.g. EXIF, GPS location), text annotations, discussions on social networks, etc. [3,22,31,41]. The multi-modal approach promises to improve the performance of retrieval systems on two levels: first, the limitations of any given modality should be reduced in the confrontation with other viewpoints on a candidate object's relevance; second, a

well-designed multi-modal system should allow a complex evaluation of objects'
relevance with acceptable costs, exploiting parallel processing of individual modalities and advanced filtering for fast and precise identification of candidate objects.
To meet these expectations with a working search system, two principal questions
need to be answered: (1) which data sources to select for a given application and
how to extract maximum relevant information from them, and (2) how to combine
these pieces of information effectively and efficiently.

Both these issues have been studied intensively in recent years and many solutions have been proposed for different use scenarios. However, a lot of work still
remains to be done before the principles of multi-modal retrieval are sufficiently
understood. One of the open problems concerns the practical applicability of different techniques that have been proposed for combining multiple modalities in
the retrieval process. Although several studies that compare multiple techniques
in equal settings have been published [2,11,30,47,63], none of them provides a
systematic comparison of different multi-modal retrieval methods in the context
of large-scale retrieval. Yet, the scalability aspect is extremely important in the
Big Data era.

1.2   Our Contributions

Reflecting on this situation, the objective of this paper is to provide a systematic
overview of existing multi-modal retrieval methods and analyze their properties
with a special attention to their applicability for interactive large-scale searching.
In the second part of the paper, we implement and experimentally evaluate
selected fusion techniques over two large image datasets. The main contributions
of the paper are the following:

- *Formal model of multi-modal retrieval:* We formally define the concept of
  modality and present a theoretical model of both mono-modal and multi-
  modal similarity-based retrieval, thus providing a solid foundation for our
  discussion of individual retrieval techniques.
- *Extended categorization of approaches to multi-modal retrieval:* Existing studies of multi-modal data management have established two basic categories of
  modality fusion techniques – the *early fusion* and the *late fusion*. Having analyzed a number of recent research works, we identify several additional aspects
  that are relevant for the practical applicability of multi-modal retrieval.
- *Analysis of modality fusion options for large-scale image retrieval:* Focusing
  on the specific task of large-scale image retrieval, we analyze its requirements
  and identify eligible fusion techniques.
- *Experimental evaluation of diverse approaches to large-scale image search:*
  Using a general framework for similarity-based data management and two
  large sets of real-world image data, we implement the selected techniques
  and perform extensive experiments that allow us to compare these methods
  in terms of retrieval precision as well as processing costs. Using the experimental data, we derive some interesting insights that can be used for future
  optimization of multi-modal search systems.

The rest of this paper is organized as follows. Section 2 provides a formal background for the discussion of multi-modal retrieval techniques, which is followed by a survey and categorization of existing techniques in Sect. 3. In Sect. 4, we focus on the specific task of web-like image retrieval, discuss its requirements, and identify applicable techniques. Section 5 introduces our experimental framework and describes the implementation of selected methods. Section 6 details the evaluation procedure and experimental settings, the evaluation results are then reported in Sect. 7. Finally, Sect. 8 summarizes our findings.

2   Formal Model

Before we start analyzing possible approaches to modality fusion, let us formalize the basic concepts and processes that take part in the multi-modal retrieval. In this section, we first briefly review the basics of similarity-based searching model, which is a suitable abstraction of the retrieval process that covers all search systems in practical use. Next, we define a mono-modal retrieval model and then extend it to embrace multiple modalities.

2.1   Similarity Search

Similarity-based data management is a generic approach that allows to organize and search any data for which a measure of similarity between individual objects can be defined [98,99]. The similarity of objects is typically expressed by the inverse concept of a *distance* (dissimilarity) measured by a suitable *distance function*. The distance function can be applied to any pair of objects from a given domain and produces a positive number or zero; the zero value is returned for identical objects, higher values correspond to a growing dissimilarity between objects. Noticeably, this definition can also accommodate the exact-match paradigm (used in traditional databases) by assigning a fixed non-zero distance to all non-matching object pairs (so-called *trivial distance function*).

Let $\mathcal{X}$ be a collection of objects to be organized and $\mathcal{D}_{\mathcal{X}}$ be the domain of objects from $\mathcal{X}$. The similarity-based data retrieval exploits the "query-by-example" principle, where the query is defined by one or several reference objects $q_1, \ldots, q_n \in \mathcal{D}_{\mathcal{X}}$ and a similarity condition that needs to be satisfied by qualifying objects from $\mathcal{X}$. In this text, we limit our attention to the most typical query type – the *k nearest neighbor (kNN) query*, which retrieves the k objects that are most similar to a single reference point q. Nearest neighbor queries appear in many information retrieval tasks; apart from text search, kNN queries can be used to recognize a song from a fragment recording [35], track objects in videos [56], automatically cluster and annotate images [100], etc. Developing efficient and effective algorithms for kNN queries is thus a very important issue.

2.2   Single Modality Data Management

Let us now examine more closely the dataset $\mathcal{X}$, which contains objects of some generic data type $\mathcal{D}_{\mathcal{X}}$ (e.g. a vector, binary image, music recording, etc.). In many cases, objects from $\mathcal{D}_{\mathcal{X}}$ are very complex and not sufficiently structured to allow meaningful similarity evaluations. Images in particular can be seen as structured for storage and display, but are totally unstructured according to semantic content. Therefore, some suitable aspect of $\mathcal{D}_{\mathcal{X}}$ needs to be identified and used to represent each object for the purpose of data organization. We call each such aspect a *modality*, thus naturally extending the meaning of this term that originally referred to a physical representation of some information (e.g. text, video and sound capturing the same event). In the context of image retrieval, a typical example of a modality is a color histogram [62].

A modality $\mathcal{M}$ can be formally represented by an ordered pair $(p_{\mathcal{M}}, d_{\mathcal{M}})$ of a *projection function* $p_{\mathcal{M}} : \mathcal{D}_{\mathcal{X}} \rightarrow \mathcal{D}_{\mathcal{M}}$, where $\mathcal{D}_{\mathcal{M}}$ is a domain of modality $\mathcal{M}$, and a *distance function* $d_{\mathcal{M}} : \mathcal{D}_{\mathcal{M}} \times \mathcal{D}_{\mathcal{M}} \rightarrow \mathbb{R}_0^+$. The projection function can be applied on any object $o \in \mathcal{X}$ to extract a *feature descriptor* $o.f_{\mathcal{M}} \in \mathcal{D}_{\mathcal{M}}$, while the function $d_{\mathcal{M}}$ evaluates the distance between any two descriptors, i.e. the dissimilarity of the respective objects as seen in the view of modality $\mathcal{M}$.

Let $SE_{\mathcal{M}}$ be a mono-modal search engine that uses a single modality $\mathcal{M}$ for data organization. Typically, $SE_{\mathcal{M}}$ stores each object $o \in \mathcal{X}$ as a pair $(o.f_{\mathcal{M}}, o)$ and uses $o.f_{\mathcal{M}} = p_{\mathcal{M}}(o)$ to search for the data object o. The search engine $SE_{\mathcal{M}}$ may employ one or several index structures $I_{\mathcal{M}}^1, \ldots, I_{\mathcal{M}}^n$ that organize the descriptors of objects in $\mathcal{X}$ [12,79,99]. A similarity query over $SE_{\mathcal{M}}$ is defined by a query object $q_{\mathcal{M}}$, which needs to be from the domain $\mathcal{D}_{\mathcal{M}}$ (clearly, such query can be easily extracted from a more user-friendly query object $q_{\mathcal{X}} \in \mathcal{D}_{\mathcal{X}}$, as depicted in Fig. 1). The kNN query is then defined as follows:

$$kNN_{\mathcal{M}}(q_{\mathcal{M}}, \mathcal{X}) = \{\mathcal{R} \subseteq \mathcal{X}, |\mathcal{R}| = k \wedge \forall x \in \mathcal{R}, y \in \mathcal{X} \setminus \mathcal{R} :$$
$$d_{\mathcal{M}}(q_{\mathcal{M}}, p_{\mathcal{M}}(x)) \le d_{\mathcal{M}}(q_{\mathcal{M}}, p_{\mathcal{M}}(y))\}$$

2.3   Multi-modal Data Management

Although different sophisticated modalities have been proposed for images and other types of complex data, experience shows that each modality has some limitations that prevent it from fully answering to users' needs [5]. Some modalities do not sufficiently capture the user-perceived similarity of the original objects (e.g. the color histogram), other are highly computationally demanding (e.g. various local visual features) or not available in all situations (e.g. descriptive text). To overcome this problem, multi-modal data management systems employ a set of modalities $\mathcal{M}_1, \ldots, \mathcal{M}_n$ that are relevant for the given data domain $\mathcal{D}_{\mathcal{X}}$ and the target applications. The modalities can be combined in many different ways to provide more complex representations of objects from $\mathcal{X}$ and to evaluate their similarity on a higher semantic level.

To describe the functionality of a multi-modal system, we need to introduce additional notation. Let $p_{\widehat{\mathcal{M}_{i_1}, \ldots, \mathcal{M}_{i_m}}}$ be a multi-modal projection function that transforms an object $o \in \mathcal{X}$ into a multi-modal descriptor $o.f_{\widehat{\mathcal{M}_{i_1}, \ldots, \mathcal{M}_{i_m}}}$; trivially, $o.f_{\widehat{\mathcal{M}_1, \mathcal{M}_2}}$ can be obtained by concatenation of $o.f_{\mathcal{M}_1}$ and $o.f_{\mathcal{M}_2}$, but more

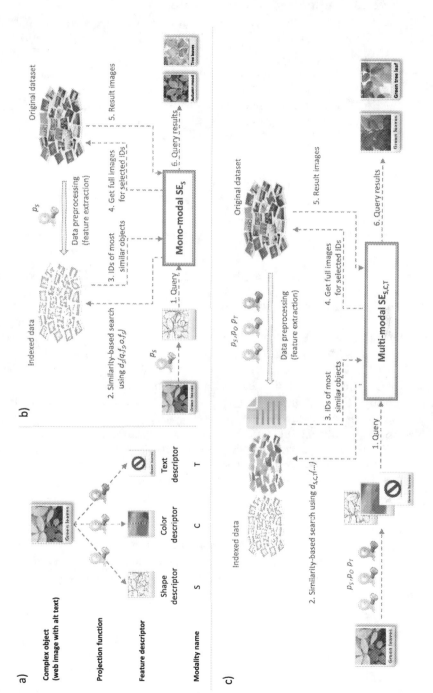

Fig. 1. Web image search example: (a) Modalities, (b) single-modality retrieval, (c) multi-modal retrieval.

sophisticated techniques are also available. Similarly, let $d_{\widehat{\mathcal{M}_{i_1},...,\mathcal{M}_{i_m}}}$ be a multi-modal distance function that evaluates the dissimilarity of objects with respect to multiple viewpoints; again, $d_{\widehat{\mathcal{M}_{i_1},...,\mathcal{M}_{i_m}}}$ can be defined in many ways, which will be discussed later.

Now, we are able to define a multi-modal search engine $SE_{\mathcal{M}_1,...,\mathcal{M}_n}$ that recognizes a set of modalities $\mathcal{M}_1,...,\mathcal{M}_n$. $SE_{\mathcal{M}_1,...,\mathcal{M}_n}$ is characterized by a set of projection functions π and a set of distance functions δ that can be used to organize objects from $\mathcal{X}$. Set π contains all supported projection functions over $\{\mathcal{M}_1,...,\mathcal{M}_n\}$; similarly, δ contains all supported distance functions. $SE_{\mathcal{M}_1,...,\mathcal{M}_n}$ may further exploit a set of multi-modal index structures $\iota_{\widehat{\mathcal{M}_{i_1},...,\mathcal{M}_{i_m}}}$, which can be used to retrieve candidate objects relevant with respect to the particular modalities engaged.

A query $Q = (q, d_Q)$ over $SE_{\mathcal{M}_1,...,\mathcal{M}_n}$ is defined by a query object q and a distance function d_Q. The query object q can be specified as $q_\mathcal{X} \in \mathcal{D}_\mathcal{X}$, by a single modality descriptor $q_{\mathcal{M}_i} \in \mathcal{D}_{\mathcal{M}_i}$, or as a combination of several modality descriptors $(q_{\mathcal{M}_{i1}},...,q_{\mathcal{M}_{im}})$. The query distance d_Q needs to be taken from the set δ of supported distance functions.

3   Categorization of Approaches

Having defined the multi-modal search paradigm, we can now proceed with a more detailed study of different projection and distance functions and the specific techniques of modality fusion. At the same time, we introduce a new categorization of existing multi-modal search methods in this section. Some of the observations presented here have been inspired by discussions of fusion techniques in multimedia processing survey studies [5,14,28,47] and also by several research works that deal with information fusion in different domains [13,75,76]. However, to the best of our knowledge no other taxonomy of fusion methods exists that would take into account all the factors discussed here.

Our categorization is defined by several dimensions of the fusion that we believe to be significant for large-scale retrieval. These dimensions are not orthogonal but rather interconnected, so that a single design decision often influences several of the properties we study. However, we prefer to analyze the individual aspects separately to see more clearly how the different types of solutions work and what are their strengths and weaknesses. The dependencies between individual dimensions will naturally be mentioned in the discussions and summarized at the end of this section.

3.1   Integration of Modalities

The fundamental idea of multi-modal search paradigm is to exploit several complementary modalities $\mathcal{M}_1,...,\mathcal{M}_n$ to describe complex data objects and evaluate their similarity. During data processing and query evaluation, these modalities need to be combined together to produce the overall similarity measure d_Q requested for a particular query Q. The fusion process may take into account the individual data descriptors $f_{\mathcal{M}_1}, \ldots, f_{\mathcal{M}_n}$, the respective distance functions $d_{\mathcal{M}_1}, \ldots, d_{\mathcal{M}_n}$, or both. In this section, we focus on the semantics of different approaches to modality integration.

Among the existing solutions, we can distinguish two classes of methods that differ significantly with regard to the relative importance assigned to individual modalities during the retrieval process. In the *symmetric fusion* paradigm, all modalities are considered to be equally important for the data management and are utilized in all phases of query processing. In *asymmetric fusion*, some of the modalities are treated as more influential and are used to organize and pre-select data, while the remaining modalities are only used for query result refinement. The choice between these two options, and the subsequent selection of integration parameters, depends on various properties of the input modalities, the target application characteristics, and efficiency requirements.

Symmetric Fusion. In solutions that follow the symmetric fusion paradigm, all modalities are considered independent and can be processed in parallel until the moment of fusion, when all of them are merged together. Even though the contribution of each modality can be increased or decreased by a particular setting of the fusion mechanism, it is important that all modalities are used for indexing and searching of the whole dataset $\mathcal{X}$. The following sections present possible implementations of this fusion type.

Feature fusion. Feature (or descriptor) fusion is an integral part of early fusion strategies, which combine modalities $\mathcal{M}_1, \ldots, \mathcal{M}_n$ prior to data indexing. The joining of modalities is applied on the level of descriptors, where individual mono-modal descriptors $o.f_{\mathcal{M}_1}, \ldots, o.f_{\mathcal{M}_n}$ of a given data object are merged into a single complex descriptor $o.f_{\widehat{\mathcal{M}_1, \ldots, \mathcal{M}_n}}$. This descriptor is provided by a suitable multi-modal projection function $p^{FF}_{\widehat{\mathcal{M}_1, \ldots, \mathcal{M}_n}} : \mathcal{D}_{\mathcal{X}} \to \mathcal{D}_{\widehat{\mathcal{M}_1, \ldots, \mathcal{M}_n}}$, and the similarity of two objects is evaluated by a multi-modal distance function $d^{FF}_{\widehat{\mathcal{M}_1, \ldots, \mathcal{M}_n}} : \mathcal{D}_{\widehat{\mathcal{M}_1, \ldots, \mathcal{M}_n}} \times \mathcal{D}_{\widehat{\mathcal{M}_1, \ldots, \mathcal{M}_n}} \to \mathbb{R}_0^+$.

For a simple feature fusion, individual mono-modal descriptors can be straightforwardly concatenated to form the multi-modal descriptor. In the first multi-modal solutions for ImageCLEF retrieval tasks [28] or video retrieval [84], the concatenated descriptors were perceived simply as points of a multi-dimensional vector space and standard L_p metrics were applied to measure their distance. However, this approach may degrade the performance of multimedia content analysis algorithms, especially when the features are independent or heterogenous [84]. Therefore, most systems that employ feature concatenation combine it with the distance aggregation approach that will be discussed in the following section.

If training data is available for a given retrieval task, it is possible to engage more advanced feature fusion strategies. These define p^{FF} by mining semantic relationships between modalities and identification of data characteristics that are most important with respect to a given data set and/or retrieval task [31, 32, 36, 57, 71, 72, 82, 90, 92]. As detailed in [5], the most common semantic fusion methods include SVMs, Bayesian models, neural networks. The resulting feature space typically has a lower number of dimensions than the input ones, therefore the feature fusion also serves as a dimensionality reduction technique. A suitable distance function can also be determined by the semantic analysis [94].

Distance aggregation. Alternatively, it is possible to perform symmetric fusion by combining partial distances of object $o \in \mathcal{X}$ measured by $d_{\mathcal{M}_1}, \ldots, d_{\mathcal{M}_n}$, using a suitable aggregation function $d^{AGG}_{\mathcal{M}_1, \ldots, \mathcal{M}_n} : (\mathbb{R}_0^+)^n \to \mathbb{R}_0^+$. The aggregated distance can be combined with previously described feature concatenation in early fusion systems, however its main use is in late fusion architectures where each modality is indexed separately. As will be discussed later, some properties of the aggregation function (e.g. monotonicity) may be crucial for the selection of the late fusion method. In the late fusion phase, it is also possible to combine object ranks from previous retrieval phases instead of the actual distances. Recent study [70] suggests to use both the ranks and distances during the fusion.

Similar to feature fusion, there exist several categories of distance aggregation methods. The first category is composed of so-called *blind* fusion functions [67], where fixed rules are applied regardless of individual distance function value distributions. Examples of such aggregations include non-weighted min, max, sum, product, or geometric mean [28,67]. The second class contains weighted linear and non-linear aggregation functions, the most popular of which is definitely the weighted sum of $d_{\mathcal{M}_1}(p_{\mathcal{M}_1}(o), p_{\mathcal{M}_1}(q)), \ldots, d_{\mathcal{M}_n}(p_{\mathcal{M}_n}(o), p_{\mathcal{M}_n}(q))$ [8,55,93]. Other possible options include weighted product, sum of logarithms, sum of squares, sum of k lowest distances, etc. [5,24,54,102]. Aggregation parameters such as the weights of individual modalities can be determined by domain experts or dataset analysis and machine learning [8,93]. Alternatively, users can personalize the search by setting the respective weights manually, if the system architecture supports flexible aggregations (see Sect. 3.3). In [49,102], the authors attempt to determine optimal fusion coefficients dynamically for individual queries without user interaction. Also, it is often necessary to normalize the individual distances before the aggregation, which is studied in [7]. Finally, the most complex aggregation functions engage probabilistic or regression models of distance distributions [5].

Asymmetric Fusion. Asymmetric fusion strategies constitute a complement to the symmetric solutions. Here, the modalities $\mathcal{M}_1, \ldots, \mathcal{M}_n$ are not considered equal but instead, one or several of the modalities are chosen as dominating or *primary*. Let us suppose that the modalities are ordered in such a way that $\mathcal{M}_1^P, \ldots, \mathcal{M}_m^P$ are the primary ones. These modalities are used in data indexing phase to organize dataset $\mathcal{X}$, and in a search session to pre-select a set of candidate objects $CS_{\mathcal{M}_1^P, \ldots, \mathcal{M}_m^P}$. This candidate set is then subjected to further evaluation, where *secondary* modalities $\mathcal{M}_{m+1}^S, \ldots, \mathcal{M}_n^S$ as well as the primary ones may be exploited. Noticeably, such solution typically results in an approximate retrieval, where the query result $\mathcal{R}$ is evaluated as follows:

$$\mathcal{R} = kNN_{\mathcal{M}_1,...,\mathcal{M}_n}(Q, CS_{\mathcal{M}_1^P,...,\mathcal{M}_m^P}), \text{where}$$

$$CS_{\mathcal{M}_1^P,...,\mathcal{M}_m^P} = \kappa NN_{\mathcal{M}_1^P,...,\mathcal{M}_m^P}(Q', \mathcal{X})$$

Here, the κ denotes the size of the candidate set $CS_{\mathcal{M}_1^P,...,\mathcal{M}_m^P}$ and Q' the query object transformed into the domains of values of the primary modalities. For obvious reasons, this approach is also denoted as incremental data *filtering*. Parameter κ significantly influences both the evaluation costs and the precision of results, therefore its value needs to be chosen carefully [4].

The motivation for applying the asymmetric fusion may be threefold: (1) the primary modalities are more important for the user – this is typical e.g. for location-aware applications; (2) the asymmetric solution is chosen because of efficiency issues – e.g. text search is a very efficient method that is often used to pre-select the candidate set for further processing; or (3) some of the modalities may not be available at the beginning of the query evaluation but emerge later by means of (pseudo)-relevance feedback. In the first two situations, the primary and secondary modalities can be fused in any of the ways mentioned above. A typical asymmetric fusion system is composed of a text-based primary search (possibly over several text features joined by feature fusion) and a re-ranking phase, during which distance aggregation over several modalities is applied [11,28]. In addition to this, most of the recent asymmetric fusion solutions exploit the pseudo-relevance feedback principle, which allows to introduce *context-aware* modalities in the second retrieval phase. These are defined by projection and distance functions that take into account the properties of the actual candidate set $CS_{\mathcal{M}_1^P,...,\mathcal{M}_m^P}$ and the relationships between objects in this set. The idea of context-aware modalities is based on the assumption that objects relevant to a given query should be similar to each other, while the less relevant ones are likely to be outliers in a similarity graph of objects from $CS_{\mathcal{M}_1^P,...,\mathcal{M}_m^P}$. This assumption is exploited by many clustering-based distance measures [39,40,61,68,103], distances based on random walks in the similarity graph [44,45,52,64,74,89,101], and several other contextual distance measures [43,70]. More detailed discussion of re-ranking techniques can be found in surveys [2,60].

3.2   Fusion Scenarios

By the term *modality fusion scenario*, we denote the sequence of actions that are undertaken by the system during data organization and query processing in order to combine the modalities. The fusion scenario is a principal characteristics of multi-modal systems that strongly influences the overall efficiency and effectiveness. Traditionally, multi-modal approaches are divided into two classes denoted as *early fusion* and *late fusion*. In this section, we take a closer look on individual solutions within each of these classes, and define a more fine-grained categorization of late fusion methods.

Early Fusion: Data Preparation and Indexing. Under the early fusion paradigm, modalities $\mathcal{M}_1, \ldots, \mathcal{M}_n$ are combined prior to data indexing. After initial data analysis, the search system employs a single fused projection function $p_{\widehat{\mathcal{M}_1,...,\mathcal{M}_n}}$ and a distance measure $d_{\widehat{\mathcal{M}_1,...,\mathcal{M}_n}}$, which can be understood as a new fused modality. Early fusion is also denoted as *data fusion, feature fusion,* or a *joint features model,* because it happens on the feature level, before any decisions concerning the similarity of objects are taken. The early fusion is in principle a symmetric approach. Any of the fusion techniques surveyed in Sect. 3.1 can be employed to provide $p_{\widehat{\mathcal{M}_1,...,\mathcal{M}_n}}$ and $d_{\widehat{\mathcal{M}_1,...,\mathcal{M}_n}}$, the best results are naturally achieved when semantic analysis of relationships between modalities is used [28, 31, 32, 36, 87].

A great strength of the early fusion paradigm is the fact that the fusion process can exploit rich information about the whole dataset $\mathcal{X}$ (in contrast to late fusion methods which typically work with pre-filtered data), and the modality fusion is performed off-line. This allows to thoroughly analyze the data, construct optimal fused projection and distance functions, and build an optimal index structure for the new modality. On the other hand, a major disadvantage of early fusion solutions is the limited flexibility of the resulting search system. The combination of modalities is usually fixed in the index and cannot be adjusted to accommodate particular user's preferences. Even though some progress has been made towards providing index structures that support multiple distance functions [18, 23], the flexibility is still very limited. Moreover, sophisticated early fusion methods that analyze semantic relationships between modalities require high-quality training data, which is often difficult to obtain, and substantial computational resources, which may become a limitation of scalability.

Late Fusion: Query Evaluation. In a multi-modal search system that exploits late fusion, modalities $\mathcal{M}_1, \dots, \mathcal{M}_n$ are not fused in advance, but only during query evaluation. This approach can be perceived as an on-request fusion – a late fusion system typically supports mono-modal retrieval over some of the available modalities as well as different settings of multi-modal searching. The resulting flexibility of searching is one of the most important benefits of late fusion.

In modern retrieval systems, the query evaluation is often a complex and possibly iterative process. As depicted in Fig. 2, there are several common query processing phases that differ in the amount and type of information that is exploited there. In the following sections, we briefly describe each of these phases and discuss modality fusion techniques that can be implemented in individual phases to refine the query $Q = (q, d_Q)$ and to identify relevant objects from $\mathcal{X}$.

Query specification and preprocessing. In the beginning of the retrieval process, users need to express their information need as a query. This is composed of a (multi-modal) query object q (i.e. an example image and a set of keywords) and a distance function d_Q to be used for selection of similar objects. Before the query is submitted to the search system, different preprocessing techniques may be applied to refine, disambiguate, or expand the query [6, 19].

In the context of multi-modal query preprocessing, the synergy between modalities can be exploited for both query disambiguation and expansion. Typically, the preprocessing introduces an auxiliary query, which may be evaluated

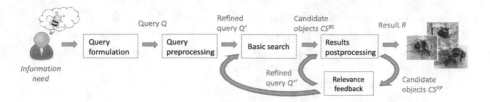

Fig. 2. Phases of query evaluation.

over the target dataset or some external knowledge base (e.g. WordNet [34] or ImageNet [27] for image-and-text query preprocessing). The disambiguation process is used to refine mono-modal descriptors provided by users and thus replace the query object q by q' [1,58], whereas query expansion retrieves additional modalities from external resources, producing a more complex query object q' that requires a new distance function d'_Q [22,86].

Basic search. A fundamental part of any query evaluation is the *primary* or *basic search (BS)*, during which a candidate result set CS^{BS} is selected from the whole dataset $\mathcal{X}$. Depending on the strategy of the search engine, CS^{BS} may be either directly presented as the final result, or submitted to a postprocessing phase. In the latter case, CS^{BS} is usually several orders of magnitude larger than the requested result set.

In late fusion systems, the dataset $\mathcal{X}$ is typically preprocessed (indexed) using one or several separate modalities. Let independent indexes $I_{\mathcal{M}_{i1}}, \ldots, I_{\mathcal{M}_{im}}$ be available in $SE_{\mathcal{M}_1, \ldots, \mathcal{M}_n}$. During the basic search phase, some of these can be utilized for standard mono-modal retrieval and produce intermediate results on which the fusion will be applied in a latter processing phase. Alternatively, modality fusion can be implemented during the basic search phase, both in a symmetric and asymmetric manner.

The symmetric basic-search-phase fusion is best represented by the Threshold Algorithm [33], which works as follows. For each modality $\mathcal{M}$ to be fused, there needs to exist an index from which individual objects $o \in \mathcal{X}$ can be retrieved one by one, ordered by their increasing distance $d_{\mathcal{M}}(p_{\mathcal{M}}(q), p_{\mathcal{M}}(o))$ from the query object in the view of modality $\mathcal{M}$. Apart from this *sorted access* to objects, there also has to be a *random access* method that can access any object from $\mathcal{X}$ and retrieve its aggregated distance from the query, taking all modalities in consideration. The Threshold Algorithm then proceeds in iterations: in each iteration, the next object is retrieved from each index and the aggregated multi-modal query distance d_Q^{AGG} is computed for each retrieved object. After each iteration, the intermediate query result is updated to contain the best objects seen so far, and a stopping condition is evaluated that decides whether better results can be found among the yet unseen objects. The stopping conditions compares the aggregated distance of the most dissimilar object in the intermediate result with the *threshold value* (lower bound) on the distance of yet unseen objects, which is computed by applying the aggregation function on the highest partial distances seen so far in each of the mono-modal sorted lists. Provided that the aggregated distance function d_Q^{AGG} is monotonous, the algorithm guarantees that the most relevant objects from $\mathcal{X}$ with respect to d_Q^{AGG} are found. However, this method can run into performance problems since the number of objects from $\mathcal{X}$ that may need to be accessed is not known in advance. Therefore, approximate implementations have also been studied [9,33].

For asymmetric basic-search-phase fusion, it is necessary to utilize a specialized index structure constructed in such way that the data is organized by one modality but can be searched by a combination of several. This can be achieved by extending a standard mono-modal index with additional information about secondary modalities and adjusting the retrieval algorithm so that it takes these modalities into account when pruning the search space and identifying candidate objects. Solutions of this type have been studied mainly in the context of geo-textual data processing. For instance, the IR-tree [25] extends the standard R-tree spatial index to store both spatial and text information about points of interest. Non-leaf nodes of the IR-tree contain summarized information about text data in respective subtrees, which allows a search algorithm to prune the search space efficiently with respect to both textual and spatial modalities. Any monotone aggregation function can be then used to compute the query distance. Several other geo-textual indexes are analyzed in [21], a more generic but approximate solution with metric-based index was proposed in [15].

Result postprocessing. When the postprocessing phase is implemented, its task is to re-evaluate the similarity between the query and the objects in CS^{BS}, using more complex measures of similarity. No more objects are accessed in the postprocessing phase than those in CS^{BS}, therefore the postprocessing is often denoted as *result ranking* or *re-ranking*.

According to [28], postprocessing-phase fusion is the most frequent type of multi-modal image search, and the same trend can be observed in other multimedia retrieval fields. The main advantages of this solution are its low processing costs, the possibility to apply fusion on top of well-established mono-modal index structures, and no limitations on the form of the aggregated query distance. Postprocessing fusion is also very often combined with pseudo-relevance feedback, which allows to exploit context-aware modalities.

When CS^{BS} is provided by multiple indexes/modalities, the postprocessing fusion is symmetric and approximates the Threshold Algorithm. Instead of accessing all potentially relevant objects from $\mathcal{X}$, only a fixed number of top-ranking objects is retrieved from each index, merged, and re-ranked. Examples of symmetric postprocessing fusion include text-and-visual fusion in [28], combination of different visual modalities [20], or a fusion of multiple text-based search results [54].

However, the more typical type of postprocessing fusion is asymmetric combination of modalities. One modality with low processing costs and good selectivity is chosen for indexing and basic search, while the remaining ones are utilized during re-ranking. Most commonly, text is used as the primary modality [4,28,44,64,81,89], but some solutions that utilize content-based retrieval as the primary modality also exist [17,53,65,80]. A more detailed survey of re-ranking mechanisms and comparison of selected techniques can be found in [2, 11, 60].

Relevance feedback. Relevance feedback is a result refinement mechanism that assumes interactive searching, where users repeatedly provide their opinion on the relevance of candidate objects [77]. In *pseudo-relevance feedback* variant, user opinion is replaced by assumption that candidate objects from the last iteration are likely to be relevant and their properties can be used to predict the properties of the desired answer. With both interactive and automatic evaluation, the feedback loop may be repeated several times. In each iteration, either the query object or the query distance measure is updated. The refined query is then reintroduced either to the basic search, or the result postprocessing phase.

In the context of modality fusion, relevance feedback may be utilized to obtain values of some modalities that are not present in the query specification, to refine the values of available modalities, or to adjust the query distance function to better suit the user's information need [53, 61, 85, 88, 95–97]. The most frequent pseudo-relevance feedback methods are based on candidate set clustering and random walks in a candidate objects' similarity graph, as discussed in Sect. 3.1.

Comparison of Early and Late Fusion. While state-of-the-art research literature provides many examples of both early and late fusion methods, there are not many guidelines for deciding which approach is more suitable for a given application. The effects of early and late fusion on retrieval result quality have been compared in several studies, but the results are not very conclusive. Some authors find the early fusion to be superior since it allows complex semantic analysis of the data [30, 84], others conclude that late fusion can provide better results in many situations [24, 28]. In principle, early fusion is likely to provide good results if the user/application needs are well understood and good training data is available, which is satisfied e.g. for well-defined classification tasks [48]. On the other hand, late fusion should be preferred in general-purpose retrieval where users are expected to interact with the system and adjust the evaluation of similarity to their preferences. Late fusion is also a natural implementation for asymmetric integration of modalities. Finally, some authors propose to combine early and late fusion to achieve the best results [50].

3.3 Flexibility

As suggested in the previous section, one of the big challenges of searching in broad data domains is the fact that it is impossible to define a universal similarity measure that would be suitable across different queries and user needs. This introduces the need for flexible retrieval methods that would allow users to influence the choice of modalities and the manner in which they are combined. As we have observed in the descriptions of the fusion scenarios, not all modality fusion techniques allow users to adjust the combination. Typically, early fusion approaches do not support flexible searching, whereas some late fusion architectures are highly adaptable. We propose to distinguish the following three levels of flexibility.

Zero flexibility. In zero flexibility systems, the selection of modalities as well as their combination is fixed. This applies for most early fusion systems [3, 8, 32, 36, 72, 82, 90, 92].

Aggregation flexibility. In this case, the selection of modalities is fixed, but users can influence the aggregation function. The aggregation flexibility can be either *full*, or *partial*. In the latter case, the set of supported aggregation functions is limited by some required properties (e.g. monotonicity is needed for [23, 33]). Full aggregation flexibility is provided by most postprocessing fusion solutions [4, 44, 60, 89].

Feature flexibility. Again, we distinguish between a *full* and *partial* feature flexibility. For full flexibility, the modalities to be fused need not be known in advance, since users can introduce additional modalities during query specification. The system has to be able to embrace the new modalities without rebuilding the whole search infrastructure, which is easily achieved in postprocessing fusion. In case of a partial feature flexibility, adding a new modality needs to be processed off-line and may require adaptations of the infrastructure, but does not necessitate a complete rebuild of the search system. This is satisfied by asymmetric indexing structures such as the IR-tree [21, 25].

3.4   Precision

The precision of any search result can be analyzed from two different perspectives: (1) a *distance-based* or *objective* perspective analyses the result precision with respect to the selected data representation and the query distance function d_Q, whereas (2) a *user-perceived*, *subjective*, or *semantic* perspective takes into account the users' satisfaction with the result. The second view determines the real usability of the respective search system, but depends on multiple factors – the selection of modalities, quality of data capturing and feature extraction, definition of the distance function, and the objective precision of the actual retrieval – and can only be assessed by user-satisfaction studies. In this section, we focus only on the distance-based precision, which can be objectively measured.

The objective retrieval precision of 100% can be always achieved by exhaustive checking of all objects in $\mathcal{X}$. However, in large-scale searching some approximations are usually applied during the query evaluation to decrease the computation costs. These approximations may not result in any noticeable deterioration of user-perceived result quality, as the similarity-based searching is (semantically) approximate by nature. Still, the distance-based approximation ratio should intuitively not be too large if we do not want to risk decreasing user satisfaction. In the multi-modal retrieval, we can identify two types of distance-based approximations: those that regard the processing of individual modalities, and approximations of the actual fusion that can be applied when late fusion strategies are used. Single-modality retrieval approximations are analyzed in a survey study [69], which identifies several important aspects of approximation strategies. In the following, we study the same aspects for fusion approximations.

Applicability of a given technique on different data domains. The applicability of fusion solutions is very wide in case of postprocessing fusion (e.g. [4, 44, 60, 89]), whereas basic search fusion is more restricted. Specifically, basic search fusion mechanisms either pose limitations on the aggregation function (e.g. the Threshold Algorithm [33]) or are suitable only for specific data and distance function (e.g. the geo-textual indexes [21, 25]).

The principle of achieving approximation. From the implementation point of view, most of the fusion approximations fall into the category of *reducing comparisons* – the similarity of objects is not evaluated for all candidates that are potentially relevant, but only for such objects that are considered most promising in a given processing phase.

Result quality guarantees. Considering the quality of the results, existing fusion techniques either guarantee 100% fusion precision (early fusion, the Threshold Algorithm) or give no guarantees on quality apart from reporting experimental results (postprocessing fusion techniques).

User interaction with the system. The majority of approximate fusion techniques allow users to influence the trade-off between retrieval costs and precision, e.g. by setting the size of CS^{BS}.

3.5   Efficiency and Scalability

Retrieval efficiency and search system scalability are clearly crucial qualities of any system designed for big data processing. In multimedia retrieval, there are two major issues that need to be addressed: the costs of data preprocessing, and the efficiency of query evaluation. Depending on a selected fusion scenario, multi-modal retrieval introduces additional costs to one or both of these phases.

Data preprocessing. In the data preprocessing step, descriptors of primary modalities first need to be extracted from all objects in $\mathcal{X}$. This complexity of the extraction process is linear with respect to the size of $\mathcal{X}$, with the actual costs depending on the selection of modalities – when sophisticated content-based descriptors are used, the extraction process can be very computationally intensive [8]. In early fusion scenarios, the extracted descriptors are immediately analyzed and fused. The costs of this phase depend on the specific fusion technique employed, but the complexity of semantic fusion techniques is in general super-linear with respect to the size of $\mathcal{X}$. Finally, index structures for either the original or the fused descriptors are created [12, 79, 99].

Even though the data preprocessing phase is evaluated off-line, its complexity may become a bottleneck of the overall system scalability. Efficient extraction of descriptors for very large data is considered a challenging task nowadays [98], so the choice of primary modalities should be made carefully. To the best of our knowledge, complex early fusion has never been implemented in very large scale.

Query evaluation with early fusion. As discussed earlier, query evaluation in early fusion systems is equal to mono-modal query evaluation. After the extraction of query descriptors, which requires constant time, relevant objects from $\mathcal{X}$ are identified in the index. The complexity of index retrieval is usually strongly sub-linear or even constant, depending on the level of approximation applied [66].

Query evaluation with late fusion. In case of late fusion, additional processing is added to the query evaluation costs. The actual fusion complexity is determined by the number of objects that are considered during fusion. As discussed in Sect. 3.2, in basic search fusion the number of objects may be unlimited and the fusion may thus degrade to linear complexity with respect to the size of $\mathcal{X}$. On the other hand, the number of objects entering postprocessing fusion is always limited. The postprocessing costs may be high with respect to the size of CS^{BS}, but are constant with respect to the size of $\mathcal{X}$. Furthermore, the efficiency of late fusion is influenced by the choice between symmetric and asymmetric integration of modalities. Symmetric fusion may exploit parallel processing, whereas asymmetric fusion typically tries to minimize processing costs by utilizing cheap and highly selective modalities first.

3.6   Axis Correlations and Other Aspects

In the previous sections, we have defined five axes that can be used to classify multi-modal retrieval techniques. As already mentioned, these axes are not orthogonal; on the contrary, a single design decision typically determines several of the axes. The correlations between individual axes were discussed in the descriptions of individual axes. To complete our analysis, Table 1 presents an overview of meaningful combinations of individual approaches.

The five classification criteria that we have introduced represent important characteristics of large-scale multi-modal retrieval, but are by no means exhaustive. Many other aspects are worth attention and need to be considered carefully to design a multi-modal search system. The *selection of modalities* is extremely important – it is necessary to choose such a set of modalities that provides complementary information and does not require too costly processing [5,63]. *Individual application domains* may require different modalities and pose various restrictions on evaluation costs, precision and flexibility. The *level of user participation* may also vary; in general, users do not like to provide much input during the query processing, but in some cases intensive interaction can be expected. *Additional information sources* such as ontologies or general web data need to be studied, collected or created, cleaned, and maintained [37,38]. Finally, the *synchronization of modalities* is vital for modalities with a time dimension, e.g. sound or video [5].

Table 1. Multi-dimensional classification of fusion techniques.

Fusion strategy	Flexibility	Approxim.	Scalability	Examples
Symmetric early fusion				
Simple early fusion	zero	none	medium	[3,8,84]
Semantic early fusion	zero	none	medium or high	[31,32,36,57,71,72, 82,87,90,92,94]
Multi-metric indexing	partial aggreg. f.	none	medium	[18,23]
Symmetric late fusion				
Threshold algorithm (basic search phase)	partial aggreg. f. partial feature f.	none or guaranteed	low	[33]
Symmetric postprocessing	full aggreg. f. partial feature f.	not guaranteed	high	[5,20,24,54,67,78]
Asymmetric late fusion				
Asymmetric indexing (basic search phase)	partial aggreg. f. partial feature f.	none	medium	[15,21,25]
Asymmetric postprocessing	full aggreg. f. full feature f.	not guaranteed	high	[4,11,17,39,40,43– 45,52,53,61,64,65,68, 70,73,74,80,81,85,88, 89,95–97,101–103]

4   Large-Scale Multi-modal Image Search

In the previous section, we have surveyed fundamental characteristics of multi-modal searching, taking into account a number of diverse methods that have been proposed for different situations. The presented categories provide us with basic guidelines that can be used to select possible solutions for a given application. However, the multi-modal retrieval is a complex task with many factors that influence the search results, thus true usefulness of any method cannot be determined unless it is experimentally verified in context of the target use case and modalities. Each such evaluation also provides new data that allow the scientific community to study relationships between information needs, modalities, and retrieval techniques.

Accordingly, the second part of this paper is devoted to an experimental evaluation of techniques applicable for interactive large-scale image search, which is a principal component of many popular applications, e.g. web galleries, social networks, etc. Specifically, we focus on the fusion of text and visual modalities in this context. In a typical browsing scenario, a user sees an image for which he or she would like to get similar ones. The usual way to provide the results is to execute a textual search based on the annotation of the original image. However, since the user selected a particular image, the visual content of the image is also important. Thus a multi-modal search combining the textual and visual aspect search is likely to produce better results. Even though search engines with such functionality already exist, their design is often based on assumptions and expectations that have not been rigorously defined and studied. To address this situation, we perform an extensive evaluation of different approaches to image-and-text retrieval and analyze the results.

4.1   Review of Requirements

First, let us briefly analyze the basic characteristics of web image searching. Web search, as opposed to retrieval from specialized resources, is often used by people who do not know precisely what they are searching for. These users are looking for inspiration or some general information (i.e. "browsing") rather than performing a "targeted search" for a specific item [26,46]. User's preferences tend to become more focused during a search session, when the results that are found influence the user [98].

The implications of this behavior are two-fold. On one hand, user's uncertainty about the desired result relaxes the requirements for objective precision – the results need to be relevant, but not necessarily the most relevant items that exist for a query that in itself is often just an approximate expression of user's information need. On the other hand, there are strong requirements concerning search efficiency and flexibility. Efficiency is crucial for user's convenience, especially when a search session consists of more than one query-response cycle. As for flexibility, we have already debated that it is impossible to define a universally applicable model of similarity for a broad-domain searching. Even though current search engines provide only limited means of adjusting the retrieval semantics, the flexibility of searching is becoming one of the most important features that are required e.g. for personalized searching.

4.2   Task Specification

For the purpose of experimental evaluation, we define the large-scale image retrieval task as follows. We assume a k-nearest-neighbor search, where the user issues a multi-modal query and expects k relevant images. We only consider a single iteration of a query session. To keep the evaluation task feasible, we only employ the two most popular image search modalities – the textual similarity of image keywords, and the visual similarity of image content. We assume that each query consists of a visual example and one or several keywords. Such queries naturally appear in web searching – a user may e.g. employ a standard keyword-based retrieval to search for images, then select a suitable visual representant and continue searching with both modalities.

4.3   Selection of Eligible Techniques

Having established the desired characteristics of a successful web image retrieval technique, we can use them to filter out unsuitable approaches and select promising techniques for further examination. Due to the flexibility requirement, we can directly rule out most early fusion solutions and focus on the late fusion techniques, which are by design suited for flexible searching. As discussed in Sect. 3.2, late fusion is realized during query evaluation, which may be composed of multiple phases. In this paper, we limit our attention to the two central ones that are crucial for the overall effectiveness and efficiency: basic search and postprocessing. Basic search is inevitably a part of each retrieval solution, while postprocessing is the most frequent strategy of result refinement. Considering these two phases and the two possible approaches to modality combination (see Sect. 3.1), we obtain four basic search strategies depicted in Fig. 3: symmetric basic-search fusion realized by TA, asymmetric basic-search fusion that exploits some specialized index structure, symmetric postprocessing that approximates TA, and standard asymmetric postprocessing.

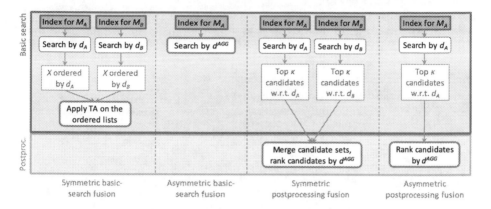

Fig. 3. Possible late fusion scenarios.

In most of the existing image search systems, the choice between these options was based on implementation convenience and rather vague assumptions about the efficiency and effectiveness of these methods. Even though some of these systems provide good results [44,89], the lack of rigorous performance evaluations makes it difficult to decide what factors participate in the success. Therefore, we decided to conduct a series of experiments that would allow us to quantify the performance of individual techniques and assess their usefulness.

5   Experimental Framework

To perform such a broad range of experiments and provide as fair comparison as possible, we have decided to implement all the retrieval methods using the same framework and run the experiments on the same hardware. In this section, we provide more information about the selected modalities that we have compared, the specific indexing techniques that have been utilized for efficient retrieval, and the parameters of the given techniques that have been examined.

5.1   Specification of Modalities

As stated earlier, a modality $\mathcal{M}$ is defined by a projection function $p_{\mathcal{M}}$ and a distance function $d_{\mathcal{M}}$. For the textual modality $\mathcal{M}^T$, we follow the traditional text retrieval paradigm – $p_{\mathcal{M}^T}$ extracts the keywords from a given multimodal object and performs standard normalization (stemming, stopword-filtering), $d_{\mathcal{M}^T}$ computes the cosine distance with *tf-idf* weighting [6]. The visual modality $\mathcal{M}^V$ can be represented by various types of global or local visual descriptors. Currently, global descriptors produced by deep convolutional neural networks (e.g. DeCAF [29]) represent state-of-the-art for visual similarity evaluation. However, at the time of our experiments the extraction of such descriptors for large data collections was prohibitively expensive. Therefore, we use the MPEG-7 [62] global descriptors in our experiments, which represent a reasonable compromise between retrieval quality and extraction costs. In particular, we employ a fixed combination of five MPEG-7 visual descriptors (Color Layout, Color Structure, Scalable Color, Edge Histogram, Homogeneous Texture) together with a distance function that is computed as a weighted sum of the partial distances evaluated by individual descriptors (for details, see [55]). The MPEG-7 descriptors are fused prior to data indexing (early fusion) and are regarded as a single visual descriptor in further discussions.

5.2   Implementation of the Fusion Methods

Most of the proposals of techniques for information retrieval are accompanied by experimental evaluations, therefore some implementation of the techniques can be acquired from their authors. However, the quality and reusability of the implemented prototypes vary greatly, the efficiency is heavily affected by the programming language that was employed, and the input and output data formats are usually specific to a given technique. On the other hand, in our complex experimental settings the most fair measure of efficiency is the wall-clock time. Therefore, we have decided to implement all the necessary techniques using our Java-based framework MESSIF [10], for which we already have several good implementations of state-of-the-art retrieval techniques.

For the visual similarity search, we have used the M-index [66] technique – a dynamic disk-based indexing approach that employs pivot-permutation approach along with various forms of metric dataspace pruning techniques to achieve online response times even on datasets with tens of million objects. For the text search, we have adopted the Lucene search engine [59] that was embedded in the MESSIF framework. Lucene provides fast text retrieval using classical tf-idf paradigm with several effectivity enhancements. Lucene is also able to provide online responses for tens of million indexed documents, which is our target dataset size.

In order to evaluate a multi-modal search, the aggregation function for combining the respective modalities must be provided. The modular design of the MESSIF library allows to plug in any user-specified function for the computation. In our case, we use a function that first normalizes the partial distances of each candidate object from a given modality and then uses a weighted sum to combine the partial distances. The influence of a given modality thus can be adjusted by providing weights for the summation. However, providing correct weights can be difficult for a user, therefore the weights can also be automatically learned on a sample collection for which a ground-truth is known.

Following from the analysis of large-scale image search task needs in Sect. 4, our comparison of multi-modal aggregation focuses on late fusion techniques. Specifically, we consider the symmetric basic-search fusion, asymmetric basic-search fusion, symmetric postprocessing fusion, and asymmetric postprocessing fusion. In case of asymmetric solutions, we consider that both $\mathcal{M}^T$ and $\mathcal{M}^V$ can be used as the primary modality. The following paragraphs detail the implementation of individual techniques:

Symmetric basic-search fusion. This fusion technique is implemented by the standard Threshold Algorithm [33]. The indexes $I_{\mathcal{M}^T}$ and $I_{\mathcal{M}^V}$ provide the sorted access for the TA input while the MESSIF storage module provides a fast random access for retrieving the missing features need for computing the multi-modal distance d^{AGG}. The storage serves the data from a disk using a B-tree index built for the object identifiers.

Asymmetric basic-search fusion. This approach is implemented by the *inherent fusion* technique [15], an approximate asymmetric late fusion method that computes the aggregated similarity of objects directly during the selection of the candidate set CS^{BS}. In particular, if the objects stored in a mono-modal index $I_{\mathcal{M}_1}$ contain feature descriptors for all other modalities (even though they are not used to build the index itself), the MESSIF library allows the user to alter the index searching procedure so that objects to be visited are identified by $d_{\mathcal{M}_1}$ but all visited objects are ranked directly by d^{AGG}. The number of objects to be visited is determined by the approximation parameter κ. Although no quality guarantees are given, this approach allows to compute the query distance function and the final candidate ranking efficiently for a large set of candidates identified by $d_{\mathcal{M}_1}$. In contrast to postprocessing asymmetric late fusion, the candidate identification and ranking can be run in parallel and thus much larger set of objects (typically by several orders of magnitude) can be visited within the same time limit.

Symmetric postprocessing fusion. The postprocessing symmetric late fusion utilizes two sets of candidate objects, $CS^{BS}_{\mathcal{M}^V}$ and $CS^{BS}_{\mathcal{M}^T}$, retrieved from separate mono-modal indexes $I_{\mathcal{M}^T}$ and $I_{\mathcal{M}^V}$. Both $CS^{BS}_{\mathcal{M}^V}$ and $CS^{BS}_{\mathcal{M}^T}$ contain $\kappa/2$ objects, so that κ objects altogether are visited in the postprocessing phase. The objects from both basic-search results are merged and the d^{AGG} is computed using the MESSIF random-access storage. The top k ranking objects are then reported. This is in fact an approximation of the TA algorithm, where the sorted accesses are not incremental but provided completely as bulks. Note that the threshold constraint might not be satisfied, since the inspection of the sorted access lists might not be deep enough. Therefore, the effectiveness might be lower but the execution is much faster.

Asymmetric postprocessing fusion. Finally, standard re-ranking is used to represent the asymmetric postprocessing fusion. The candidate set CS^{BS} of size κ is retrieved by one mono-modal index, and the candidates are ranked by the d^{AGG}.

In comparison with the inherent fusion, this approach computes the multi-modal ranking only after the whole result is returned by the primary index.

6   Evaluation Plan

The objective of the experimental study is to evaluate both the efficiency and effectiveness of selected image retrieval methods in uniform conditions. In particular, we are interested in the following aspects: (1) applicability of precise retrieval techniques in large-scale searching, (2) effect of approximation on user satisfaction, (3) selection of method(s) with the best relevance-cost trade-off, and (4) identification of factors that influence the retrieval quality. With these objectives, we have designed the experiments as follows.

6.1   Datasets, Queries and Ground Truth

Even though the need for common benchmarking platforms is well recognized, there are only few datasets that can be used for image search evaluation [26]. In our particular case, we need a large collection of image-and-text data, accompanied with a ground truth for general multi-modal retrieval. To the best of our knowledge, no such testbed is publicly available apart from the Profiset platform[1] that we have introduced recently to enable large-scale retrieval evaluations [16]. The Profiset collection contains 20M high-quality images provided by the Profimedia photostock site[2]. Each image is accompanied by a rich and mostly error-free keyword annotation in English. Furthermore, the Profiset provides a set of 100 test queries, each of which is composed of a single example image and a short keyword description. The topics comprise a selection of the most popular queries from Profimedia search logs and several queries that are known to be either easy or difficult to process in content-based searching. A few examples are shown in Fig. 4.

The Profiset platform does not provide a complete ground truth for the test queries, but offers tools for collecting a *partial ground truth*, i.e. relevance assessments for selected result objects. Our partial ground truth has been formed as follows: each result found by any tested method has been evaluated by at least two human judges, who have marked it as *highly relevant, partially relevant*, or *irrelevant* with respect to a given query. These categories have been transformed into relevance percentage (100%, 50%, and 0%, respectively) and averaged, thus forming the relevance value of the given result object. More details about the ground truth collection process can be found in [16].

Although the Profiset provides a suitable test environment, the evaluation results may be biased by the particular properties of this dataset. Therefore, we also employ a second testbed obtained from a different type of application. The CoPhIR test collection[3] contains images downloaded from the Flickr web gallery,

---

[1] http://disa.fi.muni.cz/profiset.
[2] http://www.profimedia.com.
[3] http://cophir.isti.cnr.it/.

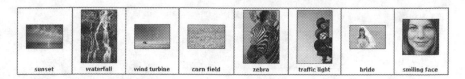

Fig. 4. Query objects.

accompanied by user-provided tags of unguaranteed quality. A 20M subset of the CoPhIR collection was randomly selected to make it comparable with the Profiset. The same set of test images and ground truth collection process have been used as with the Profiset testbed.

6.2   Performance and Quality Measures

For each experiment E, we measure the evaluation costs and the quality of the retrieved set of objects. Since all experiments are run in identical conditions, we can utilize wall-clock time as the measure of costs. Result quality is evaluated on both *distance-based* and *user-perceived* level (see Sect. 3.4). Let R_E be the result set returned in experiment E. The distance-based metric *relative error on distance at k (rED(k))* [99] compares R_E to a precise result R_{TA} provided by TA (as discussed in Sect. 3.2, it can be proved that TA finds the best k objects in terms of distance-based precision). Specifically, *rED(k)* compares the distances of objects at k-th position (d^k) in R_E and R_{TA}: $rED(k) = d^k_{R_E}/d^k_{R_{TA}} - 1$. The user-perceived quality is measured by the *Normalized discounted cumulative gain at k* $(NDCG(k))$, computed as a sum of user-provided relevance values of the k best objects from R_E normalized by their rank [42]. The $NDCG$ metric is applied in two modes: *natural NDCG* $(NDCG_N)$ is computed using multi-valued relevance assessments provided by users, whereas for *strict NDCG* $(NDCG_S)$ the relevance assessments are transformed into binary values so that only the results denoted as *highly relevant* are considered relevant. $NDCG_S$ thus represents a more demanding user.

To guarantee maximum fairness, all experiments were run on the same single machine with 8 CPU cores and 32 GB RAM. In order to assess the scalability, some of the experiments were restricted to a single CPU.

6.3   Retrieval Parameters Settings

The parameters of the specific techniques, as described in Sect. 5.2, are summarized in Table 2. Mono-modal text search and content-based search constitute the baselines. For the approximate techniques, different values of the approximation parameter κ were tested. We should also notice that for asymmetric fusion with text as the primary modality, inherent fusion was not applied. The reason is that text-based retrieval is very efficient, thus re-ranking with $\kappa = 30000$ can be used to perform text-based fusion comparable (in terms of approximation strategy) to visual-based inherent fusion.

Table 2. Overview of tested methods.

Method name	Fusion type	Approx. parameter κ	Abbreviation
Text search			Text
Content-based search			Visual
Threshold Algorithm	Symmetric, basis-search		TA
Approximate TA	Symmetric, postprocessing	100, 500, 2000, 30000	TA100, TA500, TA2K, TA30K
Visual-based inherent fusion	Asymmetric, basic-search	30000, 100000	VIF30K, VIF100K
Visual search with re-ranking	Asymmetric, postprocessing	100, 500, 2000	VR100, VR500, VR2K
Text search with re-ranking	Asymmetric, postprocessing	100, 500, 2000, 30000	TR100, TR500, TR2K, TR30K

As discussed earlier, a crucial requirement for wide-domain searching is fusion flexibility, which is supported by all the above-listed methods. However, to avoid unnecessary confusion we only consider a single d^{AGG} in the experiments. A fixed weighted sum of the text- and visual-induced distances is used, the respective weights being chosen in a separate set of experiments so that average result quality is maximized.

7　Evaluation Results

As stated earlier, one of the main objectives of the experimental evaluation is to compare the precision and costs of various approaches to multi-modal image retrieval, and to select the most suitable solution for large-scale image searching. Accordingly, the global effectiveness and efficiency of individual methods and the trade-off between these two characteristics are analyzed in the first part of this section. Afterwards, we present an additional analysis of the collected data that examines several factors specific for combining text and visual modalities of images.

7.1　Effectiveness and Efficiency: Overall Trends

An overall evaluation of experimental results in terms of both retrieval costs and result relevance is provided in Fig. 5. In the following subsections, we examine individual graphs to answer the questions formulated in Sect. 6.

Applicability of precise retrieval. The costs graph in Fig. 5a clearly shows that precise late fusion, depicted in the rightmost bar, is not applicable in interactive large-scale searching. The response times are extremely high for TA, which is the only precise late fusion solution suitable for text and visual modalities that allows

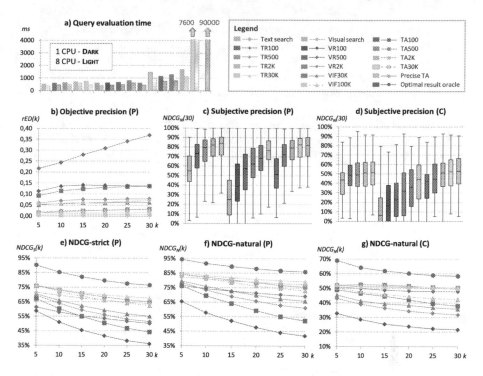

Fig. 5. Retrieval costs and precision for different search methods. (*Note that the graphs are color-coded.*)

flexible query evaluation. The TA costs depend on the number of objects that need to be accessed, for which there is no theoretical bound. Our experiments have confirmed that for real data, such as ours, the number of visited objects is indeed very high.

Influence of approximation. Since precise evaluation is too costly, an approximation is a vital concept to apply for interactive retrieval. Fortunately, we have been able to verify the generally accepted assumption that a certain level of distance-based imprecision does not result in any noticeable deterioration of result quality as perceived by users, which is illustrated by Figs. 5b–g. However, it is important to select the approximation parameters appropriately.

Individual graphs in Fig. 5 depict different aggregated metrics of result relevance measured over Profiset (P) and CoPhIR (C) collections. Figure 5b shows the objective result precision measured by rED, other graphs display the $NDCG$ metric of users' satisfaction. Quartile distribution of $NDCG$ for $kNN(30)$ query is shown in Figs. 5c–d, which provide comparison of effectiveness for all tested methods. Figures 5e–g illustrate the development of average result relevance for various result sizes, using only a selection of methods to maintain readability. We can observe that there is an almost perfect agreement in the ordering of methods by rED and $NDCG$, with a single notable exception of text-based asymmetric fusion with a very rough approximation. This method provides poor results in terms of rED, but is considered rather good by users. This phenomenon is probably caused by users' preference for semantic relevance, which will be discussed more thoroughly later.

Considering the approximations, we can observe that for small candidate set size κ the quality of results is considerably worse than that of TA, especially when visual modality is used as the primary one. However, with sufficiently large κ the approximate techniques are comparable to or even slightly better than TA in terms of user satisfaction. The observed dependence between the result quality and candidate set size is roughly logarithmic. The largest improvements can be seen for visual-based asymmetric fusion where the trends suggest that even better results could be achieved if κ was higher. For text-based and symmetric fusion it seems that the optimum κ has been reached.

From the efficiency point of view, there are no large differences between the costs of asymmetric text-based and visual-based methods with the same κ, whereas the TA-based solutions are considerably more expensive. This is caused by the need to access two independent index structures which are not optimized for mutual cooperation. Subsequently, we do not consider symmetric fusion to be applicable for κ larger than a few thousand objects. On the other hand, both asymmetric variants are capable of processing 30000 candidate objects in about 0.5 s on moderately strong hardware, which we consider to be perfectly acceptable.

Optimal method selection. The relevance results reveal that general trends of fusion effectiveness are very similar for both tested collections. All approximate late fusion techniques under consideration – text-based asymmetric fusion, visual-based asymmetric fusion, and approximate TA – are capable of achieving comparable result quality. However, the text-based asymmetric fusion slightly outperforms the other approaches in all quality measures, and requires less processing time to achieve a given level of relevance. This clearly makes it the most eligible method for both our datasets. Approximate TA comes as a close second in terms of result quality at any fixed approximation level, but its costs are prohibitive for the more precise variants. Visual-based approaches need to examine significantly more objects to achieve the same level of relevance, which is partly balanced by efficient inherent fusion implementation (Fig. 5a).

The success of text-based methods is not surprising for the Profiset collection, which contains high-quality image annotations. We have also expected the text-based fusion to be less effective for the CoPhIR dataset than for Profimedia, as the quality of textual information in CoPhIR is significantly lower. However, we have assumed that the other approaches would be less influenced by the change of datasets. The absolute relevance values for text-based fusion are indeed about 30% lower as compared to the Profiset, but the same applies for all results and the ordering of methods with respect to retrieval precision remains unchanged. Currently, we see at least three possible causes of such behavior: (1) human perception of relevance is more semantically-oriented than visually-oriented, therefore a text search result not visually similar to the query is more likely to be regarded relevant than vice versa (this corresponds to the observation made about the disproportion in rED and $NDCG$ relevance evaluations); (2) visual content descriptors and distance measures that were applied are not mature enough to capture the features important for users; and (3) the CoPhIR collection exhibits worse quality than the Profiset not only in the textual component but also in the quality of photos – in terms both of technical aspects (blur or other types of imaging noise) and relevance of content (many of the CoPhIR photos are difficult to interpret, do not attract the user, etc.). We believe that the observed results are influenced by all these factors, however a more detailed model than ours would be needed to determine their roles more precisely.

The fact that semantics is very important to users can also be observed in the difference between the evaluations by strict and natural $NDCG$. The ranking of methods by $NDCG_N$ is slightly different that ranking by $NDCG_S$. In particular, the highly approximate solution $TR100$ ranks higher by $NDCG_N$ than by $NDCG_S$, which supports our hypothesis that users appreciate semantic relevance even if the visual component is not sufficiently close to the query.

7.2   Uncovering Deeper Roots of Relevance

Even though the general findings in the previous section appoint the text-based asymmetric fusion as the most suitable search method, this approach is not optimal for all queries. In fact, about 40% of queries would be better answered by a different method for Profiset and 50% for CoPhIR. The red line denoted as "optimal result oracle" in Figs. 5e–g shows the relevance level that could be achieved if the optimal method was chosen for each individual query. Unfortunately, it is very difficult to decide which fusion technique is the most suitable one for a given query. Our data shows that the effectiveness of methods differs from query to query, and often even for the same query when evaluated over two different datasets. To gain more insight into the behavior of multimedia retrieval, we study the experimental results from several less traditional perspectives.

Semantic categories. The first aspect we examine are the query topics. In our experience, simple content-based retrieval works well on concepts like "sunset", "clouds", and other natural scenes, therefore we assume that some correlations could exist between the query topic and the effectiveness of individual fusion techniques (e.g. visual-based asymmetric fusion is expected to work well for pictures of nature, text-based for activities). Therefore, we have defined several categories that comprise popular search topics, and sorted our query objects into them. The less typical queries which do not fit into any category are not considered now.

In Fig. 6, we can see the effectiveness of selected methods for individual categories. The results do not show the expected relationships between categories and fusion behavior – although "nature" queries seem to be more visually-oriented than others in Profiset, this is not confirmed by CoPhIR. We conclude that semantic categories alone cannot be used to decide which fusion method to apply.

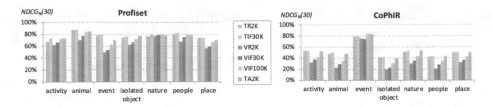

Fig. 6. Result relevance in different categories.

However, sorting the queries into categories has revealed other interesting details. Queries from the "event" category are better answered in CoPhIR than in Profiset, which contradicts the general observations presented in Sect. 7.1. We hypothesize that the observed phenomenon is caused by a higher occurrence of event-related images in CoPhIR, which was obtained from a photo-sharing site that is likely to contain such photos. The data indicate that the popularity of a given topic in the target database plays an important role for both the overall result quality and the applicability of individual search methods – whereas text-based search is clearly dominant for event queries in Profiset, visual-based fusion provides better results in CoPhIR.

Text-based relevance. As shown in Sect. 7.1, methods that rely primarily on the text retrieval outperform the visual-based ones in a general case. To better understand the cases when the text modality misses relevant objects that the visual one is able to provide, we study the influence of the density of text descriptions on the retrieval effectiveness.

We have divided all query objects evenly into 4 groups based on the selectivity of the query text. Figure 7 shows the effectiveness of the selected methods in both the Profiset and CoPhIR collections, expressing the selectivity on x-axis by the total number of results possibly matching the query text. Note that the CoPhIR collection has only about a tenth of potential results as compared to the Profiset, which is caused by sparser annotations of the CoPhIR images. We can observe that for queries with more discriminative text (lower number of potential results) the text retrieval is distinctly more successful than methods that use primarily the visual search. However, for broader-term queries the visual similarity is becom-

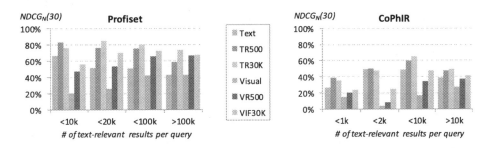

Fig. 7. Effectiveness versus text selectivity.

Table 3. Retrieval of objects without text.

Method name	# of no-text results	# of relevant
Visual	136	27
VR500	98	12
VIF30K	25	3
TA	1	0
TA500	63	7
TA30K	4	0

ing more important, e.g. for the group of queries with the lowest text selectivity – matching from 100,000 to 1.3 million objects – the visual-based asymmetric methods provide the same quality of results as text-based.

Next, we focus on the case where the text modality is not present in the target objects, thus the potentially relevant objects cannot be found by text search. This is only observable in the CoPhIR dataset where 28% of objects contains only an automatic file name or no text at all. In the well-annotated Profiset collection, there are no images without text. Table 3 provides the numbers of results with no textual information returned by a respective method along with a number of those results that were considered (highly) relevant by users. Note that methods based on text search are not included since they cannot find such objects. We can observe that most no-text objects are retrieved by the visual-only method followed by the visual search with text re-ranking. As expected, the number of results without text decreases for larger candidate sets, since the no-text objects are penalized by text-ranking. Interestingly, the visual-based methods are able to find relevant text-free results in about two thirds of the evaluated queries, and these results represents up to 6% of the total returned relevant results.

Visual-based relevance. Having analyzed the strengths and weaknesses of the text modality, let us now focus on the visual. Visual modality is inherently more problematic than text because of the semantic gap problem, and the fact that there is no strict differentiation between potentially relevant and irrelevant objects. However, these problems get reduced as the search space becomes denser. The improvement of visual search results with growing dataset size has been empirically observed in [8]. Google uses near-duplicate search for image annotation [91], which proves that in the web-scale searching the space is already dense enough. Since our previous analysis shows that text-based searching is reaching its limits for discriminating relevant objects in dense collections, we believe visual-based (or eventually also TA-based) solutions are better suited for such situations.

Although the density of our datasets is not high enough for the described phenomenon to apply, we can see some indications in Fig. 8 that the distribution of objects in the search space is important. The average relevance of results obtained by approaches based on visual search reaches its maximum for queries that have low average distances of result sets, which corresponds to a higher density of the search space in the neighborhood of the respective query.

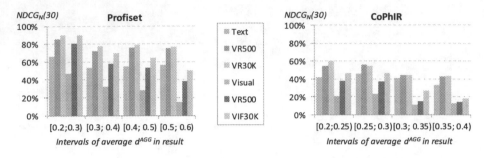

Fig. 8. Result relevance in relation to distance.

8 Summary and Discussion

The presented study is devoted to both theoretical and practical aspects of multi-modal retrieval. In the first part, we have laid formal foundations for a systematic study of fusion techniques, and presented a new, comprehensive categorization of existing solutions. In the second part, we have focused on interactive large-scale image retrieval with text and visual modalities. In this context, we have compared two mono-modal search methods and four multi-modal late fusion techniques with different settings. The evaluation has been performed on two real-world datasets that are orders of magnitude larger than data usually employed in fusion evaluations. In particular, user-perceived relevance of more than 170,000 query-result pairs has been manually evaluated. This data allows us to study various aspects of image retrieval, including effectivenes, efficiency, and scalability. Let us now summarize the most important findings.

Our first conclusion concerns the applicability of individual late fusion solutions in large-scale multi-modal searching. We have found that precise flexible fusion is extremely costly on real-world data, while results of the same user-perceived quality can be obtained by efficient approximate solutions. Approximate solutions are thus more suitable. To maximize the chance of obtaining high-quality results, the approximation parameter κ should be chosen as high as efficiency limits allow. The observed dependence between the result quality and the candidate set size is roughly logarithmic.

For text-and-visual datasets of size and quality comparable to ours, text-based asymmetric fusion is very likely to provide optimal results in the majority of cases. Text-based searching is very strong, since it expresses semantics, it is also highly discriminative (there is a clear distinction between relevant and not-relevant objects), and the text searching is fast. Moreover, our experimental data shows that users tend to be satisfied with semantically relevant results even if the visual component is not sufficiently close to the query. If the quality of text information in a given collection is known to be low, symmetric late fusion stands as the most suitable solution, as it can best balance the strengths and weaknesses of both the modalities. However, the approximation then needs to be more rough because the processing costs are higher.

The data from our experimental evaluation also allowed us to study the suitability of individual fusion methods for different queries. While the text-based asymmetric fusion performed best on average on our data, it was far from being optimal for all queries. For nearly half of the queries, the result quality would be better if a different fusion method was chosen. A typical example are queries for which there are too few or too many text-relevant results, which would be better answered by visual-based asymmetric fusion. Our analysis discovered that the suitability of any given method is determined by both the specific query and the dataset properties. In particular, we studied the following aspects:

– Semantic categories: Classifying queries into semantic categories such as *nature*, *object*, etc. is alone not sufficient to decide which fusion method to apply. However, our data suggest that the popularity of a given topic within the dataset could be used to assess the suitability of fusion methods. In particular, the more popular topics tend to form dense subspaces that can be better searched by visual-based asymmetric fusion.
– Query text selectivity: As mentioned earlier, the text similarity is a highly effective tool for identifying candidate objects as long as the number of text-relevant objects is not too high or too small. In case of broad-term queries with many relevant results the text prefiltering may not select the best candidate set. On the other extreme, objects without text descriptions cannot be found by text-based methods.
– Visual selectivity: We have discovered that visual-based fusion methods are most suitable for queries that have low average distances between objects in the result sets, which corresponds to a higher density of the search space in the neighborhood of the respective query.

These observations could be used in future to improve the quality of multi-modal searching by dynamically choosing an optimal fusion method for a given query and dataset. The decision process would be based on statistics about the dataset and the properties of a given query. There is an intuitive parallel between such fusion optimization process and the query optimization performed by standard relational databases systems – in both cases, data statistics is used to estimate the best approach for query processing. However, the RDBS optimization aims at reducing the evaluation costs, whereas in fusion optimization we are mainly concerned with result quality. Based on the above-listed observations, we propose to utilize the following information as an input for the fusion optimization:

– Statistics of semantic categories: Using a suitable ontology of query topics and state-of-the-art classification methods, the dataset can be preprocessed so that individual objects are sorted into (possibly overlapping) semantic categories. On top of these, different statistics can be collected, including the category size, its visual density, and the number of no-text objects.
– Statistics of query text selectivity: Information about the selectivity of frequent text queries can be collected in advance or gradually at runtime.

To the best of our knowledge, the fusion optimization has not been considered before. It offers several new problems that can be studied in future, e.g. proposing algorithms for optimal fusion strategy selection, collecting and maintaining the statistics, or further data analysis to determine additional useful data properties.

Acknowledgments. This work was supported by the Czech national research project GA16-18889S. Computational resources were provided by the CESNET LM2015042 and the CERIT Scientific Cloud LM2015085.

References

1. Abu-Shareha, A.A., Mandava, R., Khan, L., Ramachandram, D.: Multimodal concept fusion using semantic closeness for image concept disambiguation. Multimedia Tools Appl. **61**(1), 69–86 (2011). doi:10.1007/s11042-010-0707-8
2. Ah-Pine, J., Csurka, G., Clinchant, S.: Unsupervised visual and textual information fusion in CBMIR using graph-based methods. ACM Trans. Inform. Syst. **33**(2), 9:1–9:31 (2015). doi:10.1145/2699668
3. Andrade, F.S.P., Almeida, J., Pedrini, H., S.Torres, R.: Fusion of local and global descriptors for content-based image and video retrieval. In: Alvarez, L., Mejail, M., Gomez, L., Jacobo, J. (eds.) CIARP 2012. LNCS, vol. 7441, pp. 845–853. Springer, Heidelberg (2012). doi:10.1007/978-3-642-33275-3_104
4. Arampatzis, A., Zagoris, K., Chatzichristofis, S.A.: Dynamic two-stage image retrieval from large multimodal databases. In: Clough, P., Foley, C., Gurrin, C., Jones, G.J.F., Kraaij, W., Lee, H., Mudoch, V. (eds.) ECIR 2011. LNCS, vol. 6611, pp. 326–337. Springer, Heidelberg (2011). doi:10.1007/978-3-642-20161-5_33
5. Atrey, P.K., Hossain, M.A., El-Saddik, A., Kankanhalli, M.S.: Multimodal fusion for multimedia analysis: a survey. Multimedia Syst. **16**(6), 345–379 (2010). doi:10.1007/s00530-010-0182-0
6. Baeza-Yates, R.A., Ribeiro-Neto, B.A.: Modern Information Retrieval - The Concepts and Technology Behind Search, 2nd edn. Pearson Education Ltd., Harlow (2011)
7. Barrios, J.M., Bustos, B.: Automatic weight selection for multi-metric distances. In: Proceedings of the 4th International Conference on Similarity Search and Applications (SISAP 2011), pp. 61–68 (2011). doi:10.1145/1995412.1995425
8. Batko, M., Falchi, F., Lucchese, C., Novak, D., Perego, R., Rabitti, F., Sedmidubsky, J., Zezula, P.: Building a web-scale image similarity search system. Multimedia Tools Appl. **47**(3), 599–629 (2010). doi:10.1007/s11042-009-0339-z
9. Batko, M., Kohoutkova, P., Zezula, P.: Combining metric features in large collections. In: 24th International Conference on Data Engineering Workshops (ICDE 2008), pp. 370–377 (2008). doi:10.1109/ICDEW.2008.4498347
10. Batko, M., Novak, D., Zezula, P.: MESSIF: metric similarity search implementation framework. In: Thanos, C., Borri, F., Candela, L. (eds.) DELOS 2007. LNCS, vol. 4877, pp. 1–10. Springer, Heidelberg (2007). doi:10.1007/978-3-540-77088-6_1
11. Benavent, X., Garcia-Serrano, A., Granados, R., Benavent, J., de Ves, E.: Multimedia information retrieval based on late semantic fusion approaches: experiments on a wikipedia image collection. IEEE Trans. Multimedia **15**(8), 2009–2021 (2013). doi:10.1109/TMM.2013.2267726
12. Blanken, H., de Vries, A., Blok, H., Feng, L.: Multimedia Retrieval. Data-Centric Systems and Applications. Springer, Secaucus (2007)

13. Bossé, É., Roy, J., Wark, S.: Concepts, Models, and Tools for Information Fusion. Artech House, Inc., Norwood (2007)
14. Bozzon, A., Fraternali, P.: Chapter 8: multimedia and multimodal information retrieval. In: Ceri, S., Brambilla, M. (eds.) Search Computing. LNCS, vol. 5950, pp. 135–155. Springer, Heidelberg (2010). doi:10.1007/978-3-642-12310-8_8
15. Budikova, P., Batko, M., Novak, D., Zezula, P.: Inherent fusion: towards scalable multi-modal similarity search. J. Database Manag. **27**(4), 1–23 (2016). doi:10.4018/JDM.2016100101
16. Budikova, P., Batko, M., Zezula, P.: Evaluation platform for content-based image retrieval systems. In: Gradmann, S., Borri, F., Meghini, C., Schuldt, H. (eds.) TPDL 2011. LNCS, vol. 6966, pp. 130–142. Springer, Heidelberg (2011). doi:10.1007/978-3-642-24469-8_15
17. Budikova, P., Batko, M., Zezula, P.: Similarity query postprocessing by ranking. In: Detyniecki, M., Knees, P., Nürnberger, A., Schedl, M., Stober, S. (eds.) AMR 2010. LNCS, vol. 6817, pp. 159–173. Springer, Heidelberg (2012). doi:10.1007/978-3-642-27169-4_12
18. Bustos, B., Kreft, S., Skopal, T.: Adapting metric indexes for searching in multi-metric spaces. Multimedia Tools Appl. **58**(3), 467–496 (2012). doi:10.1007/s11042-011-0731-3
19. Carpineto, C., Romano, G.: A survey of automatic query expansion in information retrieval. ACM Comput. Surv. **44**(1), 1:1–1:50 (2012). doi:10.1145/2071389.2071390
20. Chatzichristofis, S.A., Zagoris, K., Boutalis, Y., Arampatzis, A.: A fuzzy rank-based late fusion method for image retrieval. In: Schoeffmann, K., Merialdo, B., Hauptmann, A.G., Ngo, C.-W., Andreopoulos, Y., Breiteneder, C. (eds.) MMM 2012. LNCS, vol. 7131, pp. 463–472. Springer, Heidelberg (2012). doi:10.1007/978-3-642-27355-1_43
21. Chen, L., Cong, G., Jensen, C.S., Wu, D.: Spatial keyword query processing: an experimental evaluation. In: The Proceedings of the VLDB Endowment (PVLDB), pp. 217–228 (2013). doi:10.14778/2535569.2448955
22. Chen, Y., Yu, N., Luo, B., wen Chen, X.: iLike: integrating visual and textual features for vertical search. In: 18th International Conference on Multimedia (ACM Multimedia 2010), pp. 221–230 (2010). doi:10.1145/1873951.1873984
23. Ciaccia, P., Patella, M.: Searching in metric spaces with user-defined and approximate distances. ACM Trans. Database Syst. **27**(4), 398–437 (2002). doi:10.1145/582410.582412
24. Clinchant, S., Ah-Pine, J., Csurka, G.: Semantic combination of textual and visual information in multimedia retrieval. In: Proceedings of the 1st International Conference on Multimedia Retrieval (ICMR 2011), p. 44 (2011). doi:10.1145/1991996.1992040
25. Cong, G., Jensen, C.S., Wu, D.: Efficient retrieval of the top-k most relevant spatial web objects. Proc. VLDB Endowment (PVLDB) **2**(1), 337–348 (2009). doi:10.14778/1687627.1687666
26. Datta, R., Joshi, D., Li, J., Wang, J.Z.: Image retrieval: Ideas, influences, and trends of the new age. ACM Comput. Surv. **40**(2), 5:1–5:60 (2008). doi:10.1145/1348246.1348248
27. Deng, J., Dong, W., Socher, R., Li, L.J., Li, K., Li, F.F.: ImageNet: a large-scale hierarchical image database. In: IEEE Computer Society Conference on Computer Vision and Pattern Recognition (CVPR 2009), pp. 248–255 (2009). doi:10.1109/CVPRW.2009.5206848

28. Depeursinge, A., Müller, H.: Fusion techniques for combining textual and visual information retrieval. In: ImageCLEF. The Kluwer International Series on Information Retrieval, vol. 32, pp. 95–114. Springer, Heidelberg (2010). doi:10.1007/978-3-642-15181-1_6

29. Donahue, J., Jia, Y., Vinyals, O., Hoffman, J., Zhang, N., Tzeng, E., Darrell, T.: Decaf: a deep convolutional activation feature for generic visual recognition. In: Proceedings of the 31st International Conference on Machine Learning (ICML 2014), pp. 647–655 (2014). http://jmlr.org/proceedings/papers/v32/donahue14.html

30. Dong, Y., Gao, S., Tao, K., Liu, J., Wang, H.: Performance evaluation of early and late fusion methods for generic semantics indexing. Pattern Anal. Appl. **17**(1), 37–50 (2013). doi:10.1007/s10044-013-0336-8

31. Eickhoff, C., Li, W., Vries, A.P.: Exploiting user comments for audio-visual content indexing and retrieval. In: Serdyukov, P., Braslavski, P., Kuznetsov, S.O., Kamps, J., Rüger, S., Agichtein, E., Segalovich, I., Yilmaz, E. (eds.) ECIR 2013. LNCS, vol. 7814, pp. 38–49. Springer, Heidelberg (2013). doi:10.1007/978-3-642-36973-5_4

32. Escalante, H.J., Montes, M., Sucar, L.E.: Multimodal indexing based on semantic cohesion for image retrieval. Inform. Retrieval **15**(1), 1–32 (2012). doi:10.1007/s10791-011-9170-z

33. Fagin, R.: Combining fuzzy information: an overview. SIGMOD Rec. **31**(2), 109–118 (2002). doi:10.1145/565117.565143

34. Fellbaum, C. (ed.): WordNet: An Electronic Lexical Database. The MIT Press, Cambridge (1998)

35. Fu, Z., Lu, G., Ting, K.M., Zhang, D.: A survey of audio-based music classification and annotation. IEEE Trans. Multimedia **13**(2), 303–319 (2011). doi:10.1109/TMM.2010.2098858

36. Ha, H., Yang, Y., Fleites, F., Chen, S.: Correlation-based feature analysis and multi-modality fusion framework for multimedia semantic retrieval. In: Proceedings of the 2013 IEEE International Conference on Multimedia and Expo (ICME 2013), pp. 1–6 (2013). doi:10.1109/ICME.2013.6607639

37. Hemayati, R., Meng, W., Yu, C.: Semantic-based grouping of search engine results using wordnet. In: Dong, G., Lin, X., Wang, W., Yang, Y., Yu, J.X. (eds.) APWeb/WAIM -2007. LNCS, vol. 4505, pp. 678–686. Springer, Heidelberg (2007). doi:10.1007/978-3-540-72524-4_70

38. Hoque, E., Strong, G., Hoeber, O., Gong, M.: Conceptual query expansion and visual search results exploration for web image retrieval. In: 7th Atlantic Web Intelligence Conference (AWIC 2011), pp. 73–82 (2011). doi:10.1007/978-3-642-18029-3_8

39. Hörster, E., Slaney, M., Ranzato, M., Weinberger, K.: Unsupervised image ranking. In: 1st ACM Workshop on Large-Scale Multimedia Retrieval and Mining (LS-MMRM 2009), pp. 81–88 (2009). doi:10.1145/1631058.1631074

40. Hsu, W.H., Kennedy, L.S., Chang, S.F.: Reranking methods for visual search. IEEE Multimedia **14**(3), 14–22 (2007). doi:10.1109/MMUL.2007.61

41. Jain, R., Sinha, P.: Content without context is meaningless. In: International Conference on Multimedia (ACM Multimedia 2010), pp. 1259–1268. ACM (2010). doi:10.1145/1873951.1874199

42. Järvelin, K., Kekäläinen, J.: Cumulated gain-based evaluation of IR techniques. ACM Trans. Inform. Syst. **20**(4), 422–446 (2002). doi:10.1145/582415.582418

43. Jegou, H., Schmid, C., Harzallah, H., Verbeek, J.J.: Accurate image search using the contextual dissimilarity measure. IEEE Trans. Pattern Anal. Mach. Intell. **32**(1), 2–11 (2010). doi:10.1109/TPAMI.2008.285

44. Jing, Y., Baluja, S.: VisualRank: applying PageRank to large-scale image search. IEEE Trans. Pattern Anal. Mach. Intell. **30**(11), 1877–1890 (2008). doi:10.1109/TPAMI.2008.121

45. Khasanova, R., Dong, X., Frossard, P.: Multi-modal image retrieval with random walk on multi-layer graphs. In: IEEE International Symposium on Multimedia (ISM 2016), pp. 1–6 (2016). doi:10.1109/ISM.2016.0011

46. Kherfi, M.L., Ziou, D., Bernardi, A.: Image retrieval from the World Wide Web: Issues, techniques, and systems. ACM Comput. Surv. **36**(1), 35–67 (2004). doi:10.1145/1013208.1013210

47. Kludas, J., Bruno, E., Marchand-Maillet, S.: Information fusion in multimedia information retrieval. In: Boujemaa, N., Detyniecki, M., Nürnberger, A. (eds.) AMR 2007. LNCS, vol. 4918, pp. 147–159. Springer, Heidelberg (2008). doi:10.1007/978-3-540-79860-6_12

48. Krizhevsky, A., Sutskever, I., Hinton, G.E.: ImageNet classification with deep convolutional neural networks. In: 26th Annual Conference on Neural Information Processing Systems (NIPS 2012), pp. 1106–1114 (2012). http://papers.nips.cc/paper/4824-imagenet-classification-with-deep-convolutional-neural-networks

49. Lai, K., Liu, D., Chang, S., Chen, M.: Learning sample specific weights for late fusion. IEEE Trans. Image Process. **24**(9), 2772–2783 (2015). doi:10.1109/TIP.2015.2423560

50. Lan, Z., Bao, L., Yu, S.-I., Liu, W., Hauptmann, A.G.: Double fusion for multimedia event detection. In: Schoeffmann, K., Merialdo, B., Hauptmann, A.G., Ngo, C.-W., Andreopoulos, Y., Breiteneder, C. (eds.) MMM 2012. LNCS, vol. 7131, pp. 173–185. Springer, Heidelberg (2012). doi:10.1007/978-3-642-27355-1_18

51. Lew, M.S., Sebe, N., Djeraba, C., Jain, R.: Content-based multimedia information retrieval: State of the art and challenges. TOMCCAP **2**(1), 1–19 (2006). doi:10.1145/1126004.1126005

52. Li, J.: Reachability based ranking in interactive image retrieval. In: Proceedings of the 38th International ACM SIGIR Conference on Research and Development in Information Retrieval (SIGIR 2015), pp. 867–870 (2015). doi:10.1145/2766462.2767777

53. Li, J., Ma, Q., Asano, Y., Yoshikawa, M.: Re-ranking by multi-modal relevance feedback for content-based social image retrieval. In: Sheng, Q.Z., Wang, G., Jensen, C.S., Xu, G. (eds.) APWeb 2012. LNCS, vol. 7235, pp. 399–410. Springer, Heidelberg (2012). doi:10.1007/978-3-642-29253-8_34

54. Liu, Y., Mei, T., Hua, X.S.: CrowdReranking: exploring multiple search engines for visual search reranking. In: 32nd Annual International ACM SIGIR Conference on Research and Development in Information Retrieval (SIGIR 2009), pp. 500–507 (2009). doi:10.1145/1571941.1572027

55. Lokoč, J., Novák, D., Batko, M., Skopal, T.: Visual image search: feature signatures or/and global descriptors. In: Navarro, G., Pestov, V. (eds.) SISAP 2012. LNCS, vol. 7404, pp. 177–191. Springer, Heidelberg (2012). doi:10.1007/978-3-642-32153-5_13

56. Ma, D., Yu, Z.: New video target tracking algorithm based on KNN. J. Multimedia **9**(5), 709–714 (2014). doi:10.4304/jmm.9.5.709-714

57. Magalhães, J., Rüger, S.: An information-theoretic framework for semantic-multimedia retrieval. ACM Trans. Inform. Syst. 28(4), 1–32 (2010). doi:10.1145/1852102.1852105

58. May, W., Fidler, S., Fazly, A.: Unsupervised disambiguation of image captions. In: Proceedings of the First Joint Conference on Lexical and Computational Semantics (SemEval 2012), pp. 85–89, June 2012. http://dl.acm.org/citation.cfm?id=2387636.2387652

59. McCandless, M., Hatcher, E., Gospodnetić, O.: Lucene in Action: Covers Apache Lucene V. 3. 0. Manning Pubs Co Series, Manning (2010)

60. Mei, T., Rui, Y., Li, S., Tian, Q.: Multimedia search reranking. ACM Comput. Surv. **46**(3), 1–38 (2014). doi:10.1145/2536798

61. Mironica, I., Ionescu, B., Vertan, C.: Hierarchical clustering relevance feedback for content-based image retrieval. In: 10th International Workshop on Content-Based Multimedia Indexing (CBMI 2012), pp. 1–6 (2012). doi:10.1109/CBMI.2012.6269811

62. MPEG-7: Multimedia content description interfaces. Part 3: Visual. ISO/IEC 15938–3:2002 (2002)

63. Müller, H., Clough, P., Deselaers, T., Caputo, B.: ImageCLEF: Experimental Evaluation in Visual Information Retrieval, 1st edn. Springer, Heidelberg (2010)

64. Nga, D.H., Yanai, K.: VisualTextualRank: an extension of VisualRank to large-scale video shot extraction exploiting tag co-occurrence. IEICE Trans. Inform. Syst. **98-D**(1), 166–172 (2015). http://search.ieice.org/bin/summary.php?id=e98-d_1_166

65. Novák, D.: Multi-modal similarity retrieval with distributed key-value store. Mob. Networks Appl. **20**(4), 521–532 (2015). doi:10.1007/s11036-014-0561-4

66. Novák, D., Batko, M., Zezula, P.: Metric index: an efficient and scalable solution for precise and approximate similarity search. Inform. Syst. **36**(4), 721–733 (2011). doi:10.1016/j.is.2010.10.002

67. Oh, S., McCloskey, S., Kim, I., Vahdat, A., Cannons, K.J., Hajimirsadeghi, H., Mori, G., Perera, A.G.A., Pandey, M., Corso, J.J.: Multimedia event detection with multimodal feature fusion and temporal concept localization. Mach. Vis. Appl. **25**(1), 49–69 (2013). doi:10.1007/s00138-013-0525-x

68. Park, G., Baek, Y., Lee, H.K.: Web image retrieval using majority-based ranking approach. Multimedia Tools Appl. **31**(2), 195–219 (2006). doi:10.1007/s11042-006-0039-x

69. Patella, M., Ciaccia, P.: Approximate similarity search: a multi-faceted problem. J. Discrete Algorithms **7**(1), 36–48 (2009). doi:10.1016/j.jda.2008.09.014

70. Pedronette, D.C.G., da Silva Torres, R.: Combining re-ranking and rank aggregation methods for image retrieval. Multimedia Tools Appl. **75**(15), 9121–9144 (2016). doi:10.1007/s11042-015-3044-0

71. Pham, T.T., Maillot, N., Lim, J.H., Chevallet, J.P.: Latent semantic fusion model for image retrieval and annotation. In: Sixteenth ACM Conference on Information and Knowledge Management (CIKM 2007), pp. 439–444 (2007). doi:10.1145/1321440.1321503

72. Pulla, C., Jawahar, C.V.: Multi modal semantic indexing for image retrieval. In: 9th ACM International Conference on Image and Video Retrieval (CIVR 2010), pp. 342–349 (2010). doi:10.1145/1816041.1816091

73. Qi, S., Wang, F., Wang, X., Guan, Y., Wei, J., Guan, J.: Multiple level visual semantic fusion method for image re-ranking. Multimedia Syst. **23**(1), 155–167 (2017). doi:10.1007/s00530-014-0448-z

74. Richter, F., Romberg, S., Hörster, E., Lienhart, R.: Multimodal ranking for image search on community databases. In: Proceedings of the International Conference on Multimedia Information Retrieval (MIR 2010), pp. 63–72 (2010). doi:10.1145/1743384.1743402

75. Rokach, L.: Taxonomy for characterizing ensemble methods in classification tasks: a review and annotated bibliography. Comput. Stat. Data Anal. **53**(12), 4046–4072 (2009). doi:10.1016/j.csda.2009.07.017
76. Ross, A., Jain, A.K.: Multimodal biometrics: an overview. In: 12th European Signal Processing Conference, pp. 1221–1224 (2004). http://ieeexplore.ieee.org/abstract/document/7080214/
77. Rui, Y., Huang, T., Ortega, M., Mehrotra, S.: Relevance feedback: a power tool for interactive content-based image retrieval. IEEE Trans. Circuits Syst. Video Technol. **8**(5), 644–655 (1998). http://ieeexplore.ieee.org/abstract/document/718510/
78. Safadi, B., Sahuguet, M., Huet, B.: When textual and visual information join forces for multimedia retrieval. In: International Conference on Multimedia Retrieval (ICMR 2014), p. 265 (2014). doi:10.1145/2578726.2578760
79. Samet, H.: Foundations of Multidimensional and Metric Data Structures. Computer Graphics and Geometric Modeling. Morgan Kaufmann Publishers Inc. (2005)
80. Santos, J.M., Cavalcanti, J.M.B., Saraiva, P.C., Moura, E.S.: Multimodal re-ranking of product image search results. In: Serdyukov, P., Braslavski, P., Kuznetsov, S.O., Kamps, J., Rüger, S., Agichtein, E., Segalovich, I., Yilmaz, E. (eds.) ECIR 2013. LNCS, vol. 7814, pp. 62–73. Springer, Heidelberg (2013). doi:10.1007/978-3-642-36973-5_6
81. Santos, E., Gu, Q.: Automatic content based image retrieval using semantic analysis. J. Intell. Inform. Syst. **43**(2), 247–269 (2014). doi:10.1007/s10844-014-0321-8
82. Siddiquie, B., White, B., Sharma, A., Davis, L.S.: Multi-modal image retrieval for complex queries using small codes. In: International Conference on Multimedia Retrieval (ICMR 2014), p. 321 (2014). doi:10.1145/2578726.2578767
83. Smeulders, A., Worring, M., Santini, S., Gupta, A., Jain, R.: Content-based image retrieval at the end of the early years. IEEE Trans. Pattern Anal. Mach. Intell. **22**(12), 1349–1380 (2000). doi:10.1109/34.895972
84. Snoek, C., Worring, M., Smeulders, A.W.M.: Early versus late fusion in semantic video analysis. In: 13th ACM International Conference on Multimedia (ACM Multimedia), pp. 399–402 (2005). doi:10.1145/1101149.1101236
85. Sugiyama, Y., Kato, M.P., Ohshima, H., Tanaka, K.: Relative relevance feedback in image retrieval. In: International Conference on Multimedia and Expo (ICME 2012), pp. 272–277 (2012). doi:10.1109/ICME.2012.161
86. Tollari, S., Detyniecki, M., Marsala, C., Fakeri-Tabrizi, A., Amini, M.-R., Gallinari, P.: Exploiting visual concepts to improve text-based image retrieval. In: Boughanem, M., Berrut, C., Mothe, J., Soule-Dupuy, C. (eds.) ECIR 2009. LNCS, vol. 5478, pp. 701–705. Springer, Heidelberg (2009). doi:10.1007/978-3-642-00958-7_70
87. Tran, T., Phung, D., Venkatesh, S.: Learning sparse latent representation and distance metric for image retrieval. In: IEEE International Conference on Multimedia and Expo (ICME 2013), pp. 1–6. IEEE (2013). doi:10.1109/ICME.2013.6607435
88. Uluwitige, D., Chappell, T., Geva, S., Chandran, V.: Improving retrieval quality using pseudo relevance feedback in content-based image retrieval. In: Proceedings of the 39th International ACM SIGIR Conference on Research and Development in Information Retrieval (SIGIR 2016), pp. 873–876 (2016). doi:10.1145/2911451.2914747
89. Wang, L., Yang, L., Tian, X.: Query aware visual similarity propagation for image search reranking. In: ACM Multimedia 2009, pp. 725–728 (2009). doi:10.1145/1631272.1631398

90. Wang, W., Yang, X., Ooi, B.C., Zhang, D., Zhuang, Y.: Effective deep learning-based multi-modal retrieval. VLDB J. **25**(1), 79–101 (2016). doi:10.1007/s00778-015-0391-4

91. Wang, X.J., Zhang, L., Ma, W.Y.: Duplicate-search-based image annotation using web-scale data. Proc. IEEE **100**(9), 2705–2721 (2012). doi:10.1109/JPROC.2012.2193109

92. Wei, Y., Song, Y., Zhen, Y., Liu, B., Yang, Q.: Heterogeneous translated hashing: A scalable solution towards multi-modal similarity search. ACM Trans. Knowl. Discov. Data **10**(4), 36:1–36:28 (2016). doi:10.1145/2744204

93. Wilkins, P., Smeaton, A.F., Ferguson, P.: Properties of optimally weighted data fusion in CBMIR. In: 33rd International ACM SIGIR Conference on Research and Development in Information Retrieval (SIGIR 2010), pp. 643–650 (2010). doi:10.1145/1835449.1835556

94. Wu, P., Hoi, S.C.H., Zhao, P., Miao, C., Liu, Z.: Online multi-modal distance metric learning with application to image retrieval. IEEE Trans. Knowl. Data Eng. **28**(2), 454–467 (2016). doi:10.1109/TKDE.2015.2477296

95. Xiao, Z., Qi, X.: Complementary relevance feedback-based content-based image retrieval. Multimedia Tools Appl. **73**(3), 2157–2177 (2014). doi:10.1007/s11042-013-1693-4

96. Xu, S., Li, H., Chang, X., Yu, S., Du, X., Li, X., Jiang, L., Mao, Z., Lan, Z., Burger, S., Hauptmann, A.G.: Incremental multimodal query construction for video search. In: Proceedings of the 5th ACM on International Conference on Multimedia Retrieval (ICMR 2015), pp. 675–678 (2015). doi:10.1145/2671188.2749413

97. Yang, X., Zhang, Y., Yao, T., Ngo, C., Mei, T.: Click-boosting multi-modality graph-based reranking for image search. Multimedia Syst. **21**(2), 217–227 (2015). doi:10.1007/s00530-014-0379-8

98. Zezula, P.: Future trends in similarity searching. In: Navarro, G., Pestov, V. (eds.) SISAP 2012. LNCS, vol. 7404, pp. 8–24. Springer, Heidelberg (2012). doi:10.1007/978-3-642-32153-5_2

99. Zezula, P., Amato, G., Dohnal, V., Batko, M.: Similarity Search - The Metric Space Approach, Advances in Database Systems, vol. 32. Springer (2006)

100. Zhang, D., Islam, M.M., Lu, G.: A review on automatic image annotation techniques. Pattern Recogn. **45**(1), 346–362 (2012). doi:10.1016/j.patcog.2011.05.013

101. Zhang, S., Yang, M., Cour, T., Yu, K., Metaxas, D.N.: Query specific fusion for image retrieval. In: Fitzgibbon, A., Lazebnik, S., Perona, P., Sato, Y., Schmid, C. (eds.) ECCV 2012. LNCS, pp. 660–673. Springer, Heidelberg (2012). doi:10.1007/978-3-642-33709-3_47

102. Zheng, L., Wang, S., Tian, L., He, F., Liu, Z., Tian, Q.: Query-adaptive late fusion for image search and person re-identification. In: IEEE Conference on Computer Vision and Pattern Recognition (CVPR 2015), pp. 1741–1750 (2015). doi:10.1109/CVPR.2015.7298783

103. Zitouni, H., Sevil, S.G., Ozkan, D., Duygulu, P.: Re-ranking of web image search results using a graph algorithm. In: 19th International Conference on Pattern Recognition (ICPR 2008), pp. 1–4 (2008). doi:10.1109/ICPR.2008.4761472

Author Index

Printed in the United States
By Bookmasters